THE DRAFTSMAN'S ART

Master Drawings
from the National Gallery
of Scotland

The Draftsman's Art

NATIONAL GALLERIES OF SCOTLAND

Published by the Trustees of the
National Galleries of Scotland on the occasion
of the exhibition *The Draftsman's Art: Master
Drawings from the National Gallery of Scotland* at the
National Gallery of Scotland, Edinburgh,
April 9 to June 13, 1999, subsequently shown at
The Frick Collection, New York, December 12,
2000, to February 25, 2001, and the Museum of
Fine Arts, Houston, March 20 to June 8, 2001.

ISBN 0 903598 90 6

Designed and typeset in Albertina by Dalrymple
Printed in Great Britain by BAS Printers

Cover illustration: detail from Georges Seurat,
Study for Une baignade, no. 60

Contents

Acknowledgments

Selected from one of the world's finest collections of works on paper, *The Draftsman's Art: Master Drawings from the National Gallery of Scotland* illuminates the magnificent breadth and depth of the gallery's holdings and presents a marvelous survey of five centuries of European draftsmanship. The AFA's collaboration with the National Gallery of Scotland provides a unique opportunity for American audiences to view treasures by masters such as Leonardo da Vinci, Peter Paul Rubens, François Boucher, William Blake, Jean-Auguste-Dominique Ingres, and Georges Seurat.

It has been a pleasure working with the staff of the National Gallery of Scotland on the organization of this exhibition. In particular, our gratitude goes to Timothy Clifford, director, who first proposed this collaboration along with Michael Clarke, keeper. Thanks also go to Mr Clarke for expertly overseeing the project and making the inspired selection of works, and to Katrina Thomson, assistant keeper, prints and drawings, for assisting with the numerous logistical aspects of the exhibition.

At the AFA, I want to thank Thomas Padon, director of exhibitions, for his valuable oversight of the project; Suzanne Ramljak, curator of exhibitions, for developing and supervising the project from its inception; and Michael Miller, curator of exhibitions, for overseeing the logistics of the tour. Working diligently with Ms Ramljak and Mr Miller were Margaret Calvert and Rebecca Friedman, curatorial assistants. Karen Convertino, registrar, expertly attended to the myriad of details involved in traveling the exhibition; Lisbeth Mark, director of communications, oversaw the promotion and publicity of the project; and Brian Boucher, interim head of education, created the educational materials.

Lastly, I wish to recognize the two museums participating in the exhibition tour: The Frick Collection, New York, and the Museum of Fine Arts, Houston. It has been a pleasure to work with them again.

SERENA RATTAZZI
Director, American Federation of Arts

Foreword

It is a particular pleasure for the National Gallery of Scotland to exhibit eighty of its finest master drawings in two such prestigious institutions. We are delighted that the American public will have this opportunity to appreciate our fine drawings by not only the great names such as Leonardo, Raphael and Seurat, but also many excellent examples by lesser-known masters. We also hope this selection will be seen as a testimony to our vigorous policy of acquisition in recent years, dedicated to ensuring that our collection's international status is maintained and enhanced.

The catalogue is very much a collaborative effort by the curatorial staff at the National Gallery of Scotland, supplemented by Dr Colin Bailey who has kindly contributed entries on some of the German drawings, and by Dr Stephen Lloyd of the Scottish National Portrait Gallery who has written the entry on Cosway. Valerie Hunter, the Print Room Assistant, has taken care of many of the more practical tasks associated with the exhibition, and Daniel Parker has also helped in a number of ways. All of us would wish to acknowledge the expert contributions of our colleagues in the Conservation Department, John Watson and Graeme Gollan. They have worked in close collaboration with our Registrar's Department, headed up by Anne Buddle. The publication has been seen to press by Janis Adams and designed, with his customary flair, by Robert Dalrymple.

We are delighted to have worked with the American Federation of Arts in bringing this exhibition to the United States. In particular, we thank their director, Serena Rattazzi, and her colleagues Thomas Padon, director of exhibitions, and Suzanne Ramljak and Michael Miller.

Above all, we wish to express our heartfelt thanks to Sam Sachs II and Peter C. Marzio, distinguished directors of The Frick Collection, New York and the Museum of Fine Arts, Houston, respectively, for their hospitality in welcoming *The Draftsman's Art*.

TIMOTHY CLIFFORD
Director, National Galleries of Scotland

MICHAEL CLARKE
Keeper, National Gallery of Scotland

Introduction

The National Gallery of Scotland, which was founded in 1850 and first opened its doors to the public in 1859, is certainly best known for its world-class collection of paintings. It also houses, however, the major drawings collection in Scotland, which ranges in date from the Early Renaissance to the end of the nineteenth century. Most of the major names of European art are represented and, in the case of the Scottish school, the intention is to create as comprehensive a holding as possible.

The concise statistics of the collection are as follows. There are over 20,000 works on paper, of which just under 14,000 are drawings (with sketchbooks counted as one item), and approximately 7,000 prints. As far as drawings are concerned, the numerical percentage breakdown of the various national schools reveals 62% to be Scottish, 12% Italian, 11% English, 7% Dutch and Flemish, 3% French, 2% German and Swiss, and 3% miscellaneous. To date, permanent collection catalogues have been published on the Scottish (1960), Italian (1968), Netherlandish (1985) and German schools (1991). Significant selections from the collection have been exhibited outside Edinburgh at Colnaghi, London (1966), Hazlitt, Gooden and Fox, London (1985 and 1994) and in a touring exhibition shown at Washington and Fort Worth (1990–1), the latter accompanied by an exemplary catalogue by Hugh Macandrew. Needless to say, the earlier permanent collection catalogues are now in need of substantial revision and the English and French school catalogues have still to appear. Balanced against this is the much greater degree of good, elementary record-keeping and stock-taking now possible in the age of the computer, and significant progress has already been made in recording all of the graphics collection in this manner.

We live, even more than our ambitious nineteenth-century predecessors (soon to be left more than a century behind!), in an era dominated by exhibitions and their concomitant demands. There may be no more Universal Exhibitions, but the latter part of our century has seen a glut of highly specialised shows, many of them devoted to the more arcane areas of graphics scholarship. Indeed few, if any, areas of art offer richer pickings for the connoisseur than the field of Old Master drawings where the intimacy of intuition and appreciation between creator and viewer is so profound. Many of our more outstanding drawings have been lent to prestigious and informative exhibitions and our knowledge of our drawings has increased accordingly. This present catalogue, then, seems a highly appropriate vehicle in which to present a stimulating anthology of some of our greatest treasures to a wider public than just the habitual users of the Print Room, and to focus attention on what continues to be, with the limited funds available, a very vigorous policy of acquisition in the drawings field.

In its early days, however, the graphics collection at the National Gallery grew more by stealth than intention. Known somewhat disparagingly as the 'black and white collection' it was viewed merely as an adjunct to the collection of paintings and was essentially neglected. It was only as a result of the 1945 National Galleries of Scotland (Care of Prints and Drawings) Order that a separate Department of Prints and Drawings was established at the Gallery the following year. The collection was housed in the west end of the city centre in Ainslie Place, entirely separate from the main Gallery, and available to the public only by limited appointment. It also remained essentially unsorted for many years until Keith Andrews began his remarkable and pioneering ordering of the collection, a Herculean labour to which tribute has been paid many times elsewhere and which is quite rightly repeated here. The brief history of the collection prior to Keith Andrews's appointment to the Gallery in 1958 has already been elegantly sketched by Hugh Macandrew in his 1990 catalogue. Suffice it to repeat that the collection draws its strength from four principal founding sources: the Lady Murray of Henderland Bequest of 1860 (based on the collections of the painter Allan Ramsay and his son General John Ramsay); the William Findlay Watson Bequest of 1881 (an antiquarian bookseller from Edinburgh whose main interests were in Scottish literature and topography); the Henry Vaughan Bequest of Turner watercolours of 1900 (which can only be shown in January and can not be lent); and the David Laing Bequest, much of which was

J. M. W. Turner, *Heriot's Hospital, Edinburgh, c.*1818
National Gallery of Scotland, D5447

J. M. W. Turner, *Edinburgh from Calton Hill, c.*1818
National Gallery of Scotland, D5446

transferred from the Royal Scottish Academy in 1910 with further deposits from that source in 1966 and 1974. Like Watson, Laing was an Edinburgh bookseller and in 1837 was appointed Librarian to the Writers to the Signet. A member of the Society of Antiquaries and a friend of Sir Walter Scott, Laing's keenest interest was in Scottish history and his extensive quest for manuscripts and papers throughout Europe led him to purchase a significant number of Old Master drawings and prints as well. His collection is of particular importance for the Netherlandish School holdings of the Gallery – of the 924 drawings included in Andrews's 1985 catalogue, 739 were formerly owned by Laing.

An important later bequest was that of 56 English watercolours and other drawings from the estate of Miss Helen Barlow, received in 1976. Half of these came from the collection of her distinguished father, Sir Thomas Barlow Bart., physician to Queen Victoria, King Edward VII and King George V, and the other half collected by herself, enthused as she was by her father's love of English watercolours. Apart from her many family connections with Edinburgh, Miss Barlow also wished her collection to travel north on account of the care with which she perceived the Gallery looked after the aforementioned Vaughan Bequest. Certainly, her collection forms an admirable complement to the Vaughan Turners.

If the first hundred years or so of the Gallery's history with regard to the graphic arts can be classified as one of passive recipience of the largesse of others, the policy since the 1960s has been one of an enterprising pursuance

of what that eminent Victorian Scot, Samuel Smiles, termed 'Self-Help'. The process was begun by Andrews with judicious purchases across a wide range, many of them from the London-based dealers Calmann and Colnaghi, and often for relatively modest amounts. A significant arrival was the group of drawings by Pietro Testa from the Oppé collection in 1973. The pace quickened towards the end of Andrews's Keepership (1958–85) with the acquisitions of major sheets by De Gheyn, Menzel (no.41), Ingres (no.53), Seurat (no.60), and Poussin's great drawing of *The Dance to the Music of Time*. More recently, outstanding acquisitions have included Raphael's *A Nude Woman Kneeling with her Left Arm Raised* from Chatsworth, acquired in 1987, and his *Study for the Madonna of the Fish* (no.3), bought in 1992, one year after Leonardo's *Study of Paws* (no.1) entered the collection. The Italian school was further strengthened in 1991–2 with the purchase of drawings by Parmigianino (no.4), Pietro da Cortona, Baciccio (no.18), Bernini and Cirro Ferri from the collection at Holkham Hall. In this instance the Gallery, mindful as others of the problems surrounding past dispersals from Chatsworth, joined a consortium of major British museums which banded together to acquire a significant group of drawings, all originally collected in the eighteenth century by Thomas Coke, Earl of Leicester. These were then distributed among the various partners of the consortium and thereby kept in Britain to the benefit of the national heritage.

A deliberate strand to our collecting policy over the last ten years or so has been the building up of our collection of French drawings, prompted by a desire to ensure it becomes a more worthy complement to the Gallery's outstanding holding of French paintings. A number of relevant examples are included in this exhibition, among them sheets by Boucher (no.44), Jeaurat (no.45), Girodet (no.52), and Ingres (no.56).

Last year we were fortunate enough to acquire two fine watercolours of Edinburgh by Turner, *Edinburgh from Calton Hill* and *Heriot's Hospital, Edinburgh* (illustrated opposite), both of them commissioned to be engraved as illustrations to Sir Walter Scott's *The Provincial Antiquities and Picturesque Scenery of Scotland* which was published in parts between 1819 and 1826. We were greatly assisted in this, as in a number of the purchases already discussed, by both the National Art Collections and the Heritage Lottery Funds. Indeed, without the major financial aid provided by such bodies we would be unable to contemplate further major additions to the collection.

Since 1978, with the opening of a new Print Room in the underground extension to the Gallery, visitors have been able to study our graphics collections in relative comfort and the conditions in which the collections are stored have been greatly improved. Furthermore, since the late 1980s, two rooms on the main floor of the Gallery have been refitted with variable lighting so that they may accommodate larger displays of graphics than were hitherto possible in the Gallery. At the time of writing, a further underground area is under consideration, linking our building to that of the neighbouring Royal Scottish Academy. It has been suggested that this additional area could be constructed with corridor space suitable for additional graphics display areas. As we gradually acquire more, and highly justified, exhibiting space for our hidden treasures, it is both amusing and salutary to recall that from the Gallery's opening in 1859 there have been works of graphic art continually on display in the building. Unfortunately, the cast list remained unchanged for too long and the unwitting victims of this doubtless well-intentioned measure were a group of watercolours by Hugh 'Grecian' Williams (1773–1829), presented by the artist's widow, Robina in 1860. For around half a century these were on permanent display in one of the small octagon rooms on the main floor. Their faded, ruined state today constitutes a sad testimony to the injurious effects of excessive light on watercolours (or indeed any works of art on paper). The following selection of drawings is therefore offered for serious, but of necessity temporal, contemplation and enjoyment.

MICHAEL CLARKE
Keeper, National Gallery of Scotland

CATALOGUE

The contributors to the catalogue
are denoted by their initials at the end
of each entry:

CB   Colin Bailey

MC   Michael Clarke

TC   Timothy Clifford

SL   Stephen Lloyd

JLW   Julia Lloyd Williams

KT   Katrina Thomson

AWL   Aidan Weston-Lewis

Measurements are given in centimetres,
height preceding width.

Leonardo da Vinci
1. *Studies of a Dog's Paw* (recto and verso)

ANCHIANO (NEAR VINCI) 1452–1519 AMBOISE

The archetypal 'universal artist', Leonardo was a painter, sculptor, architect, engineer, inventor, writer, musician, and natural scientist. Due to political vicissitudes, the demands and range of his commitments and his own perfectionism, very few of his undertakings were ever fully realised, although among these are two of the most famous works of art ever painted, the *Last Supper* (Sta Maria delle Grazie, Milan) and the *Mona Lisa* (Louvre, Paris). From about 1469 until at least 1476 Leonardo trained in the workshop of the Florentine painter and sculptor Andrea del Verrocchio, and became a member of the Compagnia di San Luca in 1472. Most of Leonardo's output before 1480 consisted of small-scale devotional works. An altarpiece of the *Adoration of the Magi* for San Donato a Scopeto (now Uffizi, Florence), was unfinished when he departed for Milan in 1481–2 to work for Ludovico Sforza. There he produced designs for architecture, pageants, weapons, and for a bronze equestrian statue of Francesco Sforza (never cast). The *Portrait of Cecilia Gallerani* (Cracow), the first version of the *Madonna of the Rocks* (Louvre) and the badly damaged *Last Supper* date from this period. From 1500–1508 he was mainly in Florence, where he worked on several Madonna compositions and the mural of the *Battle of Anghiari* (lost) for the Palazzo della Signoria. By early 1508 he was back in Milan, then under French control, where he probably completed the second version of the *Madonna of the Rocks* (National Gallery, London) and designed an equestrian monument to Gian Giacomo Trivulzio (again unrealised). From late 1513–16 he was mainly in Rome in the service of Giuliano de' Medici, and probably worked on several compositions begun earlier, including the *Virgin and Child with St Anne* and the *Mona Lisa* (both Louvre). His final years (1517–19) were spent in the service of Francis I in France, where he worked on costume and masque designs and yet another unexecuted equestrian monument. Hundreds of surviving drawings, annotated diagrams and notebooks testify to Leonardo's ceaseless invention and fascination with the world around him, and his desire to understand its underlying structures and processes.

Fig.1 Leonardo da Vinci, *A Bear Walking*
Metropolitan Museum of Art, New York
(Robert Lehmann Collection)

D 5189

Metalpoint on paper coated with a pale pink preparation: 14.1 × 10.7
Inscribed in black chalk at lower right of recto: *Leonard de V[…]*;[1] an illegible inscription partly cut off at lower left.

The species of animal to which these paws belonged has been the subject of some debate. When the drawing was first published they were stated to be bear's paws, presumably because the sheet has a common provenance with a study of a *Bear's Head*,[2] and because there is a series of drawings by Leonardo in the Royal Library representing what is certainly a dissected bear's paw.[3] However, the paws here under discussion are undoubtedly canine, and the uncertainty has more recently centred on whether they are those of a wolf or a dog. It is now possible to state with some confidence that they are seven studies of the left forepaw of some breed of domestic dog, possibly a large hound such as a deerhound.[4] The residual dew claw part way up the leg, which distinguishes the front from the hind legs in dogs, is visible in most of the studies.

Evidently drawn from a living dog, the repeated treatment of the same motif viewed from different angles is typical of Leonardo's analytical approach to the natural world. One senses the draughtsman simultaneously recording the surface forms and textures and exploring the way in which these reflect the underlying structure and mechanics. We know from a fragmentary treatise on anatomy, probably dating from the mid-1490s, that Leonardo was planning a comparative study of the feet of various animals ('Then I will discourse of the hands of each animal to show in what ways they vary'), and the present drawing has often been associated with this project. However, it is almost casual in its presentation when compared to some of Leonardo's more systematic and genuinely scientific anatomical studies, such as those of the dissected bear's foot mentioned above (c.1490), several densely annotated, measured drawings of the proportions of horses,[5] and the *Studies of a Skull* at Windsor, one of which is dated 1489.[6] It seems more likely, in fact, that the Edinburgh drawing dates from the end of Leonardo's first Florentine period, around 1480.[7]

Leonardo achieved an unprecedented range of effects using metalpoint, an exacting technique which had traditionally been exploited mainly for its precision and refinement. Notwithstanding the undoubted accuracy of the present studies, the handling is varied and by no means every mark is literally descriptive, the most obvious exceptions being the areas of Leonardo's characteristic left-handed parallel hatching. Some passages are remarkably free and sketchy, reinforcing the impression that they were drawn from life. In his notes for his projected treatise on painting, Leonardo specifically recommended that budding artists should carry around with them a small notebook of prepared paper to record (by implication, in metalpoint) 'men's postures and actions';[8] as a dry medium, metalpoint would have been well suited to such impromptu sketching. The modest dimensions of this sheet, and the presence of one slightly rounded, well-thumbed corner (at the upper left of the recto),[9] suggest that it could originally have formed part of such a sketchbook. Other drawings on similar paper with which it might be associated include the above-mentioned *Bear's Head*, a study of a *Bear Walking* (fig.1),[10] and, less directly, three studies of horsemen associated with the *Adoration of the Magi*.[11] The stylistically comparable sketches of *A Dog and Two Cats* in the British Museum are drawn on a sheet almost identical in size to the Edinburgh one, but coated with a cream-coloured preparation.[12]

A W L

PROVENANCE
Sir Thomas Lawrence (L 2445A); Samuel Woodburn; his sale Christie's, 4 June 1860, no.1039B; Lt. Col. Norman Colville (by 1937); purchased by private treaty with the aid of the National Art Collections Fund 1991.

EXHIBITED
Leonardo da Vinci, Palazzo dell'Arte, Milan, 1939, no.45; *Leonardo da Vinci Quincentenary Exhibition*, Royal Academy of Arts, London, 1952, nos 32–3; *Leonardo da Vinci*, Hayward Gallery, London, 1989, no.37; Edinburgh 1991, no.69; *Leonardo da Vinci: The Mystery of the 'Madonna of the Yarnwinder'*, National Gallery of Scotland, Edinburgh, 1992, no.14; Edinburgh / London 1994, no.31; *Treasures for Everyone: Saved by the National Art Collections Fund*, Christie's, London, 1997.

Palma Vecchio (Jacopo Nigreti)
2. Self-Portrait

SERINA (BERGAMO) 1479 / 80(?)–1528 VENICE

A native of the village of Serina (or Serinalta) north of Bergamo, Palma's putative birth date of 1479 / 80 is based on Vasari's statement that he was forty-eight at the time of his death, which is documented to July 1528. Nothing is known for certain about his training or early production, and hypothetical reconstructions have connected him variously with the workshops of Giovanni Bellini, or the Santacroce family, or Andrea Previtali, a fellow Bergamask resident in Venice between about 1500 and 1511.[1] He is first recorded in Venice in 1510, and this is also the date inscribed on a *Portrait of a Man* in the Borghese Gallery in Rome, which is unanimously considered to be an early work by him. However, by then – if Vasari is to be relied upon – Palma must have been painting for at least a decade, whether as an assistant in another workshop or as an independent master, so the issue of his early training must for the present remain open. His first securely documented work is the altarpiece of the *Assumption of the Virgin* for the Scuola di Santa Maria Maggiore (now Accademia, Venice), for which he received a payment in February 1513. Thereafter, Palma's name appears fairly regularly in Venetian documents. In addition to painting the standard repertoire of altarpieces, portraits and a few mythologies, Palma, in parallel with Titian, was responsible for popularising two distinctly Venetian themes: the wide format *sacra conversazione*, consisting of the Virgin and Child with Saints and / or donors in a landscape setting; and half-length, eroticised portraits of women, usually blonde and baring a breast, and sometimes in the guise of a mythological deity. Palma's business evidently flourished, for in 1523 and again in 1527 he was purchasing property on the Venetian mainland. He was a member of two Venetian confraternities, the Scuola Grande di San Marco (1513) and the Scuola di San Pietro Martire (by 1525).

Fig.2 Palma Vecchio, *Self-portrait*
Formerly Contini-Bonacossi Collection, Florence

D 5296
Black and white chalk on blue paper; the lower left corner made up: 25.7 × 18.4
Inscribed on the verso in pen and ink, in a seventeenth-century(?) hand: *H.° 473 / del Palma Vechio dipinto da / lui In Serinalda / nella palla di S. Giovanni Batt.ª / nel studio Arconati / # / 2.*[2]

The inscription on the back of the sheet, which states that this head was painted by Palma in the altarpiece of St John the Baptist in his home village of Serinalta, is so specific as to lend it credibility.[3] However, no corresponding figure appears in either of the artist's surviving polyptychs painted for Serina, and no altar there is known to have been dedicated to John the Baptist.[4]

The drawing gives every appearance of being a self-portrait, although scholarly opinion has been divided over this issue.[5] The *contrapposto* pose can readily be understood in terms of the artist gazing over his right shoulder into a mirror while recording his impressions on a sheet of paper directly in front of him. It is precisely this placement of the shoulders more or less at right angles to the surface plane which distinguishes this drawing from Palma's painted portraits, in which the torsos are invariably less sharply angled into the picture space. The sitter's gaze is also penetrating and acutely analytical in a manner frequently encountered in self-portraits, a natural consequence of artists staring intently in the mirror at their own eyes in order to draw them accurately.

The question of the reliability of Vasari's statement that Palma died aged forty-eight now enters the equation. For if it is agreed that this is a self-portrait, and that the features are those of a man of about thirty, a birth date of 1479 / 80 would imply that it was drawn around 1510. The features, with broad cheekbones, heavy jaw, finely chiselled nose and sensitive mouth, are compatible – once allowance is made for the passage of time – with two probable self-portraits from late in Palma's career, one sketched on the back of a *Portrait of a Woman* formerly in the Contini-Bonacossi Collection (fig.2), the other in the train of the Magi in an altarpiece of the *Adoration of the Magi with St Helen* commissioned in 1525 (fig.3).[6] The latter is not now generally accepted as a self-portrait,[7] although it was in the past, and the connection with the present drawing is compelling.[8] More equivocal, although not impossible, is the identity of this sitter with the beardless man in a problematic portrait in Munich which Vasari, in both editions of his *Life* of Palma Vecchio, described at length as a *Self-portrait*.[9]

The only other drawing by Palma with which the present portrait can meaningfully be compared is a *Head of a Woman* in the Louvre.[10] Although this sheet, like the Edinburgh one, has been dated to the 1520s, it has also been pointed out that very similar female heads appear in a succession of paintings by Palma, beginning with the early *Virgin and Child with Saints Jerome and Helen* at Rovigo.[11] If, as has been generally assumed, the Louvre drawing was studied from the life, it would seem logical to place it chronologically at the beginning of this sequence, before any of the painted renditions. It could thus be argued that its stylistic similarites with the study in the Louvre support an early dating for the Edinburgh *Self-portrait*.

AWL

PROVENANCE
Sir Peter Lely (L 2093; only the 'P' registered clearly); Keith Andrews, Edinburgh (by 1962), by whom bequeathed to the Gallery 1989.

EXHIBITED
Sixteenth Century Italian Drawings from British Private Collections, Merchant's Hall, Edinburgh, 1969, no.50; *Disegni Veneti di Collezioni Inglesi*, Fondazione Giorgio Cini, Venice, 1980, no.11; *The Genius of Venice*, Royal Academy of Arts, London, 1983, no.D 33; Edinburgh / London, 1994, no.34.

Fig.3 Palma Vecchio, *Adoration of the Magi* (detail)
Pinacoteca di Brera, Milan

Raffaello Sanzio (Santi), called Raphael
3. *Study for the 'Madonna of the Fish'*

URBINO 1483–1520 ROME

During a career which lasted barely twenty years, Raphael rose from modest beginnings to the summit of his profession, rubbing shoulders with the most elevated of patrons. He probably exerted a more enduring influence on the course of European painting than any other single artist. He trained first under his father Giovanni Santi, a successful painter employed at the Montefeltro court in Urbino. Raphael, too, painted portraits and exquisitely finished small panels for the court. In about 1502 he contributed designs for Bernardino Pinturicchio's decorations in the Piccolomini Library, Siena. His first major public works (1500–7) were a succession of altarpieces for churches in Città di Castello and Perugia. The style of these indicates that Raphael studied with his best-known master, Pietro Perugino, in about 1502–4 rather than earlier, as Vasari indicated. From 1504–8 Raphael was based in Florence, where he studied the works of Leonardo and Michelangelo, and painted a series of Holy Families and portraits. In 1508 he was called to Rome by Pope Julius II, and embarked on his celebrated fresco decorations in the papal apartments at the Vatican, commencing with the Stanza della Segnatura, followed by the Stanza d'Eliodoro and the Stanza dell'Incendio. He established a busy studio, and the final room, the Sala di Costantino, together with the Vatican Logge, was largely executed by assistants. Meanwhile he had designed cartoons for an important tapestry series to be hung on the walls of the Sistine Chapel. Other major commissions of Raphael's Roman years included altarpieces – the *Sistine Madonna* (Dresden) and the *Transfiguration* (Vatican) – and frescoes (*Galatea* and the *Psyche Loggia*) in the suburban villa of Agostino Chigi. Raphael was made an official architect to St Peter's by Pope Leo X in 1514. His most notable architectural projects were the Chigi Chapel in Sta Maria del Popolo and the Villa Madama and its garden loggia. Raphael died of a fever aged just thirty-seven and was buried in the Pantheon.

Fig.4 Raphael and workshop, *The Madonna of the Fish*
Museo Nacional del Prado, Madrid

D 5342

Brush and brown wash, heightened with white, over black chalk; laid down: 26 × 21.2

This elaborate *modello* is an advanced preparatory study for an altarpiece known as the 'Madonna of the Fish' in the Prado (fig.4).[1] It was painted by Raphael and his assistants in about 1512–14 for the chapel of the Del Doce family in San Domenico, Naples.[2] The fish of the title (scarcely visible in the drawing) is suspended on a string by the young Tobias who, supported by the Archangel Raphael, gingerly approaches the enthroned Virgin and Child. Tobias is balanced at the right by a lion, attribute of St Jerome, who appears behind reading a large volume. A grand sweep of drapery, drawn to the left to reveal a glimpse of landscape, forms the backdrop.

A drawing of great technical refinement, this is one of very few sheets by Raphael executed entirely with the brush over a chalk sketch. He may have chosen this technique because it allowed him to study effects of light and shade equivalent to those which might prevail in the dark chapel for which the altarpiece was destined, a consideration which may also have influenced its monumental design. This was evidently the first altarpiece commission for which Raphael delegated the major share of the execution to his studio, and the drawing would have served as a precise model for his assistant(s) to follow. As if to ensure that his intentions would not be misunderstood, the alteration in the black chalk to St Jerome's position was originally masked by a film of white heightening, now almost completely transparent. The drawing corresponds closely to the finished altarpiece, although the raised dais and throne in the latter are viewed frontally rather than from an angle. This change was made at a late stage, on the surface of the painting itself, for the receding perspective lines of the throne, corresponding to those in the *modello*, are just visible in the underdrawing of the painting as revealed by infra-red reflectography.[3]

The present study was preceded by a life-drawing in the Uffizi, Florence, in which Raphael determined the basic composition by posing four of his *garzoni* (studio hands) as a *tableau vivant* on a temporary stage erected in the workshop.[4] Only the pose of the infant Jesus, represented by an inert bundle, was left unresolved, and this was rectified in the Edinburgh *modello*, where a nest of exploratory black chalk lines betrays Raphael's

search for a satisfactory solution.

The first mention of Raphael's altarpiece, in a letter of 1524, describes it reductively as 'the Angel with Tobias', and specifies that it was in the chapel of Giovanni Battista del Doce, who has been generally assumed to have ordered it. However, recently discovered documents have clarified that from 1509 to 1519 the concession for this chapel, which included burial rights and masses for the dead, was in fact owned by one Geronimo del Doce, which explains the presence of his name-saint, Jerome, in the altarpiece.[5] The inclusion of Tobias and the Archangel Raphael may be related to the funerary function of the chapel, since Tobias was associated with the burial of the dead, and Raphael was invoked as an intercessor for the safe passage of souls to heaven.[6] Ever resourceful, Raphael based the pose of these two figures on an unused design dating from some ten years previously.[7]

Once the present drawing had served its primary purpose, it was handed over to Marcantonio Raimondi (*c*.1480–*c*.1530), the printmaker with whom Raphael established a working relationship that amounted to a commercial partnership. The engraving produced under Raimondi's supervision, probably by his assistant Marco Dente da Ravenna (*c*.1493–1527),[8] broadcast Raphael's composition far and wide, and reflections of it in various media soon appeared both in Italy and north of the Alps.[9]

AWL

PROVENANCE
Commendatore Vittorio Genevosio (alias Gelozzi or Gelosi; L 545);[10] Sir Thomas Lawrence (L 2445a); Samuel Woodburn; Willem II, King of the Netherlands; his sale, The Hague, 12 August 1850, no.32, bought by the dealer L. C. Enthoven; Grand Duke Alexander of Saxe-Weimar; P. & D. Colnaghi, London; Lt. Col. Norman R. Colville, Launceston; by descent; purchased by private treaty with funds from the estates of Keith and Rene Andrews and with the aid of the National Art Collections Fund and the National Heritage Memorial Fund 1993.

EXHIBITED
Drawings by Raphael from the Royal Library, the Ashmolean, the British Museum, Chatsworth and other English Collections, British Museum, London, 1983, no.136; *Raphael: The Pursuit of Perfection*, National Gallery of Scotland, Edinburgh, 1994 (31); Edinburgh / London 1994, no.61 (London showing only); *Treasures for Everyone: Saved by the National Art Collections Fund*, Christie's, London, 1997.

Francesco Maria Mazzola, called il Parmigianino
4. *The Virgin and Child*

PARMA 1503–1540 CASALMAGGIORE

Painter, etcher and designer of engravings and woodcuts. After his father Filippo's death in 1505 he was brought up by his uncles Michele and Pier Ilario Mazzola, both painters like his father. In August 1521 he was sent to Viadana to avoid the war which threatened Parma but came back the following year and on 22 November 1522 contracted to decorate the northern apse and north transept of Parma Cathedral. This apparently was never started but, by then, he seems to have been working on side chapels in San Giovanni Evangelista, Parma, which betray the influence of Correggio who was then working in the church. In 1523–4 Parmigianino produced his first great fresco masterpiece, a room in the Rocca Sanvitale at Fontanellato, near Parma. He later departed for Rome where he remained until the city was sacked by Imperial troops in 1527. There he almost completed the *Madonna with St John the Baptist and St Jerome* intended for the Church of San Salvatore in Lauro (now at the National Gallery, London). He left Rome in 1527 for Bologna where he remained until 1530–31. On 10 May 1531, he was commissioned to decorate the eastern apse and the neighbouring vault of Sta. Maria della Steccata, Parma. On 27 September 1535, the *Fabbricieri* of the Steccata gave him a revised contract providing him with an extension of his time. He failed to comply with these revised terms and, sometime after 26 August 1539, was thrown into prison. On his release, he departed for Casalmaggiore where he died the following year.

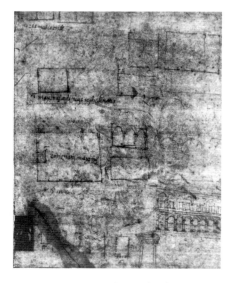

Fig.5 Parmigianino, *Architectural Studies*, verso of *The Virgin and Child*
National Gallery of Scotland

D 5196

Red and black chalk over stylus underdrawing, heightened with white; laid down: 17.1 × 13.4
Inscribed in ink at the lower right: *Parmigianino*
Verso: Architectural drawings and inscriptions by the artist are visible in strong light through the old backing. The inscriptions appear to read: *arcis medioevile / Î Maximus aedificÿs festi dinatis / Crxxoa / Î Cotignati's Maximis / Î Sirie.*

The architectural drawings on the reverse are most unusual in Parmigianino's *oeuvre* but are clearly autograph, as are the neat inscriptions in his distinctive italic hand (fig.5). Scattered over the sheet are what appear to be room plans with, lower right, an elevation of a two-storey, eight-bay building. The lower storey is arcaded, round-headed, and supported on columns, while the upper storey is articulated with blind arcading, each arcade pierced by a rectangular window supported on brackets. The proportion of these windows (9 / 7) is then assessed below, one shown with a triangular head. The artist seems not so much to be designing a building but rather establishing the position of an altarpiece in the centre of a rectangular room (centre left) and contemplating the windows and room in relation to his painting. The building is stylistically reminiscent of many in Bologna and Parma, and Mario di Giampaolo has pointed out its resemblance to the Palazzo Vescovile at Parma.[1]

This sheet is known from a large number of early copies like those in the Accademia, Venice,[2] the Musée Wicar, Lille,[3] the Victoria and Albert Museum,[4] the Uffizi, Florence (unpublished) and in a private collection, Paris.[5] In addition, there is an eighteenth-century etching after the drawing with an inscription *franc. Parme facit* in the British Museum, London.[6] Hugo Chapman noted in his entry for the Edinburgh drawing in the Christie's catalogue of 2 July 1991, 'The number of copies and the strong influence of Parmigianino may suggest that the composition derives from a prototype by the master.'

The drawing is, in reality, manifestly by Parmigianino himself, as Clovis Whitfield was the first to re-establish,[7] and his assessment has been followed by, amongst others, Mario di Giampaolo,[8] Antony Griffiths and Nicholas Turner,[9] and Hugh Brigstocke.[10] A. E. Popham, who recognised that Parmigianino's younger cousin Girolamo Mazzola Bedoli (*c*.1510–1569) made use of this sheet, came to the curious conclusion that the drawing was in fact by Bedoli

himself.[11] Not only is the style typical of mature Parmigianino at his best, but it has a basis of stylus underdrawing which is entirely typical of Parmigianino (perhaps deriving from Raphael's workshop practice) but was seldom used by Bedoli. Whitfield saw here a close connection to a series of Madonnas painted during the last years of Parmigianino in Bologna and produced a most telling relationship with *a Virgin and Child, St John and St Catherine(?)* in a British Private Collection. It also connects with a series of drawings of the Virgin and Child with her torso and legs in profile to the left, as in sheets in the Fitzwilliam Museum, Cambridge,[12] and in the Pierpont Morgan Library, New York.[13] The exquisite modelling of the Virgin's torso, with her conical breasts, and a complex pattern of folds and creases of drapery below, afford close parallels with Parmigianino's *canephore* on the ceiling of the Steccata and the draperies of the *Madonna dal Collo Lungo* (Uffizi, Florence).

T C

PROVENANCE
Thomas Coke, 1st Earl of Leicester (with his mount); by descent at Holkham Hall, Norfolk; sale Christies, London, *Old Master Drawings from Holkham Hall*, 2 July 1991, no.5, bought Thomas Agnew & Sons; from whom purchased with the aid of the National Art Collections Fund and the National Heritage Memorial Fund 1991.

EXHIBITED
Old Master Drawings from the Collection of the Earl of Leicester, Arts Council, London, 1948, no.22; *Exhibition of Old Master Drawings lent by the Earl of Leicester*, Norwich, Castle Museum and Art Gallery, 1949, no.23; *Old Master Drawings from Holkham*, Thomas Agnew & Sons Ltd., London, 1977, no.8; *Old Master Drawings from Holkham Hall*, Ashmolean Museum, Oxford, 1988; *Eighteen Old Master Drawings from the Collection at Holkham Hall, Norfolk, Acquired by a Consortium of British Museums and Galleries*, London / Birmingham / Oxford / Liverpool / Edinburgh / Cambridge, 1992–3, no.14; Edinburgh / London 1994, no.35.

Polidoro da Caravaggio
5. *Sheet of Figure Studies*

CARAVAGGIO (LOMBARDY) 1490 / 1500–1543(?)
MESSINA

His family name was Caldara. According to Vasari, he was discovered as a labourer working in the Vatican *Logge* (decorated *c.*1517–19), and later, inspired by the example of Baldassare Peruzzi, he decorated many Roman palace façades with grisaille friezes. His surviving works in Rome are few and mostly in poor condition. They include the façade of the Palazzo Milesi, via della Maschera d'Oro, the Casino del Bufalo (now removed to the Museo di Roma) and frescoes in San Silvestro al Quirinale. After the Sack of Rome in 1527, Polidoro fled to Naples and thence to Messina where, amongst various other commissions, he provided decorations for the triumphal entry of the Emperor Charles V. In Britain there are paintings by him at the Courtauld Institute, Hampton Court and a Scottish Private Collection.[1]

D 1784

Red chalk: 14.1 × 19.9 (the sheet is torn in several places and there are losses at the lower right corner and along the upper and lower margins)

Inscribed along upper right margin in pen and brown ink: *G. Ribera*

This drawing is unpublished and was always kept with the Spanish School as a putative Ribera. Indeed, this attribution was accepted by Dr Walter Vitzthum.[2] The present attribution was made by the present writer in May 1994. The style is highly characterstic of mature Polidoro drawings: compare, for instance, his two *Studies of a Man with Left Arm Raised* in the British Museum (fig.6), probably for a Crucifixion.[3] The Edinburgh sheet is preparatory for Polidoro's masterpiece, *Christ carrying the Cross,* painted just before 1534 for the church of ss. Annunziata dei Catalani at Messina, which was commissioned, as Vasari tells us, by the Consul of the Confraternity, Pietro Ansalone.[4] During an earthquake of 1783 it was moved for safety by Ferdinando Bourbon to Naples, where it remains, in the Museo di Capodimonte. It was clearly painted by Polidoro in both emulation of and in competition with Raphael's great *Way to Calvary* – the so-called *Spasimo di Sicilia* – painted for the Church of the Olivetani at Palermo, where the Ansalone family had their family chapel. The Edinburgh sheet is focused on the trumpeter who stands above and behind Christ in the centre of the composition (fig.7). Originally this figure, judging from the positioning of the fingers of the left hand, was intended to play a different musical instrument. Polidoro worried about this left hand and made two other studies of it on the same sheet. In the top left corner he studied the right hand holding a conch shell, a delightful idea but more appro-

priate for a sea triumph of, say, Neptune or Galatea. Wisely, he abandoned the conch in favour of the herald's long-horned brass trumpet. In the lower left hand corner are two studies, in profile to the left, for a companion of St Veronica, a maiden bending forward towards Christ, her right hand clasped to her breast, the left holding a pitcher of wine or water (fig.8). The sitter was clearly a local woman with her coarse features and hair parted in the middle, brushed down and tied in a kerchief. In the altarpiece, Polidoro abandons the kerchief and allows the figure to display a bare head, perhaps to counterbalance the covered head of St Veronica who, in a paroxysm of grief, holds up the vernicle displaying the features of Christ.

This sheet must have been drawn quite late in the genesis of Polidoro's ideas. He appears to have begun by painting a pastiche of Raphael's *Spasimo di Sicilia*, an oil sketch now in the Vatican.[5] He entirely reworked the composition, removing St Veronica altogether and inserting a tormenting soldier to the right of Christ in another oil sketch in the collection at Capodimonte. He then revised the composition, introducing a swooning Virgin Mary, upper left, and St Veronica in the left foreground. Then, in a drawing in the Louvre, the composition is much more nearly resolved but significantly St Veronica still has no female companion and the trumpeter blows a great curling horn. It must have been shortly after this stage that the artist decided to introduce St Veronica's companion and replaced the herald's instrument.

TC

PROVENANCE
David Laing; his bequest to the Royal Scottish Academy, 1879; transferred to the Gallery 1910.

left to right

Fig.6 Polidoro da Caravaggio, *Studies of a Man with Left Arm Raised*
British Museum, London

Fig.7 Polidoro da Caravaggio, *Christ carrying the Cross* (detail)
Museo di Capodimonte, Naples

Fig.8 Polidoro da Caravaggio, *Christ carrying the Cross* (detail)
Museo di Capodimonte, Naples

Francesco Salviati
6. *Landscape with Classical Ruins*

FLORENCE 1510–1563 ROME

Francesco de' Rossi, called Francesco ('Cecchino') Salviati, was one of the foremost exponents of the Italian *maniera* or Mannerism, a style characterised by extreme artifice, elegance, and sophistication. He was a friend of Giorgio Vasari, whose biography of him is full and for the most part accurate. He trained initially as a goldsmith, but between 1523 and 1530 was apprenticed to a succession of distinguished masters, including Bugiardini, Bandinelli, and Andrea del Sarto, none of whom had a lasting influence on his style. He adopted the surname Salviati from his early supporter, Cardinal Giovanni Salviati, with whom he lodged after his arrival in Rome in 1530–31. Resident in Rome until 1539, his most important works of this decade were an altarpiece of the *Annunciation* for San Francesco a Ripa, decorations for the entry of Charles V, and a fresco of the *Visitation* for the Oratory of San Giovanni Decollato. In 1539 he contributed to temporary decorations for the wedding of Cosimo I and Eleanora of Toledo in Florence, and then proceeded to Bologna and Venice, where he painted an altarpiece for the Chiesa del Corpus Domini and decorations in Palazzo Grimani. Back in Rome in 1541–3, he worked in the Vatican and for the Farnese family, and produced designs for prints. The period 1543–8 was spent mainly in his native Florence, where he painted an important fresco cycle in the Sala dell'Udienza in Palazzo Vecchio and altarpieces of the *Incredulity of St Thomas* (for Lyon; now Louvre, Paris) and the *Deposition* for Sta Croce. Between 1548 and 1556 Salviati executed some of his most successful and influential Roman fresco commissions, including those in the Palazzo della Cancelleria, more contributions to the Oratory of San Giovanni Decollato, a chapel in Sta Maria dell'Anima, the refectory of San Salvatore in Lauro, the *salone* of the Palazzo Ricci-Sacchetti, and the Sala dei Fasti Farnesiani in Palazzo Farnese. In 1556–7 Salviati journeyed to France, executing frescoes (destroyed) in the château of Dampierre before returning to Rome via Milan and Florence. Among his final Roman projects were one of the frescoes in the Sala Regia in the Vatican (completed by his pupil Giuseppe Porta) and the decoration of a chapel in San Marcello al Corso. Salviati had a notoriously difficult, competitive and arrogant temperament, which alienated many of his patrons and disrupted numerous commissions.

D 1026

Pen and brown ink and wash, heightened with white (partly oxidised to pink and black), on blue paper; laid down: 11 × 21.3

This intensely poetic evocation of a landscape with crumbling classical buildings colonised by vegetation is unique among Salviati's surviving drawings. Apart from the fact that it, too, includes classical ruins, his only other pure landscape drawing – a sheet in the Louvre executed entirely in red chalk – could hardly be more different in appearance.[1]

The principal, concave structure at the left in the present drawing, consisting of an arched recess or opening flanked by paired pilasters supporting an entablature, is guarded by two satyr terms on pedestals, and is loosely reminiscent of parts of the remains of Hadrian's Villa at Tivoli. A water-course descends in cascades across the middle distance, turns towards the viewer, and issues in the right foreground as a waterfall (at the point where Richardson stamped his collector's mark). Beyond the trunks which bridge the stream appear three highly schematised, gesticulating figures. The way the media are combined with the blue paper suggests that the artist may have intended this to be a nocturnal scene bathed in silvery moonlight, although the moon itself is not visible.

It has been observed that a number of similar landscape motifs appear in Salviati's frescoes in the Palazzo dei Penitenzieri, Rome, executed for Cardinal Salviati in 1552, and the Edinburgh drawing has been dated to about the same period.[2] The fact that comparable classical ruins also feature in Salviati's design for the frontispiece of Antonio Labacco's architectural treatise (first edition, 1552) has been cited in support of this late dating.[3] However, both the technique and the extreme geometric simplification of the figures in the present drawing are parallelled in two designs for tapestry borders in the Louvre which have been dated to 1541–2,[4] so a rather earlier date for the Edinburgh landscape is equally plausible.

AWL

PROVENANCE
Jonathan Richardson, Senr. (L 2183; with his mount and shelf mark, D55 / 39 / 0); David Laing; his bequest to the Royal Scottish Academy, 1879 (L 2188); transferred to the Gallery 1910.

EXHIBITED
Il Paesaggio nel Disegno del Cinquecento Europeo, Villa Medici, Rome, 1972–3, no.110; *Francesco Salviati, o la Bella Maniera*, Rome / Paris, 1998, no.126.

Taddeo Zuccaro
7. Studies of Reclining Figures

SANT'ANGELO IN VADO 1529–1566 ROME

Son of the painter Ottaviano Zuccaro, Taddeo was born in Sant'Angelo in Vado, near Urbino, in the Marche. He went alone to Rome at the age of fourteen, and embarked on an intensive study of the works of Raphael, Michelangelo, Sebastiano del Piombo and Polidoro da Caravaggio. Inspired by the latter, his earliest public works (now lost) were monochrome façade decorations, notably at the Palazzo Mattei. During the 1550s Taddeo received the important commissions to decorate the Mattei Chapel in Sta Maria della Consolazione and the Frangipani Chapel in San Marcello al Corso. He also executed secular decorations at the Castello Orsini at Bracciano and the Palazzo Mattei di Giove in Rome. In about 1559 he was employed by Cardinal Alessandro Farnese on the most important commission of his career, the decoration of the family villa at Caprarola (unfinished at his death). He was also called on to complete the important cycle of frescoes in the Sala dei Fasti Farnesiani of the Palazzo Farnese in Rome after Francesco Salviati's death in 1563, and in 1564 collaborated with Vasari and others on the decoration of the Sala Regia in the Vatican. Taddeo's mature style blended prevailing mannerist compositional and decorative principles with naturalistic observation and a more classical conception of the human form. Later in his career Taddeo frequently collaborated on large-scale decorative projects with his younger and less talented brother Federico (1540 / 41–1609), who completed several of Taddeo's commissions after the latter's premature death, and was much influenced by him.

D 3130

Pen and brown ink and wash over red chalk, the sketch at the right margin in black chalk; laid down: 23.7 × 19.9 Truncated inscription at upper right in pen and ink: *del Zuccaro feder[ico]*; and at centre right: *Ca*

Although it was inexplicably excluded from the standard monograph on Taddeo Zuccaro's drawings, this extremely vital sheet of figure studies is an entirely characteristic example of his draughtsmanship.[1] Neither the reclining figures, nor the highly schematic half-length man in armour drawn at the right edge (to view correctly, rotate the paper clockwise through 90 degrees) can be connected to any surviving painting or fresco by Taddeo. Stylistically, the drawing appears to date from relatively early in the artist's career, probably around 1550. The meandering, wiry pen lines and deftly applied films and blobs of wash recur in several other drawings generally assigned to this period, when Taddeo was principally engaged on monochrome façade decorations in the tradition popularised in Rome in the 1520s by Polidoro da Caravaggio (*c*.1499–*c*.1543).[2] The disappearance of all of Taddeo's works of this kind has, however, left us with no firm points of reference for the early development of his painting or drawing style.

The reclining poses of the principal figures, with each leaning on a supporting form to their right, has led to the suggestion that they may have been intended as designs for *sopraporta* (overdoor) decorations, to be paired with balancing figures on the opposite side.[3] Later in his career, in 1564–5, Taddeo was himself to fresco paired figures of this kind in the Sala Regia of the Vatican. However, the coupling of the male nude with a female figure behind in the present drawing – her torso and leg rendered in wash alone with brilliant economy of means – makes it unlikely that the upper sketch, at least, was

intended for this purpose. The restricted height of the picture field implied by the poses, and the relatively flat, relief-like disposition of the forms, would have been equally well suited to a narrow frieze on a palace façade.[4] On the other hand, such façade decorations were typically (though not always) martial in theme, whereas the present drawing seems more bacchic in spirit.[5] There remains the possibility, of course, that this sheet of sketches is one of Taddeo's few drawings to have been made with no preparatory function in mind. The elongation and elegant *contrapposto* of the lower female figure on the sheet are reminiscent of the figure style of Perino del Vaga (1501–47).

AWL

PROVENANCE
William Findlay Watson; his bequest to the Gallery 1881.

Battista Franco, called il Semolei
8. *The Resurrection*

VENICE(?) C.1510–1561 VENICE

Draughtsman, painter and printmaker, (Giovanni) Battista Franco was probably born in Venice around 1510.[1] According to Vasari, who knew him and who is the principal source of information about his life, Franco went to Rome at about the age of twenty, and busied himself copying antique sculpture and the works of Michelangelo, who was to remain an important influence on his style. His first recorded commissions were for temporary decorations to celebrate the entries of the Emperor Charles V into Rome and Florence in 1536. Franco remained in Florence in the employ of the Medici until 1541, when he returned to Rome. Michelangelo's recently unveiled *Last Judgement* impressed him greatly. He executed a fresco in the Oratory of San Giovanni Decollato, and by 1545 he was in the service of Guidobaldo II della Rovere in Urbino. His decoration of the vault of the Duomo there occupied him for several years, interspersed with other commissions for the Duke, including forty designs for maiolica. He also executed works for other centres in the Marche (Osimo and Fabriano) during this period. Franco was back in Rome by 1550, the date of his most important commission there, the decoration of the Gabrielli Chapel in Sta Maria sopra Minerva. In 1551 he again worked in Urbino, and probably returned to Venice the following year, where he remained. Among the prestigious commissions he received were two in San Francesco della Vigna (altarpiece of the *Baptism* for the Barbaro Chapel; decoration of Grimani Chapel, unfinished at his death), an altarpiece for San Giobbe, and decorative works in the Fondaco dei Tedeschi, the Libreria and the Palazzo Ducale. Nothing is known of Franco's artistic training, although he probably learned to engrave in the 1540s in one of the Roman workshops specialising in reproductive prints.[2] Overall, it would be reasonable to concur with a number of Franco's contemporaries that his abilities as a draughtsman and printmaker far exceeded his talents as a painter.

Fig.9 Battista Franco, *The Resurrection*
British Museum, London

D 634

Pen and brown ink, the contours incised with a stylus: laid down: 21.4 × 14.6

A good example of Franco's fluent, scrolling penwork, using a typically fine quill, this spirited drawing was reproduced faithfully, in reverse, in the artist's own etching of this subject (fig.9).[3] The two are apparently identical in scale, and so closely does the print correspond to the drawing that it seems highly likely that the latter may have been used directly in the production of the former, especially in view of the presence of incised indentations. Not much is known about the methods used in the sixteenth century to transfer designs to printing plates, but in this case two possibilities present themselves. The principal contours of the drawing could have been incised through the paper with a stylus directly into the etching ground, the resulting image clarified and reinforced with an etching needle, and the plate then bitten in the acid bath. This method would have been especially effective in transmitting to the print the vitality so evident in the drawing. Alternatively, the verso of the sheet could have been darkened and the contours on the recto then lightly incised to register the design like a carbon-copy on the surface of the etching ground. These lines would then have been gone over with the etching needle to expose the copper and the plate bitten in the normal way. It may be noted that there appears to be considerable discolouration on the verso of the sheet, especially at the margins (although, with the drawing having been laid down, it is impossible to assess this evidence fully). In either of the foregoing scenarios, the modification between drawing and print to the profile of the risen Christ, the strengthening of the radiating strokes surrounding his aura and other areas of shading, and the removal of the shield on which the foreground soldier rests, could easily have been introduced freehand directly into the etching ground.[4]

As was his wont, for this composition Franco adapted figures from other masters whose work he admired. The soldier seen from behind in the foreground of the drawing was evidently derived from one of the fallen soldiers in the *Battle of Constantine and Maxentius* in the Sala di Costantino in the Vatican, executed by Raphael's workshop around 1520.[5] The rather meaningless gesture of the helmeted soldier at the right of the drawing suggests that he too may have been borrowed from another source, and his upper half indeed corresponds quite closely, although in reverse, to another figure in the same Sala di Costantino fresco. Most significantly, because it helps us to date the print, Franco's risen Christ clearly betrays a knowledge of Francesco Salviati's *Resurrection* fresco in the Cappella della Pietà in Sta Maria dell'Anima, Rome (note, especially, the profile view of Christ's face in the final print).[6] Franco's etching, and the preparatory drawing for it, must therefore post-date the unveiling of Salviati's decorations in 1550. Although it is tempting to argue that the composition might date from prior to Franco's departure from Rome, while the various sources upon which it drew were still close at hand, it was in all likelihood executed during his final Venetian period. The few prints for which the artist used etching alone are unanimously dated to these last years.[7] It may be noted that the Edinburgh design has remarkably little in common with either of Franco's own frescoed Resurrections, in Sta Maria sopra Minerva, Rome (which Vasari implies was painted in 1550),[8] and the lunette in the Cappella Grimani in San Francesco della Vigna, Venice, dating from some ten years later (for which there is a preparatory drawing at Chatsworth and a related print).[9]

(I am indebted to Anne Varick Lauder for her help with this entry.)

AWL

PROVENANCE
Jan Pietersz. Zoomer (L 1511); Thomas Hudson (L 2432); Richard Cosway (L 629);[10] Sir Thomas Lawrence (L 2445); David Laing; his bequest to the Royal Scottish Academy, 1879 (L 2188); transferred to the Gallery 1910 (L 1969f).

Raffaellino da Reggio
9. *Design for the Decoration of a Chapel*

CODEMONDO (REGGIO EMILIA) 1550–1578 ROME

Most of what is known about the brief career of Raffaello Motta, called Raffaellino da Reggio, is contained in the short published biographies by Bonifazio Fantini (1616) and Giovanni Baglione (1642), although the information they supply is sometimes contradictory. He trained first in Reggio under the medallist Alfonso Ruspagiari, and then in Novellara with Lelio Orsi, before making his way to Rome. He may have arrived there as early as 1565–6, for Fantini states that he worked for Girolamo Muziano on the decorations executed at that time in Palazzo Montegiordano. Raffaellino had become closely associated with Federico Zuccaro by 1572, when he assisted with the latter's decorations in Sta Caterina dei Funari, and he was much influenced by Zuccaro's style (as he was equally by that of Federico's late brother, Taddeo). Among his earliest works in both Reggio Emilia and Rome were façade decorations, none of which survive. From about 1570 he executed several commissions for frescoes and altarpieces in Roman churches, the most important of which were in SS. Quattro Coronati, SS. Giovanni e Paolo and the Oratorio del Gonfalone. Raffaellino also worked, for the most part in relatively minor capacities, in several parts of the Vatican, including the Sala Regia (under Lorenzo Sabbatini, 1572–3), the Loggia of Gregory XIII (1575–7) and the Sala del Concistoro Segreto (completed 1577). He collaborated briefly and unsuccessfully with Giovanni de' Vecchi (who was jealous of his talent) in the Villa Farnese at Caprarola. The only firmly attributed oil painting by him to survive is a *Tobias and the Angel* in the Borghese Gallery, Rome. A frescoist and draughtsman of considerable talent, Raffaellino's career was cut tragically short by his premature death, aged just twenty-seven or twenty-eight.

Fig.10 Jacopo Zucchi, *Design for the Decoration of a Chapel* Christ Church Picture Gallery, Oxford

D 1475

Pen and brown ink and wash over black chalk; laid down. The mouldings of the capital and part of the base of the extreme right-hand pilaster added by a later hand in grey-black ink: 26.6 × 17.8

As an old inscription on the mount attests, this drawing, like so many of Raffaellino's, was long thought to be by one of the Zuccaro brothers, and its style is indeed close to Federico.[1] The overall design conforms to an arrangement widely adopted for small chapels in sixteenth-century Rome. A concave niche with a semi-dome above is framed by an arch flanked by tall pilasters. Into this apse-like space is inserted a rectilinear altar with an altarpiece of the *Adoration of the Magi*. The segmental pediment above is broken by a cartouche surmounted by a crown. In niches to either side appear statues, the one on the right identifiable as the Evangelist Matthew, who is inspired by an angel while writing his gospel. A glory of angels on clouds was to be painted in the vault, while the *Annunciation* appears in the spandrels on the nave wall above. Grotesque decoration is sketched on the inner pilasters.

No chapel decoration by Raffaellino exists or is recorded which corresponds to the arrangement in the drawing, but it has been linked tentatively with the much altered Ghislieri chapel (the second, originally the third, on the left) in San Silvestro al Quirinale, Rome, only the vault of which was actually decorated by Raffaellino.[2] His frescoes of the *Holy Ghost with Angels*,[3] the *Dream of St Joseph*[4] and the *Massacre of the Innocents*,[5] with small figures of *David* and *Isaiah* on the arch soffit, bear little obvious connection with the Edinburgh design, although an *Annunciation* did originally appear in the spandrels as it does in the drawing.[6] Moreover, the chapel recess as executed has a rectangular rather than concave plan and on the side walls are frescoes rather than statues.

However, the connection between Raffaellino's design and the San Silvestro chapel becomes much more compelling when account is taken of what must be a rival design for the same commission by Jacopo Zucchi (*c*.1540–96) at Christ Church (fig.10).[7] The extensive annotations on Zucchi's drawing establish that the decorations had a typological programme, paralleling scenes from the conception and infancy of Christ with prefigurations and prophecies from the Old Testament relating to the coming of the Messiah. This theme is introduced by the quotation from *Isaiah* (7:14) inscribed in the frieze above the

chapel: 'Behold, a young woman shall conceive and bear a son, and shall call his name Immanuel', which is juxtaposed with the *Annunciation* in the spandrels directly below. Zucchi's design enables us to identify the left-hand statue in Raffaellino's drawing (whose only attribute is a crown) as King David, who was regarded both as a prefiguration and a direct ancestor of Christ (*Matthew*, 1:1–17). In Zucchi's project the vault is occupied by the tablet-bearing figures of St John the Evangelist and the Prophet Hosea, flanked by blank fields destined to portray the *Nativity* and the *Flight into Egypt*. To judge from the unusual prominence given to the star in both drawings (in Zucchi's case this is reinforced by the quotation from Matthew in the central cartouche), it may have been intended to allude to the name or coat-of-arms of the unknown patron.

The refurbishment of this chapel was part of a more ambitious renovation of the church and, as one might infer from the fundamental difference in the height of the arch in the two drawings, the standard proportions of the nave chapels were evidently yet to be finalised (*pentimenti* in the black chalk underdrawing indicate that Raffaellino was initially contemplating an even higher arch).[8] The actual contract was presumably awarded jointly, for while Raffaellino frescoed the vault – including two vertical scenes similar to the blank fields indicated in Zucchi's drawing – it was Zucchi who painted the murals of the *Adoration of the Magi* and the *Circumcision* on the lateral walls below (the former resembles in significant respects the central sketch in the Christ Church project). It is not known whether the altarpiece of the *Adoration of the Shepherds* by Marcello Venusti (*c*.1512 / 15–79) was specially commissioned as part of the new refurbishment, or was a left-over from the previous decorative scheme. The integrated typological programme initially proposed for the chapel had for some unknown reason been compromised, if not entirely abandoned, although the central theme of the infancy of Christ was retained.

AWL

PROVENANCE
David Laing; his bequest to the Royal Scottish Academy, 1879 (L 2188); transferred to the Gallery 1910.

EXHIBITED
Edinburgh 1961, no.16; Edinburgh 1976, no.64; *Religious Narrative in Sixteenth Century Rome*, Snite Museum of Art, University of Notre Dame (Indiana), 1983, no.38; *The Achievement of a Connoisseur, Philip Pouncey: Italian Old Master Drawings*, Fitzwilliam Museum, Cambridge, 1985, no.54.

Agostino Carracci
10. *Landscape with Travellers Resting*

BOLOGNA 1557–1602 PARMA

Although highly accomplished as a painter, Agostino Carracci is best known as one of the leading printmakers of his generation. He executed reproductive engravings of exceptional quality after the works of many past and contemporary painters, notably Veronese and Tintoretto, as well as numerous plates of his own invention. According to Faberio, Agostino trained under the painter Prospero Fontana, and frequented the workshops of the architect and engraver Domenico Tibaldi and the sculptor Alessandro Menganti.[1] Other sources indicate that he learned to paint principally from his cousin Lodovico (1555–1619). With Lodovico and his own younger brother Annibale (1560–1609), Agostino was jointly responsible for a far-reaching revitalisation of Italian painting towards the end of the sixteenth century. This was in part effected through the informal academy which they established in Bologna around 1580. A talented musician as well as an artist, the early sources emphasise the central role Agostino played in the organisation of the academy, and in giving its activities a more intellectual and theoretical flavour. In Bologna he collaborated on three decorative projects with Annibale and Lodovico: the frescoed friezes in the Palazzi Fava and Magnani, and frescoes and canvases for the Palazzo Sampieri. He also executed a small altarpiece for Parma (dated 1586, now Pinacoteca Nazionale, Parma), and two larger altarpieces for Bologna of the *Last Communion of St Jerome* and the *Assumption of the Virgin* (both now Pinacoteca Nazionale, Bologna). His employment as an engraver took him to Rome in 1581, Venice in 1582 and again in 1587–9, and to Parma in 1586–7. He was probably the first of the Carracci to be patronised by the Farnese family, engraving the *impresa* of the newly appointed Cardinal Odoardo in 1591.[2] He later (1598–9) joined Annibale in Rome and participated in the decoration of the celebrated Gallery of the Palazzo Farnese.[3] Temperamentally very different, the two brothers quarrelled and Agostino returned to Emilia. His last project, the decoration of a room in the Palazzo del Giardino in Parma for Duke Ranuccio Farnese, was interrupted by his premature death in February 1602. The esteem in which Agostino was held by his fellow artists is reflected in the elaborate memorial service held in his honour in the Bolognese church of the Ospedale della Morte, complete with published oration, catafalque and other temporary decorations.

D 651

Pen and brown ink; laid down: 20 × 28.5
Numbered within a box at the upper right corner: XV (in an ink very close to that of the drawing); and at the lower right: 19 (in black ink).

Although undoubtedly less important than his brother for the overall development of landscape painting in Italy, Agostino's surviving landscape drawings arguably show a greater variety than those of Annibale.[4] At times the style of their landscape drawings is extremely close, making them highly problematic from the point of view of attribution. The present sheet was itself considered in the seventeenth century to be by Annibale, and was engraved as such,[5] before Agostino's hand was correctly discerned by Mariette, if not by Crozat before him, both of whom owned a great many Carracci landscape drawings. It is, in fact, a good example of Agostino's most characteristic landscape manner, dating probably from about 1590. The extensive use of parallel and cross hatching betrays his engraver's hand, although the effect is less insistent and mechanical here than it is in some of his landscapes. Comparable drawings by Agostino are at Chatsworth[6] and in the Louvre;[7] another was formerly in the Ellesmere Collection.[8]

In his 1603 funeral oration for Agostino, Lucio Faberio describes trips to the countryside during which the artist and his companions sketched from nature: 'In the country ('*alla villa*') they drew hills, fields, lakes, rivers, and anything beautiful and noteworthy that came into view'.[9] However, of all the surviving landscape drawings by Agostino and Annibale, very few give the impression that they were made outside, directly from nature.[10] Agostino's approach to landscape was coloured by his knowledge of Venetian sixteenth-century landscape drawings and woodcuts (Titian and Campagnola), and of Cornelis Cort's impressive engravings after landscape compositions by Girolamo Muziano.[11] As a prolific and highly skilled printmaker himself, Agostino would have had easy access to such prints, and almost certainly owned impressions of some of them.

The present drawing, for which a combination of quill and reed pen appears to have been used, consists of a perfectly plausible range of landscape motifs and naturalistic details, but they have been brought together in a somewhat artificial manner. Adopting a fairly high view-point, steep, rugged outcrops topped with trees frame a central vista through to a watermill in the middle distance, and at the same time isolate the resting travellers in the right foreground (traditionally identified as the Holy Family)[12] from this evidence of human habitation. Agostino seems to have been rather partial to this basic formula, for he adopted variations of it for at least two of his painted landscapes (a *Landscape with the Vision of St Eustace* in Naples, and the scene of *Refugees Fleeing to the Temple on the Capitol* in the frescoed frieze in Palazzo Magnani)[13] and for an engraving of *St Francis Receiving the Stigmata*, which he probably executed to his own design.[14]

A W L

PROVENANCE
Probably Everard Jabach;[15] Pierre Crozat (with his number at lower right);[16] his sale, Paris, 10 April–13 May 1741, where bought by Pierre-Jean Mariette (L 1852, with his mount, numbered 644); Comte Moriz von Fries (L 2903); David Laing; his bequest to the Royal Scottish Academy, 1879 (L 2188); transferred to the Gallery 1910.

EXHIBITED
Edinburgh 1993, no.13.

Felice Brusasorci
11. *The Dead Christ Mourned by Angels*

VERONA 1539 / 40–1605 VERONA

Felice Rizzi, called Brusasorci (or Brusasorzi), trained in the workshop of his father Domenico (1516–67), a successful local painter. His production was dominated by commissions for altarpieces for churches in and around his native city. The earliest of these, datable to about 1565, is the *Virgin and Child with Eight Female Saints* in ss. Trinità, Verona. Its style clearly betrays a knowledge of contemporary Florentine painting. That Felice spent some time in Tuscany early in his career is confirmed by Vasari in the second edition of his *Lives of the Painters* (1568), where he is mentioned as a promising talent. He seems to have returned to Florence on other occasions during his career and is documented there in 1597, making copies of portraits in the grand-ducal gallery. Brusasorci executed a group of accomplished portraits in his own right, dating mainly from towards the end of his life. As his career advanced, he appears progressively to have accommodated his style to the prevailing manner in Verona in the second half of the sixteenth century, dominated as it was by Paolo Veronese (1528–88) and Paolo Farinati (1524–1606). Following in his father's footsteps, he became a member of the Veronese Accademia Filarmonica in 1564, for which he occasionally executed stage sets for concerts and plays. He ran a busy workshop, and trained most of the important Veronese painters of the following generation, among them Pasquale Ottino (1578–1630), Alessandro Turchi (1578–1649) and Marcantonio Bassetti (1586–1630).[1]

D 3084

Pen and brown ink and wash over black chalk on blue paper; an unrelated blot of pink pigment below the putto with the lance at upper left: 40.6 × 34.2

This sheet is the most highly finished of the mere handful of drawings which can be securely attributed to Brusasorci.[2] Three older and seven infant angels maintain a torchlit vigil over the limp body of Christ laid out on the winding sheet. The mood is one of profound sorrow. Several of the angels wipe tears from their eyes, one wrings his hands in anguish and another peers down mournfully at Christ's body. The flying angels bear instruments of the Passion – the lance with which the centurion Longinus pierced Christ's side, the long rod used to insert a sponge soaked in vinegar into the resulting wound, and a bundle of twigs used in the flagellation. The two foreground infants contemplate nails from the cross, while in the container between them can be glimpsed the crown of thorns and the cord with which Christ was bound to the column.

The lower part of the composition was repeated, with minor variations, in Brusasorci's signed painting in the museum at Eger in Hungary (fig.11; oil on slate, 43.5 × 55cm).[3] In adapting the design to the new horizontal format, the four flying angels were omitted (although, as if in partial compensation, an additonal one was added at the right edge), and the relative scale of the two standing angels was reduced. Even before the painting at Eger was published, it had been suggested, on account of

the even film of wash applied to most of the background and the nocturnal setting, that the drawing might have been preparatory for a painting on slate.

Brusasorci, along with Paolo Farinati and Jacopo Ligozzi, was one of the first Veronese artists to experiment with slate ('*paragone*') as a painting support, and this technique became particularly associated with his pupils Ottino, Turchi and Bassetti.[4] In addition to the painting of the *Dead Christ Mourned by Angels* at Eger, there are two other treatments of this theme on slate by Brusasorci himself (Szépmüvészeti Múzeum, Budapest; Private Collection, Rovereto), and a third of studio quality (Museo del Castelvecchio, Verona).[5] Both in terms of style, and on account of the demonstrable influence this group of pictures had on his pupils, they may be dated to the last phase of Brusasorci's career (*c.*1590–1605).[6] Support for this dating is provided by the close stylistic similarities between the Edinburgh drawing and a preparatory study (Private Collection, Milan) for the upper part of Brusasorci's 'Giusti Altarpiece' in the Sacristy of Sant'Anastasia, Verona, which was commissioned in 1598.[7]

AWL

PROVENANCE
William Findlay Watson; his bequest to the Gallery 1881.

EXHIBITED
Disegni veronesi del Cinquecento, Venice / Verona, 1971, no.91.

Fig.11   Felice Brusasorci, *The Dead Christ Mourned by Angels*
István Dobó Castle Museum, Eger

Giovanni Francesco Barbieri, called il Guercino
12. *A Boy Helping his Master to Dress*

CENTO 1591–1666 BOLOGNA

Born at Cento, a small market town in the province of Ferrara, Guercino appears to have been largely self-taught, although he certainly drew inspiration from the work of such Emilian contemporaries as the Carracci (especially Lodovico) and Scarsellino. Apart from a two-year spell in Rome during the papacy of the Bolognese Gregory XV Ludovisi (1621–23), Guercino was to base himself for most of his career in his native town, until in 1642 he moved definitively to Bologna, a short distance away. From relatively early in his career, Guercino caught the attention of several important patrons – among them the papal legate of Ferrara, the Archbishop of Bologna and the Duke of Mantua – and by the mid-1620s he was declining invitations to work abroad, including one from Charles I. His relative isolation in Cento seems not to have affected business adversely; on the contrary, he was flooded with commissions from throughout Italy and beyond, and played host to some distinguished visitors. Only after his rival Guido Reni was safely dead, however, did Guercino transfer his studio to Bologna. The vast bulk of his production consisted of altarpieces and easel pictures, but he did execute frescoes in the earlier part of his career in Cento, Bologna, Rome (notably the *Aurora* ceiling in the Casino Ludovisi) and in Piacenza Cathedral (1626–7). In terms of style, Guercino progressively abandoned an early tenebrist manner dominated by dramatic lighting, saturated colours and agitated compositions, in favour of a much more idealised, classical style, with calmer and more structured compositions, greater elegance of contour, a more pastel palette and a less contrasted treatment of chiaroscuro. Guercino was one of the most accomplished and prolific draughtsmen of the seventeenth century. His drawing style underwent a less radical transformation than his painting style, and even his late drawings are imbued with a calligraphic energy and freshness of touch unrivalled by any of his Italian contemporaries. Most of Guercino's paintings are well documented thanks to his correspondence, to the account book which he maintained from 1629 onwards, and to biography in Carlo Cesare Malvasia's *Felsina Pittrice*, published in 1678.

D 1608

Pen and brown ink and wash on buff paper; laid down: 18.1 × 15

To judge from numerous surviving drawings of this kind and the testimony of his biographer Malvasia, Guercino had a keen eye for the comedy and pathos inherent in everyday actions, characters and events, and this drawing was no doubt inspired by an incident he had witnessed. The boy appears to be lacing up the man's overgarment, while the latter holds the two flaps together to assist him. The gentle humour of the scene lies in the contrast between the man's taut, haughty, 'nose-in-the-air' demeanour, quite inappropriate to the banal situation, and the seemingly eager innocence with which the boy undertakes his task. Although one senses that certain features, notably the man's mane of swept-back hair, have been deliberately emphasised, the artist has stopped short of outright caricature.

The drawing falls into a category of informal sketches and studies with no preparatory function which Guercino seems to have produced throughout his career, and which were no doubt intended for the enjoyment and amusement of the artist and his family and friends. They are among Guercino's most immediately attractive and accessible creations, and span a whole range of everyday and fantastic subjects, including kitchen and tavern scenes, outdoor spectacles, beggars, louse hunters, women drying their hair by a fire, monstrous creatures, scenes of witchcraft and exorcism, true caricatures, and a memorable parade of four urchins lined up in descending order of height.[1]

Guercino's vibrant pen and wash technique was ideally suited to injecting movement and energy into an informal sketch such as this, but its apparent spontaneity belies its sophistication. His characteristically sinuous, looping pen lines, especially visible over the boy's torso, seem to rove almost randomly over the paper searching out the desired form; they were here also put to good descriptive use, tracing the lace-ends emanating in various directions from the central knot of hands. The effect of the rich brown wash of varied degrees of dilution set off against the pale brown of the paper is especially harmonious (only rarely did Guercino use coloured papers). On stylistic grounds, the drawing would appear to date from the early to mid-1620s.

Guercino was by all accounts an extremely pleasant and charitable man, and there is no hint of malice or pomposity in his sketches of local characters and *contadini* engaged in their everyday pursuits, or indeed in his actual caricatures. It is rather a sense of the artist's genuine humanity and *joie de vivre* that emanates from this kind of drawing. In this respect he has much in common with Annibale Carracci (1560–1609), who seems to have been the first to deem such subjects from everyday life worthy of uncensorious artistic attention.[2]

AWL

PROVENANCE
Charles, 15th Earl of Shrewsbury (L 2688); David Laing; his bequest to the Royal Scottish Academy, 1879 (L 2188); transferred to the Gallery 1910.

EXHIBITED
Colnaghi 1966, no.48; Edinburgh 1993, no.32.

Pietro da Cortona
13. *David and Abigail*

CORTONA 1597–1669 ROME

Painter, architect and designer, Pietro Berrettini, called Pietro da Cortona, was one of the key figures in the development and dissemination of the Baroque style in Italy. As a creator of grand, integrated decorative schemes involving fresco, stucco-work and gilding, he was unrivalled, while his originality as an architect was matched only by that of Francesco Borromini and Gianlorenzo Bernini. After initial training in Cortona with a minor local artist, he entered the studio of the Florentine Andrea Commodi, whom he followed to Rome around 1612. Later in the decade he completed his training with Baccio Ciarpi. By 1622–3 Cortona was working for several distinguished Roman families – the Colonna, Mattei, and Sacchetti – and had become acquainted with the antiquarian and collector Cassiano dal Pozzo, for whose celebrated 'Paper Museum' he executed a number of drawings. The Sacchetti became his most important early patrons and it was they who introduced him into the circle of the newly elected Barberini pope, Urban VIII, for whom he painted frescoes at Sta Bibiana (1624–6). Cardinal Francesco Barberini helped him win the commission for an important altarpiece in St Peter's, ordered a series of tapestry cartoons, and commissioned Cortona's most celebrated work, the huge ceiling fresco of *An Allegory of Divine Providence* in the *salone* of Palazzo Barberini (1632–9). The 1630s also saw the commencement of Cortona's work for the Oratorians at the Chiesa Nuova, which culminated in the splendid frescoes in the dome, apse, pendentives and nave vault (1647–65). Cortona's most important project outside Rome was the decoration of a series of rooms in the grand-ducal apartments in the Palazzo Pitti, Florence (1637–47, completed later by his pupil Ciro Ferri). Although increasingly handicapped by arthritis, he undertook several other significant projects after his return to Rome, including the decoration of the Gallery in Palazzo Pamphili in Piazza Navona (1651–4), the design of the Gallery of Alexander VII in the Quirinal Palace, and a series of altarpieces. Cortona's most important works of architecture are the church of ss. Luca e Martina in Rome (1634–50); the remodelling of the piazza and façade of Sta Maria della Pace (1656–9); the new façade of Sta Maria in Via Lata (1658–62); and the dome of San Carlo al Corso (begun 1668). He was an active member of the Roman Academy of St Luke, serving as its *Principe* from 1634–8.[1]

D 1906

Pen and brown ink and brown and grey wash, heightened with white, over black chalk, on brownish paper; patchy staining from discoloured animal glue: 27.1 × 39
Numbered on the verso in brown ink: 305

Following the Old Testament account (*I Samuel*, 25), Abigail begs David, then exiled with his band of followers in the wilderness, to accept as a peace offering a gift of food and drink which her wealthy husband Nabal had denied them. She thus saved her family from the vengeance David and his soldiers were about to inflict. When he heard of his wife's intervention, Nabal died of shock and Abigail later became one of David's wives.

This densely worked, painterly drawing is one of the earliest sheets by Cortona to have survived, and can be dated on stylistic grounds to about 1621–4.[2] The composition and figure types are very similar to those in his small painting on copper of *The Oath of Semiramis* (Mahon Collection, London) and his frescoes in the Gallery of Palazzo Mattei di Giove (1622–3), especially the scenes representing *The Idolatry of Solomon* and *The Queen of Sheba bringing Gifts to Solomon*. The frieze-like composition, with superimposed figures crammed into a shallow pictorial space, their heads aligned within a narrow horizontal strip, is redolent of Cortona's intensive study of both classical reliefs and the façade decorations of Polidoro da Caravaggio.[3] The framing lines indicated on all four sides reinforce this relief-like character, while foliage at the left acts as a foil which defines the back plane. It was in his copies after the Antique and Polidoro that Cortona seems to have first developed the elaborate technique used here, combining chalk, pen, wash and white heightening on coloured paper. The style of the Edinburgh sheet is very similar to several other compositional drawings by Cortona dating from the early to mid-1620s. The closest parallel is with the study in the Pierpont Morgan Library, New York (Janos Scholz Collection) for the Palazzo Mattei fresco of *The Queen of Sheba bringing Gifts for Solomon*, the theme and composition of which also echo that of the present drawing.[4]

The Edinburgh drawing was made in preparation for a painting, now untraced, but which is known from a reproductive engraving dated 1784, at which time it was in the Grifoni Collection, Florence (fig.12).[5] In common with many of Cortona's narrative compositions of the 1620s, there are notable differences between the preparatory study and the final painting. Having refined the pose of David during the execution of the drawing (a significant alteration to his right leg is clearly visible as a *pentimento*), Cortona then went to the trouble of making a separate chalk study of him in this pose (Louvre, Paris), only to rethink the whole composition before taking up his brushes.[6] Such care in planning a picture no doubt reflects Cortona's inexperience at tackling multi-figured narratives, as well as his diligence. To judge from the engraving, his final painting of *David and Abigail* had much greater pictorial depth than the Edinburgh drawing and, with the introduction of a central caesura, its composition was altogether more spacious and elegant. The compact, stocky figures in the study were also elongated and refined. It was possibly the example of such Bolognese contemporaries as Guido Reni and Domenichino which inspired Cortona to relax his dependence on classical models in this way.

A W L

PROVENANCE
Presented by Lady Murray of Henderland 1860.

Fig.12 Benedetto Eredi, after Pietro da Cortona, *David and Abigail*
Bibliothèque Nationale, Paris

Florentine School, Seventeenth-Century

14. *Sheet of Studies for an Unidentified Narrative Scene*

D 766
Red chalk, pen and brown ink and brown and grey-blue washes, heightened with white (partly oxidised): 27.8 × 21.1
Inscribed at the lower right in black chalk, reinforced with pen and ink: *Matteo Rosselli.*

Despite its high quality and its idiosyncratic style, both the attribution and the subject of this colourful, densely worked drawing remain problematic. The overall effect is strikingly cinematographic, with the sheet subdivided like a storyboard into a series of framed 'stills', as if the draughtsman were moving in his mind's eye around a stage and envisaging the events from a succession of different angles. At least one scene is conceived as if the spectator were viewing it from beneath the portico of the temple itself, while in others we witness it from a low view-point at the foot of the steps.

The subject has been identified as the *Presentation of the Virgin in the Temple*, but this is unlikely to be correct, for in several of the scenes the main protagonist approaching the priest is clearly an adult rather than a child. Nor can it represent *Solomon receiving the Queen of Sheba*, for not only is the Queen's magnificent train of gift-bearers and camels absent, but the welcoming figure at the top of steps is dressed in the garb of an Old Testament high priest, rather than crowned, as King Solomon ought to be.

As for the attribution, there is little doubt that the drawing is by a Florentine artist of the early to mid-seventeenth century working in the tradition established there by Lodovico Cardi, called Cigoli (1559–1613). However, an attribution to Cigoli himself is not sustainable, although the sketches of figures in pen and ink at the top are close to his manner, as is the way in which the sheet is compartmentalised into a series of variant treatments of the same theme.[1] Two other possible candidates – Cigoli's pupil Giovanni Biliverti (1585–1644), and the latter's own eccentric pupil Bartolomeo Salvestrini (1599–1633) – also appear to be excluded on the grounds that nothing strictly comparable by them is known.[2] There remains the possibility that the old, probably seventeenth-century, inscription attributing the drawing to Matteo Rosselli (1578–1650) is reliable, although it must be said that no published drawing by Rosselli looks even remotely like this.[3] One might conclude, somewhat lamely, that this sheet is either an untypical work by a well-known artist, or a fine and distinctive sheet by a hitherto unrecognised draughtsman.

AWL

PROVENANCE
David Laing; his bequest to the Royal Scottish Academy, 1879 (L 2188, in three places); transferred to the Gallery 1910.

Francesco Albani
15. *Study for the Head of Europa*

BOLOGNA 1578–1660 BOLOGNA

With Guido Reni, Domenichino and Guercino, Francesco Albani was one of the four great exponents of Bolognese painting in the first half of the seventeenth century (the artists' biographer Francesco Scanelli dubbed them 'the Four Evangelists of modern Italian painting'). Albani trained in Bologna, initially with Denys Calvaert and then from the mid-1590s in the Carracci academy. He operated independently by 1599, when he is listed as a member of the *Compagnia dei pittori*. He executed important commissions, including a frescoed frieze in Palazzo Fava and several altarpieces, prior to his departure for Rome in 1601, where he became a senior member of Annibale Carracci's studio. Following the breakdown of Annibale's health, Albani supervised the completion of such prestigious projects as the Aldobrandini landscape lunettes and the decoration of the Herrera Chapel in San Giacomo degli Spagnuoli. He remained in Rome until 1617, where his most significant commissions included an acclaimed fresco cycle in Vincenzo Giustiniani's villa at Bassano di Sutri, a fresco in the choir of Sta Maria della Pace and a series of four landscape *tondi* with mythological staffage for Scipione Borghese (still in the Galleria Borghese, Rome). He was based in his native Bologna for the remainder of his long career and declined invitations to work at courts abroad (his paintings were especially popular in France). Relatively small-scale mythological landscapes and altarpieces for churches in and around Bologna constituted the bulk of Albani's mature output. His busy workshop competed with that of Guido Reni, and his prodigious number of pupils included such important artists as Andrea Sacchi, Pier Francesco Mola and Carlo Cignani. From the mid-1640s the quality of Albani's work took a marked nose-dive as he endeavoured to pay off an enormous debt inherited from his brother, while at the same time supporting a family of a dozen children. Although his works were highly prized during the seventeenth and eighteenth centuries, Albani's reputation, in common with that of many Bolognese *seicento* artists, suffered an eclipse during the nineteenth century from which it has never fully recovered.[1]

D 5389

Black, red, brown and white chalks on discoloured pale brown paper; some marginal insect damage; laid down: 32.2 × 23

For an artist trained in the great Carracci tradition of draughtsmanship, surviving drawings by Albani are surprisingly rare. The Uffizi, the Louvre and the Royal Library at Windsor each have a few examples, and other sheets are scattered in public and private collections in Europe and America. Having now been published several times, this study is probably Albani's best-known drawing, although in its combination of coloured chalks it is unique among the drawings by him identified to date.[2]

It has been proposed that this study may have been preparatory for the head of Europa in Albani's *Rape of Europa*, a canvas of modest dimensions (76 × 97cm) belonging to the Pitti Gallery, Florence.[3] However, the monumental scale of the drawing makes it much more likely that it was made in connection with one of the much larger treatments of this theme produced in Albani's busy studio, with varying degrees of direct involvement on the part of the master himself.[4] The study in fact corresponds closely to the head of Europa in a composition known in several versions, of which the best appears to be that in the Galleria Colonna in Rome (173.5 × 223cm; fig.13), although even this can be only partially autograph.[5] The direction of her gaze is marginally higher in the painting, her upper teeth are no longer visible and she has acquired an earring, but these are the sorts of adjustments one would expect during translation from one medium to another, and in other respects the match is almost perfect, down to the wind-swept locks of hair above Europa's proper right shoulder and the summary indication in the drawing of the neckline of her dress. The painting had been acquired by Cardinal Girolamo I Colonna by 1648, and it is highly likely that he purchased it directly from the artist when he was serving as Archbishop of Bologna (1632–45). If it is indeed the prime version of this composition, on which all the other variants, including the Pitti canvas, depend, it probably dates from the mid-1630s.[6]

Both the facial type of Europa and the handling of the drawing reveal Albani's debt to his rival Guido Reni (1575–1642), then the most sought-after painter in Italy. The fine, parallel strokes of chalk superimposed over the more blended, tonal modelling of the cheek and nose, are especially reminiscent of Reni's drawing style.[7]

PROVENANCE

Thomas Coke, 1st Earl of Leicester (with his mount); by descent at Holkham Hall, Norfolk; sale, Christie's, London, *Old Master Drawings from Holkham*, 2 July 1991 no.19, bought Flavia Ormond Fine Arts Ltd, from whom purchased 1994.

EXHIBITED

Italian Drawings, Flavia Ormond Fine Arts Ltd, at Douwes Fine Art, London, 1992, no.9.

Fig.13 Francesco Albani, *The Rape of Europa* (detail) Galleria Colonna, Rome

AWL

Pietro Testa
16. *Narcissus at the Pool*

LUCCA 1612–1650 ROME

Pietro Testa, sometimes called il Lucchesino from his birthplace, was a difficult and progressively tortured personality beset by melancholy, self-doubts and frustration at the lack of proper recognition of his talents. He was a highly skilled draughtsman, and one of the greatest etchers of the seventeenth century, although his paintings are by and large less successful. Testa probably arrived in Rome towards the end of the 1620s and busied himself copying classical antiquities. It was in this capacity that he was soon employed by the collector and antiquarian Cassiano dal Pozzo, for whom he appears to have worked for a protracted period, and through whom he met Nicolas Poussin, by whom he was much influenced. Of the hundreds of drawings Testa reportedly made for Dal Pozzo's 'Paper Museum', only a few can now be confidently attributed to him. Testa was also commissioned by the artist and writer Joachim von Sandrart to make drawn copies of classical statues in the collection of Vincenzo Giustiniani to serve as models for engravings (c.1631). It was around this time that he made his first etchings. By 1630 he had entered the studio of Domenichino (1581–1641). On the latter's departure for Naples in 1631, Testa transferred to the workshop of Pietro da Cortona, with whom, however, he soon quarrelled. On the first of two brief return trips to Lucca (1632 and 1637) Testa secured the support of an important patron, Girolamo Buonvisi, a cleric at the papal court to whom he dedicated several prints and who was the intended dedicatee of his incomplete 'Treatise on Ideal Painting' (working notes in the Kunstmuseum, Düsseldorf). As both this project and a group of allegorical etchings indicate, Testa was much given to theoretical speculation and philosophy, particularly regarding the relationship between artistic theory and practice. He received a few commissions for altarpieces in Lucca and Rome, but suffered the indignity of having some frescoes he had executed replaced within a few years by an inexperienced northerner. Following Poussin's example, his easel paintings and etchings of the 1630s illustrate mainly themes from classical mythology. As his career progressed he selected increasingly complex allegorical and historical subjects, in keeping with his growing intellectual interests and aspirations. Testa's death by drowning in the Tiber aged thirty-seven was probably suicide.

D 4991

Pen and brown ink and wash over graphite (or black chalk): 18 × 25.5
Inscribed in pen and ink on the verso: *pie[o?]tro testa 201*

Following Ovid's account in the *Metamorphoses* (Bk 3, lines 339–510), a melancholic and emaciated Narcissus is slumped on the point of death beside a woodland pool, a victim of his love for his own reflection. He is flanked prophetically by the flowering plant to which he gave his name, a stem of which he also holds in his left hand. The much reworked form at the upper right edge is Echo, the nymph whose love Narcissus had earlier shunned, but who nevertheless grieves his demise. Narcissus is shown having rent his cloak apart and beaten his chest, as described by Ovid. The face of an *amoretto*, rather than that of Narcissus, is mirrored in the pool – a resonant detail of Testa's own invention. As if to underscore the pathos of the tale, another infant aims an arrow to kindle the passion of the moribund youth for the long-suffering Echo, but it is clearly too late.

The vigour and dynamism of this characteristic pen sketch is the product of perhaps just a few minutes of creative frenzy. Testa deployed the full range of graphic shorthand at his disposal to render the varied forms and textures, and to generate some sense of space and ambience, with little concern for the pools of ink deposited sporadically across the sheet. The angular contours of Narcissus, his draperies, and the foreground dogs, are contrasted with the ubiquitous round heads of the *amoretti*, with which Testa compulsively populated his compositions.

The present study apparently corresponds closely in most respects to a large painting on canvas by Testa in an Italian private collection, which is still unpublished, and which has been dated to the mid-1630s.[1] There are also three other drawings by Testa illustrating the story of Echo and Narcissus: a study in the Louvre, which is more highly finished than the Edinburgh sheet but differs in composition (fig.14);[2] and two closely related drawings in the Hermitage, St Petersburg,[3] and a Private Collection,[4] which are both vertical in format, and in which the landscape dominates the main protagonists and the *amoretti* are all but omitted.

A cross-fertilization of ideas and motifs evidently took place with Testa's near-contemporary and thematically related composition of *Venus and Adonis*, which is known in painted and etched versions and a series of preparatory drawings (the present drawing was in fact long thought to be related to that composition).[5] Narcissus's rather effeminate pose, particularly the sharp divergence of the legs at the knees,[6] is derived from similar figures in slightly earlier paintings by Nicolas Poussin (1594–1665), such as the *Venus and Mercury* (Dulwich Picture Gallery, London), or the *Mars and Venus* (Museum of Fine Arts, Boston), while the shadowy presence of Echo at the margin of the drawing recalls the same painter's *Death of Narcissus* (Louvre, Paris).

A W L

PROVENANCE

Hugh Howard (?);[7] Sotheby's, 14 December 1932, no.30; bought A. P. Oppé; Armide Oppé; from whom purchased with the aid of the National Art Collections Fund 1973.

EXHIBITED

Seventeenth Century Art in Europe, Royal Academy of Arts, London, 1938, no.477; *Artists in Seventeenth Century Rome*, Wildenstein and Co., London, 1955, no.81; *The Paul Oppé Collection*, Royal Academy of Arts, London, 1958, no.389; *Pietro Testa (1611[sic]–1650)*, National Gallery of Scotland, Edinburgh, 1974; *Pietro Testa 1612–1650: Prints and Drawings*, Philadelphia / Cambridge (Mass.), 1988–9, no.20; Edinburgh 1991, no.73.

Fig.14 Pietro Testa, *Narcissus at the Pool*
Musée du Louvre, Paris

Pietro da Cortona
17. *Landscape with Classical Buildings and a Grape Harvest*

For biography, see cat.no.13.

D 1837

Brush and grey wash over black chalk; a few minor losses and stains; laid down: 31.1 × 47.4

This impressive drawing is one of three closely related sheets which were implausibly attributed to Andrea Locatelli (1695–1741) when they entered the Gallery's collection; two of these are now recognised as autograph works by Pietro da Cortona, while the third is distinctly weaker, and is probably by a member of his studio.[1] As with many of Cortona's landscapes, the viewpoint is relatively high, offering a panoramic vista of vineyards, buildings, woodlands and waterways, leading to mountains in the far distance. The artist has conjured up an idyllic vision of the ancient world, in which scantily-clad figures are busily gathering and treading grapes, and moving giant fermenting barrels, presided over by a bacchic herm draped with a vine. Perhaps because of the prominence of the winery at the left, the artist has here virtually dispensed with the large *repoussoir* trees which usually frame his landscapes. Indeed, the panorama as a whole is remarkably unstructured for an imaginary landscape of this period. The trellised vineyard is strung casually across the foreground, while behind classical temples, a country villa and farm buildings are half submerged in dense woodland. Somewhat incongruously, a church spire is silhouetted against the mountain in the background.[2] Little use is made of the common formula of interlocking hillsides to achieve recession, and even the river – for most landscapists a key device for leading the eye into the distance – is here merely glimpsed at the right, only to disappear behind clumps of foliage. Cortona applies the simple principles of linear and aerial perspective and superimposition to convey a convincing sense of depth. Streaks of wash in the sky to right and left subtly convey the effect of sunlight penetrating a passing shower. Less successful, perhaps, is the rather too dense cloud invading the space between the circular temple and the hillside behind, but this too confirms Cortona's recurrent interest in meteorological phenomena and their interaction with the landscape.[3]

Cortona's landscapes, including the present sheet, have almost invariably been dated to the mid- to late 1620s, the period in which he executed beautiful landscape frescoes in the chapel of the Villa Sacchetti at Castelfusano and a group of landscape oils for the same patron, Marcello Sacchetti (now divided between the Capitoline Gallery, the Galleria Nazionale, and the Vatican Museums in Rome, and the Fitzwilliam Museum, Cambridge).[4] These works are remarkable for their freshness of vision and independence from the main currents of Roman landscape painting at this time. Cortona's early interest in landscape is also attested by Giulio Mancini, who wrote a brief biography of him, probably in 1625, and who singled out a nocturnal landscape drawing for special praise.[5]

The present drawing does indeed have much in common with some of Cortona's early painted landscapes, notably the one now in the Vatican Museums, which includes two similar temples (fig.15).[6] However, the distinctive technique of this and related sheets finds no parallels among Cortona's other drawings from this early period, whereas it is matched closely by the landscape elements in two drawings by him which can be firmly dated to the 1660s.[7] It seems that Cortona's interest in landscape was in reality more enduring than has hitherto been recognised, and that landscape drawings of this kind may have been produced by him sporadically, perhaps as a form of relaxation, throughout his career. By his own testimony, as late as 1666 he was hoping to produce some landscape watercolours (*'paesi di aguarella'*) for Cardinal Leopoldo de' Medici, crippling attacks of gout permitting.[8] The artist's choice of brush and grey (or occasionally brown) wash for the execution of these drawings, and the distinctive parallel dabs with which he indicated the clumps of foliage, may well have been influenced by his early experience painting landscape frescoes.

A W L

PROVENANCE
David Laing; his bequest to the Royal Scottish Academy, 1879 (L 2188); transferred to the Gallery 1910.

EXHIBITED
Edinburgh 1976, no.58.

Fig.15 Pietro da Cortona, *Landscape with Two Temples* Musei Vaticani, Rome

Giovanni Battista Gaulli, called Baciccio
18. *The Sacrifice of Abraham*

GENOA 1639–1709 ROME

Giovanni Battista Gaulli, called Baciccio, was one of the foremost exponents of High Baroque decorative painting in Rome. His supreme achievement in this field was the extensive cycle of frescoes in the Gesù, the Jesuit mother church (1672–85). Genoese by birth and training, by 1658 Baciccio had moved to Rome, and within a few years he had become acquainted with the great sculptor and architect Gianlorenzo Bernini, who did much to foster his career. Bernini was instrumental in securing Baciccio's first major fresco commission – for the pendentives of Sant'Agnese in Piazza Navona (1666–72) – as well as the Gesù decorations mentioned already. In addition to his works in fresco, for which numerous oil sketches and *modelli* survive, Baciccio painted many altarpieces and a fine group of sacred and secular easel pictures, but it was his skill as a portraitist that initially established his reputation. His earliest paintings reflect his Genoese heritage, particularly the work of Castiglione and of Van Dyck (a highly influential resident there in the 1620s). Works from the later 1660s and early 1670s reveal his absorption of some elements of Bolognese classicism. The impact of his trip to Parma to study Correggio's frescoes in 1669 only really surfaces later in the Gesù dome frescoes. By then his mature style was fully formed, having incorporated influences from Roman Baroque painters, notably Pietro da Cortona, and above all from his mentor Bernini. With its highly charged emotionalism and agitated draperies, Baciccio's style is often characterised as a painted equivalent to Bernini's in sculpture. He became a member of the Accademia di San Luca in 1662, and served as its *Principe* in 1673–4. During the 1670s and 1680s he was widely recognised as the leading painter in Rome, although demand for his work declined during the last two decades of his career.

Fig.16 Giovanni Battista Gaulli, called Baciccio,
The Sacrifice of Abraham
High Museum of Art, Atlanta
(Gift of the Kress Foundation, 1958)

D 5328

Pen and brown ink and wash, heightened with white, over black chalk, on discoloured blue paper; laid down: 31.8 × 23.2

An angel stays the blade-wielding arm of Abraham, who was instructed by God to sacrifice his son Isaac as a test of his faith (*Genesis*, 21: 1–19). This highly resolved drawing is usually considered to be a preparatory study for Baciccio's painting (*c*.1685–95) in the High Museum of Art, Atlanta (fig.16), although it differs from that composition in numerous and significant respects.[1] A second compositional drawing of this subject, in a Private Collection, is more loosely handled and exploratory than the Edinburgh sheet (fig.17).[2] It includes the figure of God the Father surrounded by angels at the top, but in some other respects, notably the pose of Isaac, it is closer than the Edinburgh drawing to the Atlanta painting. It would not be exceptional, however, for Baciccio to have made several quite different studies for a composition before settling on a preferred option, and it is likely that a third preparatory drawing, corresponding much more closely to the painting in Atlanta, once existed. The artist would have followed this lost drawing when making more detailed studies of individual figures, one of which, a very precise squared study for Abraham, survives in the Kunstmuseum, Düsseldorf.[3]

A painted *Sacrifice of Abraham* by Baciccio is recorded (along with a *Sacrifice of Noah*, a *Lot and his Daughters*, and an *Adoration of the Golden Calf*) as part of a series of four Old Testament scenes in the post-mortem inventory (1761) of the artist's son Giulio Gaulli.[4] While this may well be the picture now in Atlanta, which is still paired with a *Sacrifice of Noah*, the possibility remains that it was differently composed, and corresponded more closely to one or other of the surviving compositional drawings. It may be noted that in a subsequent inventory, that of Giulio Gaulli's wife Marianna Tufenni (1776), a *Sacrifice of Abraham* is paired not with the *Sacrifice of Noah*, but with the '*Sacrifice of Lot*', although this could have been a simple error on the part of the compiler (Lot's drunken liaison with his daughter's would not usually be described as a sacrifice).[5] Unlike the earlier one, the latter inventory supplies dimensions, which correspond well with the two pictures in Atlanta.

From a stylistic point of view, the handling of the draperies in this drawing – with their long parallel ridges separated by deep troughs, and their arrangement into agitated masses which defy the laws of gravity – owes a particular debt to the late sculptures of Bernini.

A W L

PROVENANCE

Thomas Coke, 1st Earl of Leicester (with his mount); 5by descent at Holkham Hall, Norfolk; sale, Christie's, London, *Old Master Drawings from Holkham*, 2 July 1991, no.57; purchased under the terms of the export deferral system with the aid of the National Art Collections Fund and the National Heritage Memorial Fund 1992.

EXHIBITED

Old Master Drawings from Holkham, Thos. Agnew and Sons Ltd, London, 1977, no.66; *Eighteen Old Master Drawings from the Collection at Holkham Hall, Norfolk, Acquired by a Consortium of British Museums and Galleries*, London / Birmingham / Oxford / Liverpool / Edinburgh / Cambridge, 1992–3, no.2; Edinburgh / London 1994, no.29; *Effigies and Ecstasies: Roman Baroque Sculpture and Design in the Age of Bernini*, National Gallery of Scotland, Edinburgh, 1998, no.171.

Fig.17 Giovanni Battista Gaulli, called Baciccio,
Study for the Sacrifice of Abraham
Private Collection, London

Carlo Innocenzo Carlone
19. *Two Figures in Adoration*

SCARIA (VAL D'INTELVI) 1686–1775 COMO

Carlo Innocenzo Carlone (or Carloni) was born in Scaria, near Lake Como, into a family which had practised various branches of the arts for generations.[1] His father Giovanni Battista was an architect and sculptor, and his brother Diego Francesco a celebrated stuccoist. One branch of the family had established itself in Styria, Austria, in the mid-seventeenth century, and both Austria and southern Germany were to become important areas of activity for Carlo Innocenzo, although he executed more commissions in his native Italy than did other members of his family. According to his early biographers, Carlone trained from about 1699 with his compatriot Giulio Quaglio, whom he accompanied to Venice, and then on to Udine and Ljubljana. From about 1706–11 he was working in Rome in the studio of the Venetian Francesco Trevisani, and devoted much time to studying the great fresco cycles in the city by Pietro da Cortona, Baciccio, and Andrea Pozzo. Carlone's first securely attributed works are two altarpieces in Kirchberg am Wagram (Austria) and Passau (Germany), which are dated 1712 and 1714 respectively. By 1716 he was executing frescoes in the Belvedere Palace in Vienna, and there followed over the next twenty years a succession of important commissions, both secular and religious, in Austria, Germany, Prague, Breslau and Switzerland. From the mid-1720s the artist began regularly to return to Italy for the winter months. From 1737 he based himself permanently there, securing the following year the extensive commission to decorate the Duomo at Monza, which occupied him periodically until 1745. From the 1740s to the 1760s Carlone executed numerous fresco commissions for churches and palaces in northern Italy, notably in and around Brescia, Bergamo and at Lodi. His last German project, carried out in 1750–52, was for decorations in Schloss Brühl near Cologne. His final commission, for frescoes in the Cathedral at Asti, was undertaken when he was eighty. Both the style and quality of Carlone's work remained relatively consistent, notwithstanding his long career and enormous output. His later works, especially his oil sketches, show an almost expressionist freedom of handling and intensity of colour.

D 4689

Oil paint on paper; varnished. A few small tears (repaired) and minor surface scratches. A significant alteration to the position of the male saint's proper left shoulder and arm was painted out by the artist himself: 32 × 32.6

These vibrant figure studies are entirely typical of Carlone's oil sketches (*bozzetti*), although more often than not he chose canvas rather than paper as a support for such works. An oil sketch of this kind was in all likelihood made in preparation for part of a more fully realised painted or frescoed composition, but the present sketch has not so far been connected with a finished work by Carlone. As a consequence, the identity of the figures represented, who have no distinguishing attributes, is open to question.

Their previous identification as St John the Evangelist and the Virgin Mary at the foot of the cross is rather undermined by the visual evidence.[2] For not only is there no hint of the shaft of the cross, but St John the Evangelist would by tradition usually be dressed in red and green, and would be younger and beardless, while the Virgin would normally wear a blue mantle over a red or pink gown.[3] The pose of the female figure, especially her upper half, does, however, correspond closely to that of the Virgin in Carlone's fresco of the *Crucifixion* in the church of San Filippo in Lodi, which is datable to *c.*1752–6.[4] The male saint's blue and gold would more usually be associated with St Peter or St Joseph. The solution could be that the figures were meant to represent St Joachim and St Anne, the parents of the Virgin Mary, and their intended context may possibly have been an Immaculate Conception.[5] Being a preparatory sketch, we need not necessarily assume that the two figures would have appeared in exactly the same relation to each other in the putative final work (there could have been more space between them, for example).

In these slender, extremely elongated figures, seen from a low viewpoint, anatomical coherence is largely sacrificed in favour of a scintillating display of vibrant brushwork, glorious colour and agitated draperies, which together enhance the emotional, and devotional, intensity of the protagonists. It is this dissolution of the forms, combined with the saccharine palette (including pastel shades of lilac, green, yellow and pink), which distinguishes this sketch from the High Baroque tradition which Carlone would have experienced in Venice and Rome as a young man, and which was ultimately more firmly rooted in nature.

AWL

PROVENANCE
Herbert Horne; Sir Edward Marsh; presented through the National Art Collections Fund 1953.

EXHIBITED
Exhibition of the Herbert Horne Collection of Drawings, Burlington Fine Arts Club, London, 1916, no.8 (as Sebastiano Ricci).

Giovanni Battista Lusieri
20. *A Greek Double Urn*

ROME(?) C.1755–1821 ATHENS

Giovanni Battista ('Titta' or 'Don Tito') Lusieri was active principally as a topographical watercolourist, although some figure and animal studies survive. His earliest watercolours, from 1781, are Roman views, but by the following year he was working in Naples, which remained his main centre of activity until 1799. He was employed at the Bourbon court, became acquainted with a number of British artists working in Naples, notably Thomas Jones, and had several important British patrons, not least Sir William Hamilton, the British Ambassador there. Shortage of commissions led Lusieri to accept the official position of royal painter at Noto in Sicily. He was thus employed when in 1799 he was invited, on Hamilton's recommendation, to join Thomas Bruce, 7th Earl of Elgin, on his embassy to Constantinople. With only minor interruptions, the remaining twenty-one years of Lusieri's life were spent in Athens, where he acted as the Earl's chief excavator and agent, as well as his resident artist. He was closely involved in supervising the removal of the Parthenon marbles and their shipment back to Britain. He completed few watercolours during his years in Greece, and most of his works from this period were tragically lost in 1828 when the ship transporting them to Britain sank. In 1824, however, Lord Elgin had acquired from Lusieri's heirs a mass of unsold watercolours and drawings dating from the artist's Italian years. Lusieri's approach to landscape was remarkably free of the sentimental or romantic overtones characteristic of so many of his contemporaries. He focused instead on a painstakingly accurate transcription of visual appearances, insisting on working outdoors both for the pencil outlines and, exceptionally, for the application of colour. Coupled with his habit of working on an extremely ambitious scale, it is hardly surprising that very few finished watercolours from his hand survive. Many others were left incomplete, either as outline drawings or as partially worked up watercolours with ghostly reserves. The glowing chromatic intensity of his works was achieved through the superimposition of films of pure watercolour over light pencil outlines, without the addition of bodycolour.

Fig.18 Greek, *c*.450–400BC, *Bronze Prize Dinos*
British Museum, London

D 711

Watercolour over pencil; laid down: 26 × 30.2

Only recently has Lusieri's authorship of this striking, almost hyper-realist watercolour been established, and it is published here for the first time.[1] Due to a misleading inscription on the back of the old mount, it was previously attributed to Lady Ruthven, an amateur artist who bequeathed the drawing to the Gallery, along with another of *The South-east Corner of the Parthenon*, now also recognised as Lusieri's work.[2] She and her husband had been in Athens in 1819 and had met Lusieri, who had been resident there since 1800.[3] It is not known how the two Lusieri watercolours came into the possession of Lady Ruthven, since the artist was supposed to work exclusively for Elgin,[4] but it is probably no coincidence that at just that time Lord Elgin was taking steps to terminate Lusieri's contract.[5] The present watercolour is a work of great rarity, one of only three fully finished watercolours to have survived from the artist's twenty years' activity in Greece.[6]

Much of Lusieri's time in Lord Elgin's service was taken up with the removal, packing and transport of the Parthenon (and other) marbles from the Acropolis, and the excavation or purchase of antiquities from elsewhere in Greece. Preserved in the Elgin archives is Lusieri's letter to his patron (in French) dated Athens, 18 May 1804, in which he describes in some detail the discovery of the double urn featured in this watercolour.[7] During an enforced suspension of work on the Acropolis, in the spring of 1804 Lusieri took part of his team to investigate a tumulus in a vineyard just off the Athens to Piraeus road.[8] 'I found', he reported, 'ten feet below the general level, a very simple large white marble vase, seven feet in circumference, two feet three inches high. It contained another vase of bronze, very well worked, of four feet four inches in circumference and one foot two inches high. Inside this were found some burnt bones, on top of which was a branch of myrtle in gold with flowers and buds. The exterior vase, pressed down by the huge weight of the tomb, was broken, which prevented the other from being perfectly preserved. Next to the outer vase there was another of alabaster, absolutely beautiful and much larger than anything I have seen of this kind … '. He then went on to describe the site and the dimensions of the tumulus in more detail. Appended to this letter are outline drawings of

the double urn and the alabaster vase, the former being identical in form to the present drawing, although smaller in scale. The watercolour, too, is likely to date from relatively soon after the excavation of the tomb.

On 4 September 1811 Lusieri reported that the Earl's marbles and vases, including the bronze urn found in the great tumulus, were safely stored in magazines in Malta awaiting shipment, and they arrived in England the following year.[9] Having been stolen and then recovered, the sprig of myrtle remained with Lusieri in Athens and, despite repeated requests, Lord Elgin eventually took possession of it only long after the artist's death.[10] The two urns were part of the original group of 'Elgin Marbles' purchased in 1816 for the British Museum, where they remain.[11] The marble urn was almost certainly made expressly to contain the bronze one,[12] and it was originally accompanied by a broken lid, fragments of which have recently been identified.[13] Lusieri's highly accurate watercolour demonstrates that the bronze urn (fig.18), of a form known as a *dinos* or *lebes*, also once had a lid, now lost, and indicates that the metal has suffered some further deterioration since its excavation. The double urn features prominently in Archibald Archer's 1819 painting of the temporary installation of the Elgin Room at the British Museum, by which time the marble vase had evidently been restored, and a support for the *dinos* placed within it to allow them to be displayed together.[14] The myrtle spray was permanently reunited with the urns when it was purchased by the British Museum from the Elgin Collection in 1960.[15] Sadly, all trace of the large alabaster tear-bottle (*alabastron*) found in the tumulus has been lost.

Not recorded in the early sources is the fact that the rim of the *dinos* bears a *pointillé* inscription in Argive script which translates as 'I am one of the prizes of Argive Hera', indicating that it was awarded as a prize in the games organised in Argos in honour of that goddess.[16] It is generally dated to about 450–400BC, that is some fifty years or so earlier than the gold spray found within it. It may have been inherited by the person to whom the tumulus was raised, or that person may have died in ripe old age having won the *dinos* in his youth and acquired the myrtle in his maturity.[17]

AWL

PROVENANCE
Bequeathed by Mary Hamilton Campbell,
Lady Ruthven, 1885.

Lambert Lombard
21. *St Thomas*

LIÈGE 1505 / 6–1566 LIÈGE

Lambert Lombard was a painter and draughtsman.[1] Strongly influenced by the art of Italy and classical Rome, he was an innovator in the Netherlands in his emulation and adoption of this art in his own work. No paintings can now be attributed to him with certainty but about five hundred drawings and some eighty engravings after his designs have survived.[2] Lombard trained in Antwerp with 'Ursus', who was perhaps Jan or Arnold de Beer ('the Bear'), and then returned to Liège. His art was much influenced by the Italianising work of Jan Gossaert van Mabuse and Jan van Scorel. He is recorded as working for the prince-bishop of Liège, Erard de la Marck, from 1532 and, due to his patronage, then accompanied Cardinal Reginald Pole (1500–1558) to Rome, leaving in August 1537. He must have been impressed by the English Cardinal's retinue, renowned for its devoutness and learned humanist debate. Lombard fulfilled a commission for a (now lost) painting for the Cardinal in Rome and spent his time drawing the artefacts of the city, as well as meeting Francesco Salviati and Baccio Bandinelli. He knew Giorgio Vasari and later supplied information on Netherlandish artists for Vasari's *Vite*. Lombard returned to Liège in 1538 or 1539 and there established the first academy of art in the Netherlands, based on Italian prototypes. Lombard was listed as having 128 pupils in his career, amongst whom were painters, draughtsmen and engravers including Willem Key, Frans Floris, Hubertus Goltzius, Lambert Suavius, Lucas de Heere and Pierre Furnius. An erudite humanist, Lombard believed strongly in the importance of scholarship in the education of the artist and he drew from the model and copied ancient and modern sculpture and painting. Apart from visiting Germany in 1557, Lombard remained in the employ of the prince-bishops in Liège for the rest of his life. Lombard's biography was written by one of his pupils, Domenicus Lampsonius (1532–1598). Imitating Vasari's *Vite* (the first edition of which appeared in 1550), it was the first art-historical commentary to be published in the Netherlands, appearing in 1565, the year prior to Lombard's death.

D 2850

Pen and brown ink; laid down: 20.3 × 10.7
Signed with initials on the blade of the halberd: *LL*
Inscribed along bottom right margin: *drawn wth a Pen.*
Verso: inscribed: *drawing by Lucas van Leyden / from the Ullaston Collection / 6.*

This is a preliminary drawing for number six of the set of thirteen engravings depicting 'Christ and the Apostles', published in two editions by Christoffel Sichem I (1546–1624) and Claes Jansz. Visscher (1587–1652).[3] The Edinburgh sheet relates very closely to another drawing now in the Frits Lugt Collection, Paris, of *Christ and St Thomas the Apostle* (see fig.19).[4] The Lugt drawing, which is slightly looser in execution and style, is signed and dated 1552 and is almost identical in the pose of *St Thomas*. However, the Edinburgh drawing has more fully worked-up details, such as the screws holding the metal plate onto the shaft of the halberd (absent in the Paris drawing). It also has denser, more finished cross-hatching in the folds of the saint's toga and crisper contours of his hair and beard. The engraving of the single figure of *St Thomas* (fig.20), printed in reverse (including Lombard's monogram shown the wrong way round), portrays the halberd details mentioned above, as well as the same tree stump seen in the Edinburgh drawing (which differs from that in the Lugt sheet). For this reason it seems likely that the print was made from the Edinburgh rather than the Lugt drawing and that the Edinburgh work must slightly postdate the Lugt drawing as a final version of the design to be engraved.[5]

Lombard made a number of other studies of similar figures to the Edinburgh drawing, some representing apostles. Interestingly, the date 1552 also appears on some of these, such as that of *Two Men in Conversation* in Dresden[6] (where the man on the left has a similar profile to St Thomas), and the *Standing Man with Right Arm resting on a Tree Stump* in the Rijksprentenkabinet, Amsterdam.[7] The figure in the Amsterdam drawing seems to derive from one found at the left of an earlier composition of *The Raising of Lazarus*, dated 1544 (now in Düsseldorf).[8] Two other related drawings, also both dated 1552, can be found in Brussels[9] and Hamburg.[10] A similar single standing figure holding a spear is in a private collection.[11] There are also several sheets in the Arenberg album (Cabinet des Dessins et Estampes, Liège) which appear to be associated with this series of prints, although it is not

entirely certain if they were executed by Lombard or perhaps one of his pupils.[12]

Lampsonius recorded that his master most admired the art of Michelangelo, Mantegna and Baccio Bandinelli because they followed the example of ancient rather than contemporary art. Similarly, here Lombard chooses to portray his *St Thomas* in classical garb, the inspiration for which may have come from drapery studies made from antique sculpture, for example from figures carved on the famous sarcophagus in San Paolo Fuori le Mura, Rome.[13]

JLW

PROVENANCE
Robert Fullarton Udny (L 2248)[14]; William Findlay Watson; his bequest to the Gallery 1881.

EXHIBITED
Edinburgh 1981, no.19.

Fig.19 Lambert Lombard, *Christ and St Thomas the Apostle*
Frits Lugt Collection, Fondation Custodia, Paris

Fig.20 Lambert Lombard, *St Thomas*
British Museum, London

drawn w. a Pen

Maarten van Heemskerck
22. *Job Tormented by Satan*

HEEMSKERCK 1498–1574 HAARLEM

Heemskerck was one of the most renowned painters in Haarlem. The dissemination of his work, which was strongly permeated by his knowledge of Italian Renaissance art, had considerable influence upon artists in the Netherlands, particularly through his designs for prints, distributed through the flourishing print markets in Haarlem and Antwerp. Born in Heemskerck, a small village near Haarlem from which he took his name, the young artist studied there with the painter Cornelis Willemsz. (fl.1481–?1552) and then with Jan Lucasz. (fl.1515–20) in Delft. From 1527, he spent two years in the Haarlem workshop of Jan van Scorel (1495–1562), who had recently returned from Italy and was then one of the leading painters in the city. Heemskerck presented his *St Luke painting the Virgin* (Frans Halsmuseum, Haarlem) to the painters' Guild of St Luke in Haarlem on 23 May 1532, a leaving gift to his colleagues before following Van Scorel's example in making an artistic pilgrimage to Italy. He made many drawings of classical architecture and monumental sculpture while in Rome and was deeply influenced by the work of contemporary artists such as Raphael, Michelangelo and Giulio Romano. Heemskerck left Rome late in 1536 or early in 1537, returning to Haarlem, when he then painted the wings for an altar of *The Crucifixion* by Van Scorel for the Oude Kerk in Amsterdam (the paintings were destroyed by iconoclasts in 1566). He was commissioned to paint a triptych for the Haarlem guild of clothweavers' chapel in St Bavo in 1546 (of which only the wings survive, Frans Halsmuseum, Haarlem). Heemskerck's inventiveness and involvement in the process of printmaking resulted in about six hundred reproductive engravings, some 188 by Dirck Volkertsz. Coornhert,[1] master of Goltzius. Heemskerck escaped to Amsterdam during the siege of Haarlem, returning to the city in 1573 and providing money to help redeem some of the city treasures plundered by the Spanish. He made his will on 31 May 1572 and died two years later aged 76. He had spent most of his life in Haarlem, where he became dean of the painters' guild and a city father, and was buried there in the Church of St Bavo.[2]

D 1682

Pen and brown ink (with faint traces of black chalk underdrawing); laid down: 19.3 × 24.8
Signed and dated, lower right: *Martinus van Heemskerk / Inventor / 1562*

This is the preliminary drawing, dated 1562, for the fifth of eight engravings for the *History of Job*, the biblical tale in which the devout Job's faith in God persists, despite being challenged to the limit by calamity and affliction. These were published in three different editions probably first by Philips Galle, then Theodoor Galle and finally probably Johannes Galle.[3] The drawing for the first engraving, *Job sacrificing for the Sins of his Children*, dated 1562, is also in the National Gallery of Scotland,[4] while the drawing for the second plate, *The Sons of God present themselves before the Lord*, dated 1561, is in Utrecht's Centraal Museum.[5] The drawings for the third, sixth and eighth plates, *Job receiving the Ill-News of his Misfortunes*, *Job sitting on the Dunghill*, and *Job receiving Gifts*, all dated 1562, are now in the Boijmans Van Beuningen Museum, Rotterdam.[6] A drawing for the fourth plate, *Satan challenging the Lord to remove his Protection from Job*, also dated 1562, is in Princeton,[7] but the drawing for the seventh plate, *The Lord answering Job*, has not been traced.

It was common practice for Heemskerck to make meticulous drawings of designs which were intended to be engraved. Though Van Mander states to the contrary, it is possible that Heemskerck did at first engrave some of his own drawings.[8] Whatever the truth, this would have become increasingly infrequent as he concentrated on the brush and pen, leaving the burin to other specialists. Such drawings were painstakingly executed, made expressly to act as the pattern for the engraver who would be able to follow each line.[9] Nonetheless, Job has an extra finger on his left hand and perhaps a sixth right toe, faults smoothly rectified in the published print. Engraved by Philips Galle, the print shows the design in reverse, with four Latin verses by Hadrianus Junius. Heemskerck's signature and the date do not appear on the engraving, only the monogram 'MH'. The Edinburgh drawing appears to be very lightly incised, perhaps to avoid damaging the sheet. This was important since the meticulous nature of the drawings meant that they, as well as the prints after them, were always considered eminently collectable, attested to by the fact that many more than a hundred such drawings by Heemskerck survive.

Heemskerck here illustrates verses 7–10 in the second chapter of The Book of Job: 'So Satan went forth from the presence of the Lord, and afflicted Job with loathsome sores from the sole of his foot to the crown of his head. And he took a potsherd with which to scrape himself, and sat amongst the ashes. Then his wife said to him,"Do you still hold fast your integrity? Curse God and die." But he said to her, "You speak as one of the foolish women would speak. Shall we receive good at the hand of God, and shall we not receive evil?". In all this Job did not sin with his lips.'

The drawing shows Satan and Job on the left with Job's wife berating him on the right, as Satan flies away. It is unclear what implement Satan carries to assist his task – it is perhaps a type of medical strigil for scarifying the sores, a torture perhaps inspired by the biblical 'potsherd' scraper. (Heemskerck had already illustrated *Satan Smiting Job with Boils* in a drawing dated 1548,[10] engraved by Coornhert, which shows Satan beating Job with a bunch of twigs instead.) Heemskerck also emphasised the composition of the dunghill: a pile of pelts and discarded bits of animal, namely haunch, hooves, horns and head which resemble the jettisoned remnants of Job's sacrificial slaughter in Plate 1. The three figures in front of the background arch at the right may refer to the arrival of Job's three friends, the 'comforters' who appear in the following verse 11 and the next plate in the series.

Heemskerck's early compositions tended to be drawn in a vertical format, but during the 1550s he began to favour a horizontal layout with smaller figures and the integration of separate narrative scenes. The earlier version of *Satan Smiting Job with Boils* also shows the narrative split into the main incident of Satan and Job and the same secondary scene in the background. Though drawn in the other direction, the figures of Job and his wife in the earlier print are roughly comparable with the Edinburgh drawing. In both, the wife stands with arms outstretched and Job seated at her side.[11] However, the Edinburgh Job bows his head over clenched hands: despite his obvious suffering, he does not reproach his God.

JLW

PROVENANCE
David Laing; his bequest to the Royal Scottish Academy, 1879 (L 2188); transferred to the Gallery 1910.

EXHIBITED
Edinburgh 1961, no.11; Edinburgh / London, 1985–6, unnumbered.

Maerten van Heemskerck
inventor
1562

Stradanus (Jan van der Straet)
23. *The Virgin, St John, Mary Magdalen and two Women at the Foot of the Cross*

BRUGES 1523–1605 FLORENCE

Stradanus spent most of his life in Italy, producing sketches and tapestry cartoons for Florentine manufactories, but he was known in the Netherlands primarily as a designer of prints. Usually called by the Latin version of his name, Stradanus was first trained in Bruges by his father, the little-known painter Jan van der Straet. Following his father's death in 1535, he was apprenticed to Maximilien Franck (1490–1547) and then trained for about three years in Antwerp with the famous still-life artist Pieter Aertsen (1507 / 8–75). He became a guild master in Antwerp in 1545 but left the city shortly afterwards to travel to Italy. On his way, he worked briefly in Lyon for Corneille de Lyon and then spent six months in Venice before arriving in Florence.[1] There, he worked for the *Arazzeria Medicea*, producing tapestry designs for Cosimo I de' Medici. He appears to have worked with Daniele da Volterra and assisted Francesco Salviati in Rome for some three years, perhaps from 1550, although the visit may have taken place later.[2] In Florence, from about 1557, he produced decorative schemes for Giorgio Vasari for tapestry and fresco at the Palazzo Vecchio and painted several altarpieces for churches in Florence. He left Vasari in 1571 to set up on his own and his style became less strongly Mannerist and more uniform in handling, remaining substantially unaltered for the rest of his life. Stradanus was an officer of the *Accademia del Disegno* in 1563, 1586 and 1591. He went to Naples in 1576, apparently working for John of Austria whom he accompanied to Flanders, remaining there until John's death in 1578. He then worked in Naples and elsewhere in Italy, but lived mainly in Florence, assisted by his son Scipione (*fl.* until 1612). According to Baldinucci, it was not until Stradanus returned to Florence that he began to send back some of his designs to be engraved in Antwerp, then one of the main centres of publishing.[3] Two series of drawings for *Hunting Scenes* were engraved by Philips Galle there and published first separately, then together as a set of 104 plates in about 1596. It was through such engravings that Stradanus's work became known and influential in the Netherlands. He died in Florence and was buried in a tomb in ss. Annunziata, in the chapel of the *Compania di Santa Barbara*, the group of Netherlandish and German artists to which both Stradanus and his son belonged.

D 1072

Pen and brown ink with traces of white bodycolour on paper; laid down: 18.2 × 26.3
Signed in ink, lower centre: *Stradano.*
Verso inscribed in ink (in John Barnard's hand): *JB No 899 / 10¼ × 7 / John Stradanus was born at Bruges in the year 1536. He went early / to Italy & studied under Dan de Volterra & Salviati. he resided at / Florence where he died anno 1604. There are many fine performances / of his at Florence.*
Also inscribed in pencil: £1–1–

Stradanus had painted a *Crucifixion*, signed and dated 1569, for the Capella della Crocifissione of ss. Annunziata in Florence, called a 'large, prominent piece' by Karel van Mander.[4] Flanked by two frescoes also ascribed to Stradanus, the *Crucifixion* (still *in situ*) was engraved by Philips Galle in 1574.[5] Van Mander also mentioned an engraved series of 'two different *Passions*'.[6]

The Edinburgh sheet is a study for the preliminary drawing for plate no.33 of '*Passio, Mors et Resurrectio Dn. Nostri Jesu Christi*', the first of these 'two different *Passions*' mentioned by Van Mander, which was published by the Antwerp-based Philips Galle (1537–1612).[7] The series contained forty pages, consisting of thirty-seven scenes from the Passion (numbered plates 4–40) a frontispiece, a dedication page and a portrait of Stradanus, engraved by Philips Galle and Adriaen Collaert with Jan Wierix and Crispin de Passe.[8] The dedication was to Cardinal Ferdinando dei Medici ('*Cardinali Amplissimi*'), and it is thought that the undated series must have been published prior to 1587, the date he was made Grand Duke of Tuscany. The preparatory drawings for the plates must have been made by 1584 for Raffaello Borghini knew of '… all the mysteries of the Passion of the Saviour of the World in 40 pieces which will be seen…', when he wrote about Stradanus's designs in his book *Riposo*, published that year by Galle in Antwerp.[9]

The fullest set of drawings for these plates to survive is the group of final preparatory studies at the Uffizi, Florence,[10] while the a study for the portrait of Stradanus set in an allegorical frame is in the Lugt Collection, Paris.[11] The Edinburgh drawing is a variant of the drawing in the Uffizi which was used for the plate of *The Women weeping beneath the Cross*, printed in reverse.[12] (Our study is not for the design of the *Three Crosses* or *Crucifixion*, plate 30, as published in 1985.)[13] The Edinburgh drawing shows the Magdalene in profile at the left of Christ's cross, whereas the Uffizi work heightens the pathos by placing her behind the cross to which she clings, facing us as she looks up to Christ. Stradanus also moves the Virgin closer to the left making the Uffizi group more compact. The white heightening on our sheet appears to highlight certain areas but it has also been used to mask changes in the composition. The original lines can be seen through the white paint and the alterations the artist made can be determined: Christ's head was made smaller, the fingers of Mary Magdalene shortened and the height of the Virgin's headdress reduced. Variant designs for other plates in this *Passion* series have also survived.[14]

The second *Passion* mentioned by Van Mander consisted of twenty pages with nineteen plates and a frontispiece, engraved by Theodoor Galle, Jan Collaert, Crispin de Passe, Jan Wierix with Philips Galle presumably completing the frontispiece. Stradanus probably worked on these designs from about 1585–88, roughly the same period as the larger *Passion* series to which the Edinburgh drawing belongs.[15] Of an upright format rather than horizontal, the second series bore a long dedication to Cardinal Alessandro Medici. Stradanus had executed many commissions of frescoes, tapestries and other designs for this great Florentine family, as well as contributing to the *History of the Medici* (*Mediceae Familiae Rerum Feliciter Gestarum Victoriae Et Triumphi*) published by Philips Galle in 1583.[16]

JLW

PROVENANCE
John Barnard (L 1420). David Laing; his bequest to the Royal Scottish Academy, 1879 (L 2188); transferred to the Gallery 1910.

EXHIBITED
Some Netherlandish Drawings from the National Gallery of Scotland, Edinburgh, Hazlitt, Gooden and Fox, London, 1985–6, (leaflet) unnumbered.

Hendrick Goltzius
24. *Figure Studies*

MÜHLBRACHT 1558–1617 HAARLEM

Goltzius was one of the most talented of the Dutch Mannerists. His father Jan Goltz II was a glass painter in Duisberg by 1562. Goltzius studied first with him and then, by 1576, was training as an engraver with Dirck Volckertsz. Coornhert (1522–1590). The family moved to Haarlem in 1576 or 1577 where Goltzius settled. In 1579 he married the widow of Adriaen Matham, the mother of Jacob (1571–1631), whom Goltzius trained as an engraver. Coornhert (who had earlier moved to Haarlem) was influential in obtaining work for his former pupil from the Haarlem-born publisher Philips Galle in Antwerp, but Goltzius started printing his own works, initially mainly portraits, in 1582.[1] He later had a number of pupils to assist him, amongst whom were Jacques de Gheyn II, Jan Saenredam, Jan Muller and Jacob Matham. Karel van Mander (1548–1606) came to live in Haarlem in 1583 and became friends with Goltzius, showing him drawings by Bartolomeus Spranger (1546–1611) who had known Van Mander in Italy.[2] Goltzius was much impressed and influenced by Spranger's work, later making prints after Spranger's compositions, some of which appear to have made specifically for Goltzius to engrave.[3] Goltzius, Van Mander and Cornelis van Haarlem (1562–1638) were joined in their mutual admiration of Spranger's style, and their close collaboration from the mid-1580s until about 1591 has become known as the 'Haarlem Academy'. This was not a formal academy as such, but the group met to talk and draw from life ('*naer het leven*'), even though much of the work produced consciously eschewed naturalism. Goltzius visited Italy via Hamburg and Munich in 1590–1, travelling to Venice, Bologna, Florence, Rome and Naples. The famous artist went *incognito* to avoid social duties in order to concentrate on improving his knowledge of classical and Italian art. Although granted the equivalent of copyright in 1595 (an imperial privilege protecting each of his designs for six years after first production), Goltzius effectively gave up printmaking in about 1600 to concentrate upon painting. He was a successful and respected artist and citizen in Haarlem. Goltzius died on 1 January 1617 and was buried in Haarlem's *Grotekerk*, the Church of St Bavo.

D 4930

Pen and brown ink (with touches of grey wash in the drapery of central figures): 18.7 × 28.3
Signed and dated, lower centre: with monogram: '*HG*' (interlinked) and '*Ao 1596*'.
Verso: top centre in brown ink (as on recto): '*goode wriendt*' (vriendt?) in a contemporary hand (the artist's?). Top corners cut off diagonally and restored later. The bottom edge appears to be intact, the vertical edges of the sheet are trimmed.

Goltzius was extremely skilled as an engraver but was particularly renowned for his ability to make the lines he drew in ink on paper resemble those engraved with a burin on copper. This highly finished and painstaking technique, with its intricate hatching and swelling lines, became a trademark of his art which he even perfected on canvas, with outstanding 'pen-paintings' such as the Philadelphia Museum of Art's *Sine Cerere et Baccho, friget Venus*, apparently the work once in the collection of Rudolf II and praised by Van Mander.[4]

However, the drawing here employs very little of the complex technique found in such famous 'pen works' and is instead remarkable for its extraordinary fluency and verve of execution. Karel van Mander said of Goltzius, 'I presume no one to be so quick or certain, so able to draw a figure, even an entire scene, freehand, without any preparatory sketch, directly with the pen, with such perfection, and to such utter completion, and with such invention'.[5] Though probably referring to the more highly finished works for which Goltzius is famous, the statement holds equally true for this exceptional drawing, which has been cited as one of the five most important additions to Goltzius's graphic *oeuvre* since 1961.[6] Goltzius himself presumably regarded it as a *virtuoso* piece for he bothered both to sign and date the sketch.[7]

The drawing displays a freedom and vigour of line which is unusual in Goltzius's surviving drawings. Keith Andrews[8] stated that it relates to two studies now in Braunschweig and Besançon, which Reznicek believed may originally have come from a sketchbook, probably datable to the late 1590s.[9] An earlier drawing, dated 1593, of a seated woman, perhaps *Circe* (British Museum, London), and a drawing of another seated woman, dated 1596 (Private Collection, Basel), are also closely related in style.[10] Oddly, one of the closest stylistic links is not to another drawing but to a chiaroscuro woodcut Goltzius made of *John the Baptist* (see fig.21). The looseness of the

cross-hatching and swirling lines are comparable, despite the difference in media.[11] Reznicek suggests that this forceful style was inspired by works from Titian's studio with which Goltzius became acquainted in Italy.[12]

Goltzius has used the two figures at the lower right as an exercise in *chiaroscuro*, with which he experimented in various prints, such as his unfinished plate of *The Adoration of the Shepherds*, published by the artist's stepson, Jacob Matham.[13]

The significance of the striding figures is not clear. Goltzius engraved running women in his plate of *To Each His Own*, where Concord, Charity and Peace are shown in flight.[14] However, they differ greatly in style from this sheet which is, instead, closer in spirit to the work of Raphael's followers, such as Polidoro da Caravaggio, some of whose drawings we know Goltzius brought back from Italy (now in the Teylers Museum, Haarlem).[15]

JLW

PROVENANCE
H. M. Calmann, London; purchased 1958.

Fig.21 Hendrick Goltzius *John the Baptist*
Boijmans Van Beuningen Museum, Rotterdam

Denys Calvaert
25. *The Marriage at Cana*

ANTWERP 1540–1619 BOLOGNA

Calvaert was born in Antwerp but spent most of his professional life as a painter and draughtsman in Italy where the academy he founded in Bologna had a significant influence upon a generation of artists there. His subject-matter was almost entirely religious and ranged from large altarpieces to small highly finished devotional works, often on copper. He was inscribed in 1556–7 as a pupil of the landscape artist Christiaan van den Queeckborne (also called Kerstiaen van Queboorn, 1515–1578). Calvaert travelled to Italy *c.*1560, settling in Bologna under the patronage of the important Bolognini family. He worked first in the studio of Prospero Fontana (1512–1597) and then with Lorenzo Sabbatini (*c.*1530–1576). When the latter was summoned to Rome by Pope Gregory XIII in 1572, to join the many artists working with Giorgio Vasari on the decorations of the Sala Regia in the Vatican, Calvaert accompanied him and stayed in the city for a couple of years. He made various copies after famous works of art there, which were of sufficient quality for others to sell on as originals. This was only discovered by Calvaert on visiting the collection of Cardinal d'Este, where he identified drawings of two figures from Raphael's *School of Athens* and a nude from Michelangelo's *Last Judgement* as being by himself.[1] He returned to Bologna in 1575, where he established an academy of about ten pupils amongst whom were Guido Reni (1575–1642), Francesco Albani (1578–1660) and Domenichino (1581–1641).[2] This form of academy was to influence the rival *Accademia degli Incamminati* set up by the Carracci in Bologna around 1580 (and to which Reni, Domenichino and Albani later transferred). Figures in Calvaert's early work showed the influence of the Antwerp masters Maerten de Vos and Michiel Coxie but this was partially altered by his contact with Italian painting, firstly with Michelangelo, Sebastiano del Piombo, Raphael and Parmigianino but latterly, after his return to Bologna, with the art of Correggio and Barocci. His panoramic landscape backgrounds remained Flemish in character while his religious figures reflected a Correggesque *chiaroscuro* and classicism which was to typify Bolognese and Emilian painting of the period.

D 5122

Red chalk, red wash, heightened with white; laid down, (with top left hand corner damaged): 26 × 20.2
Signed and dated (on vertical surface of step, lower centre): *Dioniso Calva*[aert] *Fia*[mmingo] *1598*. Faint traces of black underdrawing (for example at the left edge of fireplace) and of squaring-up in red chalk (horizontally through Christ's knee and across centre of drawing, vertically through both pillars and diagonally from top right to edge of pillar).
Verso: Four slight figure studies in black chalk.[3]
Inscribed *679 | Dio Calvart | 290*

There are three known signed and dated versions drawn by Calvaert of this composition of *The Marriage at Cana* (*St John*, II).[4] The first is in red chalk (with touches of Chinese white) and is dated 1591 (British Museum, London, fig.22).[5] It was engraved in reverse in 1592 by Philippe Thomassin.[6]

The second version is the Edinburgh sheet, which is very close in size and composition but is dated 1598. The earlier sheet has twenty-seven figures whereas the Edinburgh composition has only twenty-six, omitting the head between two figures on the extreme left. (Interestingly, the residual shape of the hat of this 'lost' head is exactly filled in the Edinburgh sheet by what now becomes part of the folds of the sleeve of the turbaned man seated above.) The landscape backgrounds are different in the two drawings: the space between the two pillars at the left of the British Museum sheet is closed off by a wall, but in the Edinburgh version the space is left open, with a view across to a round tower. The Edinburgh drawing shows the curtain decorated with tassels and one less bottle in the wine cooler, while the background behind the four musicians up in the gallery is closed off and the archway beneath it almost invisible.

The third drawing is also dated 1598 (Private Collection, fig.23).[7] It is in black chalk and much larger, with four more figures, and is more elaborate in composition and execution, using many fine parallel shading lines. An extra pillar and a mezzanine to the kitchen have been added, the arch re-opened and a basket of fruit placed in the foreground. It is not clear why Calvaert re-visited his 1591 design twice in 1598. Interestingly, both the 1598 drawings are very faintly squared up and both have traces of diagonal lines, perhaps as a guide for an engraver (although no print is known of these two versions). However, despite the squaring, Calvaert probably regarded the drawings as 'finished' in their own right since he signed and dated them, and they do not seem to be studies for paintings. It is possible the two 1598 sheets represent close alternatives for a now unknown commission. In any case, such variants are not infrequent in Calvaert's work.[8]

Timothy Clifford has pointed out that Calvaert was strongly influenced in the composition of *The Marriage at Cana* by Taddeo Zuccaro's *Last Supper*, *c.*1556, frescoed on the vault of the Mattei chapel, Santa Maria della Consolazione, Rome. Calvaert's fantastical architecture and the pose of the bending man in the foreground relate closely to this work which Calvaert could have seen during his visit to Rome in the early 1570s.[9]

A drawing after the Edinburgh version (with the same landscape view, but inferior in execution), is intriguingly signed and dated '*hans brugel 1605*', in the same place where Calvaert's signature appears in our drawing.[10]

JLW

PROVENANCE
Purchased from Yvonne Tan Bunzl, London 1984.

EXHIBITED
Edinburgh / London 1985–6, unnumbered; Edinburgh 1993, no.10: Edinburgh / London 1994, no.41, repr. in colour, p.12.

left Fig.22 Denys Calvaert, *Marriage at Cana*
British Museum, London

right Fig.23 Denys Calvaert, *Marriage at Cana*
Private Collection

Sir Peter Paul Rubens
26. Calvary

SIEGEN 1577–1640 ANTWERP

Rubens was the most productive and influential artist of the Northern Baroque. He was born in Siegen in Germany, the son of a Calvinist lawyer and magistrate who had fled his native Antwerp in 1568, the year after the Duke of Alva's army was sent to enforce Catholic supremacy in the city. The family moved to Cologne in Rubens's first year and they remained there until his father's death in 1587, following which they returned to Antwerp. There Rubens converted to Catholicism and went to Latin school where he acquired an excellent knowledge of the classics. A period then spent as a page for the Comtesse de Ligne presumably refined his Latin, Dutch, French and Italian and his courtly manners. Rubens became a master of the painters' guild in 1598, having trained with Tobias Verhaecht (1561–1631) in 1591, Adam van Noort (1562–1641) in 1592 and Otto van Veen (1556–1629) from 1596–1600. He went to Italy in 1600, working in Mantua for Duke Vincenzo Gonzaga. Rubens visited Venice and Rome and was sent to Spain in 1603–4 as Gonzaga's envoy to Philip III. After some months in Genoa in 1606, he went to Rome but returned to Antwerp in 1608 due to the illness of his mother. In 1609 Rubens was appointed as non-resident court painter to the Archdukes Albert and Isabella (and then to Cardinal-Infante Ferdinand). Apart from working for the Archdukes and, from 1620, for the Antwerp Jesuit church, Rubens gained commissions from the French, Spanish and English monarchies. His output was prodigious: paintings, drawings, cartoons for tapestry, decorative schemes, designs for books and prints and architectural plans for his own house. Rubens's studio in Antwerp was run virtually on an industrial scale, facilitated by the employment of numerous assistants and pupils, including Van Dyck and Jordaens. He visited Paris three times in the first half of the 1620s in connection with the commission of the series for the Palais du Luxembourg depicting the *History of Marie de Médicis* (now in the Louvre, Paris) and was employed on a number of diplomatic missions, notably to Madrid and England between 1628–30. Rubens was married twice, and happily, to the patrician Isabella Brant in 1609, and then to her kinswoman, Helena Fourment in 1630, four years after Isabella's death. Knighted by the crowns of England and Spain, he spent less time in the studio after 1635, staying at his estate of Het Steen which inspired his finest landscapes.

D 5134

Pen and brown ink with thin brushwork and wash in blue ink over faint black chalk underdrawing (cut on the two vertical sides and probably all round):
25.4 × 24.9

This drawing was published as an early Rubens in 1985.[1] The watermark reveals that the paper was made in 1598, before Rubens's departure for Italy in 1600.[2] Keith Andrews believed that the handling was that of the young Rubens, and that any awkward passages (such as the perspective or the *pentimento* of the 'phantom' extra leg of the central horse) were explicable by the fact that the young artist was assembling his own composition by using elements from others' designs.

Copying was certainly not unusual for Rubens at this period. In his *Teutsche Akademie* of 1675, Joachim von Sandrart recalled a converstion with Rubens held on a boat from Utrecht to Amsterdam, presumably on Rubens's visit to Holland in 1627.[3] Rubens admitted how, in his earliest youth and apprenticeship years, he had drawn copies from the work of early German masters, particularly Tobias Stimmer's *Neue kunstliche Figuren biblischer Historien* (published in Basle, 1576)[4] and also Holbein's *Dance of Death* series. Rubens's drawings after Holbein[5] tend to copy whole parts of the composition faithfully, but in his drawings after Stimmer's woodcuts he takes different figures or groups out of context from the original prints and re-assembles them on the page seemingly at random, perhaps selecting them by type, such as 'bystanders' or 'costume studies'. It is likely that Rubens intended to assemble a model book of different poses, expressions and studies for incorporation into future compositions.[6]

Calvary is certainly a jigsaw of borrowings. The position of the crosses appears to have been inspired by Goltzius's print of *The Three Crosses* from his *Passion* series.[7] The horse at the right of the drawing and the two horsemen by the foot of Christ's cross are taken directly from an engraving of the *The Withdrawal of the Swiss* designed by Stradanus for a history of the Medici family (fig.24).[8] That print was also copied by Goltzius.[9] Very faint squaring can be seen on the Edinburgh drawing at the left foreground (for example, vertically through the back of the crouching figure). This was presumably employed to help copy this section of the composition onto the sheet, although no precise source for these foreground figures has been found.

Scholarly opinion remains divided on this drawing. One reservation is that, while Rubens certainly did copy different groups chosen from an artist's work (such as studies made after Stimmer's prints, mentioned above, or adaptations after Elsheimer),[10] this drawing is pieced together from widely-varying sources, apparently unique in Rubens's *oeuvre*. Andrews believed that only an artist of Rubens's breadth of invention would have been able to combine such eclectic elements from various prints of unrelated subject-matter. However, the whole composition is somehow less than the sum of its parts. This is, indeed, forgivable in a young artist and Andrews's logical argument over the drawing's composition generally fits with the pattern of Rubens's working practices as we know them at that period. Nonetheless it remains an intriguing and problematic sheet.

JLW

PROVENANCE
Inherited by Anabel Beatrice Squire Sprigge,[11] first cousin of Giles Robertson to whom given; presented to the Gallery by Giles Robertson in recognition of the Keepership of Keith Andrews 1985.

EXHIBITED
Edinburgh / London, 1985–6, unnumbered; Edinburgh / London 1994, no.47.

Fig.24 Stradanus (Jan van der Straet), *The Withdrawal of the Swiss*, plate 7 from *Mediceae Familiae Rerum Feliciter Gestarum Victoriae et Triumphi …* British Museum, London

Roelant Savery
27. Street with Houses in Prague

Roelant Savery (also Roelandt, Roeland, Saverij) painted landcapes, flower pictures and animal pieces. His landscapes in particular, known through the many prints made after them, had a significant influence on the development of the genre in the Netherlands. Roelant's family, which was Mennonite, left Spanish-dominated Flanders to settle in Haarlem in about 1585. His elder brother, the painter Jacob (or Jacques, 1565–1603), is listed as a member of the painters' guild there in 1587 but moved to Amsterdam on his marriage in 1591. Karel van Mander, who was acquainted with Roelant, stated that Jacob trained the young Roelant, who was certainly living with Jacob's family in Amsterdam when the two brothers made their wills in 1602. Following his brother's death from plague the next year, Roelant moved to Prague. There he was appointed court artist of the Emperor Rudolf II by 1604, a position he retained after Rudolf's death in 1612, working for his successor, the Emperor Mathias. Savery spent nearly ten years in central Europe, and it was a period which marked the height of his creativity and output. He returned to Amsterdam in 1613, where he worked for some five years before moving to Utrecht, probably by September 1618, becoming a member of the artists' guild there the following year. He was joined by his nephew Hans Savery II (1589–1654) who seems to have worked with him in Prague, probably as a pupil. Others who were greatly influenced by Savery included Gilles d'Hondecoeter and Allart van Everdingen. Savery declined in mental and physical health in his latter years. Despite the highly marketable nature of his work and the importance of his own art collection,[2] application was made for his bankruptcy in September 1638. He died the following year, destitute and deranged. The trustee of Savery's estate sued one of the heirs for swindling the artist, remarking that 'Apart from his art (in which he excelled), Saverij was a simple man, unassuming in all things and, especially when in drink, could easily be persuaded to sign anything'.[3]

D 1706

Pen and brown ink with coloured washes: 22.8 × 23.7
Verso: inscribed: *No. 9 / M No 8 Rol. Savery / 2+731 (6)*

Rudolf II assembled an extraordinarily talented group of international artists in Prague, amongst whom were Adriaen de Vries, Paulus van Vianen, Hans von Aachen, Hans Hoffman, Bartolomeus Spranger and Jacob Hoefnagel. The Emperor commissioned Savery to make a series of sketches of the Tyrolean Alps to record 'the marvels of nature', c.1606–7. The artist also made many drawings during his travels around Bohemia and Southern Germany. Though known for his powers of invention, Savery developed the practice of minute observation from nature, which was to have a profound influence upon his technique and style long after he left Prague in 1613. He continued to use the designs first drawn in central Europe as the basis for his compositions made many years later, after his return to the Netherlands.

Savery's large signed *Panorama of Prague*[4] provides the key for the identification of the type of buildings seen in this drawing and others like it. In the Edinburgh sheet, the artist eschews drawing grand Prague palaces and draws instead the hills beset with picturesque ramshackle houses, so foreign to the flat landscape of the Northern Netherlands and its architecture. The Gallery owns two other views of houses in Prague[5] which were also probably made shortly after Savery's arrival in the city, c.1603–5.[6] In both this drawing and *Cottages by a Manor House* (D 1707, fig.25), the fortified walls of Prague are shown on the hill in the background, seen from the southern edges of the city. The little bushes suspended from poles projecting from the roofs seen in both drawings are thought to be signs announcing the pressing of the year's new wine.

The two Edinburgh drawings show what is roughly the same view from a slightly different position. Savery would have been made this drawing from further down the road to the right, keeping the Manor House wall, seen in D 1707, at his back. This would enable the artist to see between the inn and the gable end of the next house, drawing the houses at the left of the woodpile (invisible in D 1707). There are nonetheless discrepancies between the portrayal of the inn on the left in each drawing but, whatever the differences, Savery obviously favoured experimenting with this sort of oblique view, probably manipulating what he saw in order to achieve his

artistic purpose. The pen drawing is extremely detailed with soft atmospheric colour washes, a technique which owes something to that of his brother Jacob and much to work of Paulus van Vianen. Other drawings of Prague can be found in the National Gallery, Prague, the Kupferstichkabinett, Berlin, the Museum der bildenden Künste, Leipzig, and the National Gallery of Canada, Ottawa.[7]

JLW

PROVENANCE
David Laing; his bequest to the Royal Scottish Academy, 1879 (L 2188); transferred to the Gallery 1910.

EXHIBITED
Old Master Drawings, Royal Academy, London, 1953, no.280; *Flemish Art*, Royal Academy London, 1953–4, no.554; *Roeland Savery*, Museum voor Schone Kunsten, Ghent, 1954, no.139; Colnaghi 1966, no.50; Edinburgh 1976, no.76; Edinburgh / London 1985–6, unnumbered; *Prag um 1600, Kunst und Kultur am Hofe Rudolfs II.*, Essen / Vienna, 1988, no.251, p.384 (no.252 is incorrectly cited as D 1706 – it is actually D 1707); *Rudolph II and Prague. The Court and the City*, Prague, 1997, no.L 240, p.439.

Fig.25 Roelant Savery, *Cottages by a Manor House* (D 1707)
National Gallery of Scotland, Edinburgh

Sir Peter Paul Rubens

28. *Copy of the Figure of 'Prudence' after Raphael's fresco of 'The Virtues' in the Stanza della Segnatura, Vatican, Rome*

For biography, see cat.no.26.

D 1787

Red chalk and thin brushwork (sheet composed of two pieces with 'L' shaped strip of 2.5 × 1.8cm added along left and lower margins, the whole previously laid solid on an old paper support, irregular cut edges): 18 × 21.2 Some use of bodycolour at the feet of *Prudence* and some yellowed heightening in drapery. Faintly inscribed lower right: 29

This drawing, re-worked by Rubens,[1] is a copy by an unknown artist after Raphael's central figure of *Prudentia* (Prudence) in the lunette on the window wall to the right of *The School of Athens* in the Stanza della Segnatura in the Vatican, Rome (see fig.26).[2] Raphael probably started work on the room in 1508 and this wall, the last to be painted, was completed in 1511. Signifying wise conduct, Prudence is shown with two heads, one of which is looking into a mirror. The mirror implies that the wise are able to see themselves as they really are, while the Janus-like head with its two faces indicates circumspection and the ability to see something fairly 'from both sides'.

The drawing differs in some respects from the fresco. In the copy, the artist has changed the articulation of the figure's arm, twisting the elbow so the hand rests on the knuckles instead of the palm. The sandal painted by Raphael on Prudence's right foot is omitted in the copy, which also shows more of the putto's foot. The position of the mirror is also higher in the copy, projecting beyond the putto's fingers. Presumably because of such discrepancies, Keith Andrews suggested that the copy was unlikely to

have been made directly from the fresco but, rather, from a print.[3] However, the prints so far traced which depict this design postdate this drawing.[4]

Amidst Rubens's *oeuvre* there are a great number of such copies after earlier masters, many with similar additional strips attached. It was always assumed that these copies were entirely by Rubens himself, but this failed to explain why Rubens needed to add extra strips of paper to the compositions. It is now thought that Rubens made use of copies, often contemporary ones, which he partly redrew, sometimes adding pieces of paper over those parts he wished to alter.[5] The first author of this particular red chalk drawing was probably a mid- to late-sixteenth-century Italian artist, as yet unidentified.[6]

Rubens altered drawings made by other artists throughout his career and clearly had no compunction about doing so. He corrected proof prints others made of his compositions or improved upon designs of his pupils or assistants: alterations which had a clear purpose in enabling Rubens some degree of control over the quality of the output of his studio. However, the drawing which Rubens 'corrected' here was nothing to do with protection of his 'brand' name. This type of work presents a special problem of categorisation as well as intriguing questions of intention and technique.[7] Sometimes, as in *The Israelites Wrestling with Giant Snakes* (British Museum, London), Rubens's re-working of another's copy was so extensive that it effectively became a new work in its own right.[8]

Here the changes are less dramatic but the deft

fluency of Rubens's hand is clearly evident in certain lines, re-defining contours and strengthening shadows. The most obvious alteration is that of the female profile of Prudence. Her features have been refined, the nose made neater and the brow less pronounced. Rubens added one dark double curved line which accentuates the curve of her chin and the fold of flesh into her neck. Touches of the brush accentuate the male face and deepen the relief of the drapery, while the curves of the cherub's back muscles were redrawn and also his bottom, which now bulges out onto the added strip of paper. All of Rubens's alterations here are about emphasis and articulation. Slight though they are, these small accentuations offer a fascinating insight into what Rubens considered crucial to the success of the composition in his, rather than Raphael's, terms, making the drawing his own.

This sheet once belonged to Prosper Henry Lankrink (c.1628–1692), an Antwerp artist, who assisted Peter Lely in London from the 1660s. Lankrink owned other drawings by Rubens[9] as well as Anthony van Dyck's Antwerp and Italian sketchbooks. His collection was sold in three auctions held in 1692 and 1693.[10]

JLW

PROVENANCE

Prosper Henry Lankrink (L 2090); David Laing; his bequest to the Royal Scottish Academy, 1879; transferred to the Gallery 1910.

EXHIBITED

Edinburgh 1961, no.29; Edinburgh / London 1985–6, unnumbered.

Fig.26 Raphael, *Prudence* (detail) from *The Virtues* Stanza della Segnatura, Vatican, Rome

Cornelis Cornelisz. van Haarlem
29. *Nude Figure Studies*

HAARLEM 1562–1638 HAARLEM

Cornelis Cornelisz., son of Cornelis Thomasz., was born into a moneyed Haarlem family. During the siege of the city and the Spanish occupation 1572–77, his parents left Haarlem, entrusting their house and the training of their son to the artist Pieter Pietersz. (1540 / 1–1603). Cornelis set sail for France in 1579 but, because of an outbreak of plague, turned back at Rouen and returned via Antwerp, spending a year there as a pupil of Gillis Congnet (1538–1599). In 1580 or 1581, he settled in Haarlem and ran a studio in the city where he was one of the leading exponents of the elegant Northern Mannerist style. He collaborated with the artists Goltzius and Karel van Mander from about 1583–1591 and the work that they produced during this period was enormously influential on Haarlem artists and further afield. Works like the *Titanomachia* (Statens Museum, Copenhagen),[1] painted in about 1588, are effectively Cornelis's artistic manifesto, consisting of intricate compositions (sometimes designed to shock) and striking use of colour, together with exaggeratedly twisting figures in supple, Spranger-like contrapposto. Cornelis was involved in the important scheme for decorating the Prinsenhof from about 1590–93. His painting of *The Fall of Man* of 1592 (Rijksmuseum, Amsterdam), more restrained and smoothly elegant in figure type, was influential in providing a pattern for the Haarlem ideal for male and female nudes.[2] After about 1600, Cornelis's work became less consciously mannered, both in style and subject-matter, and generally smaller in scale. Cornelis's life was rooted in Haarlem; many of his commissions came from civic establishments and corporations there. He had married a daughter of a burgomaster (inheriting a third of his estate in 1605), was a regent of the Old Men's almshouse from 1613–19 and a member of the Catholic guild of St Jacob from 1626–29. In 1611, five years after the death of his wife, Cornelis and Margriet Pouwelsdr. had an illegitimate daughter Maria, who married the silver-smith Pieter Bagijn. (Their child, Cornelis's grandson, born in 1631 or 32, was Cornelis Bega who also became an artist.) Cornelis died on 11 November 1638 and an itemised inventory of his artistic effects was made on 1 March 1639. Half this estate was left to Margriet Pouwelsdr., the other half to his only child Maria.

D 5338
Oil: 31.8 × 23.7

Despite the red chalk drawings listed as the artist's bequest to his daughter, works on paper by Cornelis van Haarlem are now extremely rare, numbering about fifteen.[3] This is rather surprising since Van Mander noted that Cornelis 'developed his talents greatly by drawing from life extraordinarily often and industriously'.[4] Certainly, the known drawings attest to an artist completely at ease in the medium, but if Cornelis did make study drawings or preliminary sketches, most would appear to have been lost.

Sheets painted in oil on paper by Cornelis are also documented. One oil-sketch, now lost, which was listed amongst 'paintings' as part of Cornelis's estate, was almost certainly a study for the animals in the background of *The Fall of Man*.[5] Painted studies of 'two naked figures on paper' and 'some sketches on oiled paper' were also mentioned as remaining in the artist's studio and probably resembled the Edinburgh sheet.[6]

It has been suggested that this drawing may also have been a study for a painting, and the woman in the upper right corner recurs as Venus in a *Venus and Mars* dated 1627.[7] However, one overriding problem with the idea of this being a preliminary study for a picture is that the missing figures are obviously already fully planned (for instance, the artist knows the exact shape of the shadow on the breast of the seated woman [top right], even though the figure who casts it is not yet clear). This implies that the figure groups are culled from completed paintings rather than studies for them. An oil-sketch of three seated figures, now in the Rijksprentenkabinet, Amsterdam,[8] supports this idea. This group was clearly a 'cut and paste' composition, assembled from the right and left sides of the painting of *The Wedding of Peleus and Thetis*, dated 1624.[9]

There are two other known oil-sketches to which the Edinburgh sheet relates: *Two Studies of a seated Woman with her Companion* (ex-Shapiro Collection, then with Colnaghi's, 1997) and *Studies of a reclining Woman and two seated Couples* (ex-Shapiro collection, sold Christie's, Amsterdam, 11 November 1996, no.19, then with Bob Haboldt, Paris). The highly-finished figures are undeniably Cornelis 'types' and all are painted in a manner consistent with the artist's style and handling of the late 1620s–30s.[10]

The verso of the Edinburgh sheet was made after the *Figure Studies*, as the latter composition is

trimmed, while the edges of *Marine View with Shipping* are intact (fig.27). The verso was thought to be by Cornelis van Wieringen (c.1580–1633), a great friend of Cornelis van Haarlem, but the technique is very different. It is more likely that this is a copy after a painting and is perhaps closer stylistically to paintings by Pieter Mulier the Elder (1600 / 10?–1670), though no exact prototype for the composition has yet been traced.[11]

The purpose and thereby the status of these oil studies is difficult to determine. All would appear to date from the late 1620s–30s but it is odd that Cornelis should have begun to make studies after his own paintings at this late date, unless they were perhaps intended to serve as 'pattern-book' examples for assistants to copy. The other possible explanation is that they were painted by one of his pupils as a studio exercise. Perhaps the verso of the Edinburgh sheet was done by a pupil for the same reason. However, the extremely high quality and finish of the figure studies would require an enormously talented student, able to mimic his master's style and technique precisely. No such prodigy is recorded and little is known about the operation of Cornelis's workshop, particularly in his later years. The fact that oil-sketches were listed as part of his studio effects at his death could finally argue for Cornelis' authorship but, whatever the truth, the sheet remains a fascinating and most unusual document of workshop practice.

JLW

PROVENANCE
Purchased from Colnaghi, London 1992.

EXHIBITED
An Exhibition of Old Master Drawings, Colnaghi's, New York and London, 1992, no.21, Edinburgh / London, 1994, no.42.

Fig.27 *Marine View with Shipping*, verso of Cornelis Cornelisz. van Haarlem, *Nude Figure Studies*
National Gallery of Scotland, Edinburgh

Jacob Jordaens
30. *Female Nude, seen from the Back*

ANTWERP 1593–1678 ANTWERP

Jordaens was a painter, draughtsman and designer of tapestries who produced religious, mythological, allegorical, historical and moralising genre scenes. He was born in Antwerp, the eldest of eleven children. His father was a cloth merchant and sold wall hangings, then mainly produced in Mechelen, which were painted to resemble more expensive tapestries and fashionable 'Spanish leather'. In 1607 Jacob became a pupil of the Protestant painter Adam van Noort (1562–1641), to whom Rubens had earlier been apprenticed in 1592. Jordaens was enrolled in the Antwerp Guild of St Luke as a *waterschilder* (watercolour painter) in 1615 and his first works were almost certainly watercolours on canvas, like the merchandise in which his father dealt, as well as designs for tapestries. Due to their fragility, none of Jordaens 'tapestry' canvases is known to have survived but his earliest known paintings are dated 1616, the year of his marriage to Adam van Noort's daughter. In 1621 he was made dean of the painters' guild and it was either in this year or 1620 that the first of his pupils was inscribed. Many more students followed though none later achieved great fame. Jordaens collaborated with Rubens as an independent assistant and worked on the important commissions for the Triumphal Arch for Philip IV and the decorations for the entry of the Cardinal-Infante Ferdinand into Antwerp following Rubens's designs 1634–5. He was one of the many employed under Rubens's direction to work on the cycle of mythologies for the Torre de la Parada (1635–8). Wealthy through inheritance, Jordaens renovated and improved a large house in Antwerp bought in 1639, which he decorated with series of his own paintings (see below). Never as appealing to aristocratic patrons as Rubens or Van Dyck, Jordaens did gain grander commissions just before and after Rubens's death. He painted works for the Queen's House in Greenwich, London, in 1639 (though the full commission was not completed), thirty-five pictures for Queen Christina of Sweden in 1648, two paintings for the Huis ten Bosch *Oranjezaal* (*in situ*) in 1649 (the year of his visit to Brussels), and work for the Amsterdam Town Hall in 1661. Though he spent many years producing religious works for the Catholics, he rejected his family's faith and became a Protestant in his later years. He joined the Dutch Reformed Church in about 1656, though he continued to paint for Catholic patrons to the end of his life in Antwerp, a city predominantly true to the Roman church.[1]

D 1696

Black, red and white chalks: 25.7 × 20.3
Inscribed in brown ink lower left: *J. Jordaens*
Verso: *Female Nude*, torso with raised right arm, seen from below.[2]

This is a study for one of the twelve signs of the Zodiac (also called *The Twelve Months*) that Jordaens painted in about 1641 for the ceiling of his own house in Antwerp.[3] The painting (fig.28) shows the nymph Adrastea milking the goat Amalthea in order to feed the infant Jupiter, a mythological scene chosen to portray the astrological sign of *Capricorn* (and the month December), which is usually represented by a goat. Jordaens's family sold the house in 1708 and, at its resale in 1764, mention was made that the 'ceiling in the large salon, representing the Twelve Signs of the Zodiac' was not included in the auction, perhaps having already been disposed of in an earlier sale together with other paintings.[4] The twelve paintings reappeared at an auction in 1802 in Paris, when they were bought by the French State to decorate the ceiling of the large gallery (now the Bibliothèque du Sénat) in the east wing of the Palais du Luxembourg in Paris, where they remain today.[5] Jordaens had previously portrayed Adrastea in his sketch for *The Infant Jupiter fed by the Goat Amalthea* (c.1630–5), and it was a subject to which he often returned.[6]

Presumably inspired by Rubens's technique, the use of '*trois crayons*' has been seen as innovative in this drawing, looking forward to the eighteenth century. Indeed, it was only on seeing the drawing when exhibited in Ottawa that the Jordaens scholar, R.-A. d'Hulst, finally revised his opinion that it was an eighteenth-century copy.[7] However, despite its effectiveness aesthetically, on comparing the drawing with the finished painting, it appears that the use of different colours may have been employed for a practical purpose as well. The red chalk lines on the sheet, it will be noted, are mainly by way of corrections to the contour of the figure. Jordaens rounds out the nymph's shoulder, lengthens her elbow and flattens the profile of her face. Where there is a confusion between two or three black lines, as in the curves of her rump or hip, it is the red chalk which determines the final outline.[8] Consequently, it is the red chalk outlines which were followed predominantly in the final painting, and the somewhat prosaic translation of Jordaens's lively lines into paint loses much of the vibrancy of this appealing study. Although it is certainly

true that Jordaens's work was of variable quality, especially in his later years (when his own failing ability and use of a large studio could sometimes produce works characterised by slack design and crude colouring), drawings such as this show the artist at the height of his powers.

JLW

PROVENANCE
David Laing; his bequest to the Royal Scottish Academy, 1879 (L 2188); transferred to the Gallery 1910.

EXHIBITED
Exhibition of Flemish and Belgian Art, 1300–1900, Royal Academy, London, 1927, no.613; *Exhibition of 17th century Art in Europe*, Royal Academy, London, 1938, no.587; *Tekeningen van Jan van Eyck tot Rubens*, Museum Boijmans Van Beuningen, Rotterdam, 1948–9, no.103; *De van Eyck a Rubens*, Bibliothèque Nationale, Paris, 1949, no.139; *Jacob Jordaens*, National Gallery of Canada, Ottawa 1968–9, no.194; Edinburgh 1986, unnumbered; *Jacob Jordaens (1593–1678)*, Koninklijke Museum voor Schone Kunsten, Antwerp, 1993, no.B.47.

Fig.28 Jacob Jordaens, *Capricorn: The Nymph Adrastea milking the Goat Amalthea*
Palais du Luxembourg, Paris

J. Jordaens.

Jacob Jordaens
31. 'As The Old Ones Sing, So The Young Ones Pipe'.

For biography, see cat.no.30.

D 1192

Pen, brown ink and watercolour with bodycolour over black chalk: 26 × 29.6
Verso: inscribed illegibly in black chalk (in a contemporary hand)

Jordaens may have started painting tapestry cartoons based on preliminary designs by other artists from the 1620s (perhaps working on the drawings for Rubens's *Life of Constantine the Great*). He produced his own designs for weaving from the 1630s, such as the series of *The History of Alexander*, *The Life of Odysseus* and *Scenes of Country Life*.[1] However, the first documented commission known for a tapestry series is marked by a contract which Jordaens signed on 22 September 1644 with the Brussels tapestry weavers Frans van Cotthem, Boudewijn van Beveren and Jan Cordys.[2] This confirmed his agreement to provide designs for a series of eight tapestries all depicting *Spreekworden* (proverbs or 'sayings'). This drawing is a preparatory study for the first of that series.

The initial drawings for tapestry cartoons were usually made on paper in watercolour and bodycolour, with preliminary studies in chalk to clarify areas of the composition. Then the design was generally transferred into a more worked-up *modello* (often in oils) which was used for the full-scale cartoon employed by the weavers. Jordaens's *modelli* could be painted on panel, paper or canvas.[3] In the design process for this particular tapestry, Jordaens made the first sketch (the Edinburgh sheet), then a *modello* on canvas (Private Collection, France) and, finally, a full-size cartoon on heavy paper (Christie's, 6–7 April 1773, no.1:2; now lost).[4] The tapestry series of *Proverbs* was woven at least three times, the earliest recorded set being bought in 1647 by the Archduke Leopold William, Governor of the Spanish Netherlands (1646–56), who purchased it from the Brussels weavers who had originally commissioned Jordaens three years earlier. The first tapestry for which our drawing was made is now in Castle Hlubóka in Bohemia, along with the other seven from the series.[5] The tapestry measures 380 × 468cm, with the signature of Boudewijn van Beveren woven into it. As Jordaens made no allowance for the reversal of the composition when woven, all the figures appear left-handed in the tapestry.

The precise subject matter for the *Proverbs* series was to 'be chosen as appropriate by Mr Jordaens for the price of eight guilders per yard'. Here Jordaens decided to illustrate a Netherlandish proverb 'Zo de Ouden Songen, Zo Piepen de Jongen' – 'As the Old Ones Sing, so the Young Ones Pipe', which had been quoted in German by Jacob Cats in his emblem book *Spiegel van den Ouden ende Niewen Tijdt* (Mirror of the Old and the New Ages) published in the Hague in 1632.[6] This admonishes parents to set a good example to their children, for what they do will be copied by their offspring. The proverb was perhaps inspired by Biblical exhortations of the sort found in *Ezekiel* 16:14, 'like mother, like daughter' and coined also by Erasmus.[7] The tradition for such moralising sayings continued to be popular in the Low Countries in the seventeenth century and many people would have been accustomed to imagery whose significance is less familiar to us nowadays. Certain elements in the drawing probably serve as emblems to elucidate the meaning further. The flagon on the table was a symbol of temperance, warning against excess, while the owl (bird of Athena, Greek goddess of Wisdom) is used to ridicule folly, probably cautioning that the children will follow a bad example just as assiduously as a good one.

For this composition, Jordaens elaborated on his own painting of the same subject of 1638 (Museum voor Schone Kunsten, Antwerp, see fig.29).[8] Jordaens made the format squarer and more suitable for a tapestry design. The drawing shows pentimenti to the left of the dog (which he had to redraw, as only the head of the animal appears in the painting). There are a number of horizontal lines right across the sheet (presumably to aid transfer). In addition to moving the cartouche further up the wall, there are faint indications, such as what appear to be extra eyes in the foreheads of both the woman and the baby, that Jordaens was going to place these figures higher up on the sheet. The opaque dark greenish-black pigment painted around the contours of this group may have been intended to mask these alterations.

JLW

PROVENANCE
Benjamin West (L 419); David Laing; his bequest to the Royal Scottish Academy, 1879 (L 2188); transferred to the Gallery 1910.

EXHIBITED
Exhibition of Flemish and Belgian Art, 1300–1900, Royal Academy, London, 1927, no.620; *Le Siècle de Rubens*, Musées Royaux des Beaux Arts, Brussels, 1965, no.334; *Tekeningen van Jacob Jordaens*, Antwerp / Rotterdam, 1966–7, no.75; *Jacob Jordaens*, National Gallery of Canada, Ottawa 1968–9, no.216.

Fig.29 Jacob Jordaens, '*Zo de Ouden Songen, Zo Piepen de Jongen*'
Museum voor Schone Kunsten, Antwerp

Roelant Roghman

32. *Castle Zuidwijk*

AMSTERDAM 1627–1692 AMSTERDAM

A painter, draughtsman and etcher of topographical and imaginary landscapes, Roghman was inspired by diverse sources from which he formed his own identifiable yet eclectic style. Roelant (or Roeland) Roghman was baptised in the Nieuwe Kerk, Amsterdam, on 14 March 1627.[1] He was the son of the engraver Hendrick Lambertsz. Roghman (died after 1647) and Maria Savery. Her father was the artist Jacob Savery (c.1565–1603), brother of the renowned painter and draughtsman Roelant Savery (1576–1639). It is likely that Roelant was named after his great-uncle who was once thought to have acted as his first master. It is certainly true that Roghman's early work shows a thorough knowledge of his great-uncle's work, but the only proper pupil Savery seems to have had was Maria's brother, Hans Savery II (1589–1654). Some of Roghman's pen and ink drawings also display the stylistic influence of Rembrandt, Gerbrand van den Eeckhout and Lambert Doomer. Houbraken stated that Roghman, with Eeckhout, was 'a great friend of Rembrandt van Rijn' (as well as recounting that Roghman had only one eye).[2] However, there are no other documents to support the theory that Roghman, nine years older than Rembrandt, was his pupil, unlike Eeckhout who was certainly in Rembrandt's studio from 1635–1640 / 1.[3] Roghman made a number of drawings and etchings in Amsterdam and in the countryside around, such as his *Treehouses along the Ij near Amsterdam* (Gemeente Archief, Amsterdam) of 1645, one of his first two known dated sheets. His most substantial undertaking was the famous series of 'Castle' drawings (see below), also amongst his earliest known works and made c.1646–7. However, little else produced by Roghman was dated and it is difficult to establish a chronology for his drawings, or his thirty-five or so paintings, by anything other than style or subject. Surprisingly little else is known about Roghman's life, though it is thought that he may have visited Italy perhaps c.1654–58. He is recorded as being in Amsterdam again in 1658. He died unmarried and was buried in Sint Anthonies Kerkhof, Amsterdam on 3 January 1692.

D 1138

Black chalk and grey wash: 30.4 × 46.8
An additional strip of paper of about 7.5cm has been added to the double sheet to the right
Signed, bottom right of centre: *RR*
Verso: inscribed in an old hand: *Suyck of Suydwyk R Rogman fecit* and *Suytweick*

Castle Zuidwijk, or 'Zuyck', is also known by the name of Obdam. The castle is no longer standing but was sited on the east of the road from Leiden to Wassenaer, north-east of The Hague. Roghman visited Leiden and its surroundings in both 1646 and 1647 but Wouter Kloek believes that the size of the paper makes it likely that the Edinburgh drawing was made on the earlier visit in 1646.[4]

This drawing belongs to a famous series of about 250 views of 150 castles, manors and country houses in the provinces of Holland, Utrecht and Gelderland which Roghman made between 1646–7.[5] The drawings, of which 222 are known today,[6] were originally thought to have been mature works (perfectly believable in view of their artistic competence) as Roghman was formerly thought to have been born in 1597 or 1620. However, his correct birth date of 1627 means that he was only aged nineteen or twenty when they were made and may have still been an apprentice. The skill in a work such as this is all the more striking when the youth of the artist is taken into account.

It is not known for what reason such an impressive series might have been commissioned. Though Roghman depicted the buildings with great accuracy and care, the common link between the sites chosen appears to be a shared historical importance rather than architectural beauty. They may have been selected as a conscious record of the past, made in a newly-independent country.[7] Roghman varied his approach in these sheets, some focusing specifically upon the architecture (as in the Edinburgh drawing) and others giving a far broader view which emphasises the landscape setting.

The purpose of the series is likely linked to its unknown patron and there has been much speculation about both. One possible name is Hillebrand Bentes Senior (1591–1652), whose son owned the drawings in 1708. He was kinsman to the publisher Dr Joan Blaeu and it has been suggested that either he or Blaeu might have commissioned the drawings with the intention of making engravings from them. However, no such print series exists. Other names have included Cornelis Bicker van Swieten (1596–1654) and Cornelis Aerssen van Sommelsdijk (1600–1662), while Michiel Plomp has put forward a convincing case for Adriaan Pauw (1585–1653) to be considered.[8] Purchaser and renovator of Heemstede Castle, where he entertained the Winter King, Marie de Médicis and Queen Henrietta Maria, the wealthy Pauw was deeply interested in architecture, as his library lists attest. As well as views of other properties owned by Pauw, there are three Roghman views of Heemstede Castle amongst the drawings. Two differ from any other sheets in the series, one being an imaginary view of Heemstede in medieval times, the other, also of Heemstede Castle, was added to the series after 1649. Finally, a drawing which possibly formed the title sheet is decorated with two peacocks ('*Pauw*' in Dutch).[9]

Roghman continued to be interested in topographical documentation and made further drawings of similar subjects in the 1650s.[10]

JLW

PROVENANCE
Albert (Hillebrand) Bentes;[11] Christian van Hoeck;[12] Anthonie van Hoeck; Jean de Wolf;[13] Cornelis Ploos van Amstel, sale Amsterdam, 3 March 1800 (Album KK); C. S. Roos;[14] David Laing; his bequest to the Royal Scottish Academy, 1879 (L 2188); transferred to the Gallery 1910.

EXHIBITED
Colnaghi 1966, no.56; Edinburgh / London, 1985–6, unnumbered.

Jan Cossiers
33. *Head of a Man*

ANTWERP 1600–1671 ANTWERP

Cossiers was an independent master before working in Rubens's studio in the 1630s. Though influenced by his time there, his art retained its own individuality with cooler colours and a keen sense of *chiaroscuro* probably derived from Northern Caravaggists such as Gerard Seghers and Theodoor Rombouts.[1] Following Rubens's death, Cossiers established himself as one of Antwerp's leading artists in the third quarter of the century. He had originally trained with his father, Anton (fl.1604–c.1646), a tempera painter in Antwerp, before becoming a pupil of Cornelis de Vos. The young artist spent an extended period travelling, leaving for Italy in 1623. He went to Rome via Aix-en-Provence, working with Abraham de Vries (1590–1650 / 62), and apparently collaborated with Hugues Martin on paintings for the Aix Confraternity of Penitents. Cossiers was in Rome in October 1624 and later returned via Aix. There he met a friend of Rubens, the humanist Nicolas-Claude Fabri de Peiresc, who wrote to Rubens in 1626 to recommend Cossiers's employment. Cossiers became a member of the painters' guild in Antwerp in 1628 or 1629 and was made a member of the 'de Violeren' rhetoricians chamber in 1632 or 1633. He married twice, first in 1630 and again in 1640: both marriages brought him considerable wealth. Despite a letter written in 1629 to De Vries by Peiresc stating that Rubens considered taking Cossiers with him on a mission to Spain, this appears not to have happened. However, Cossiers is recorded as assisting Rubens, along with many other colleagues, on the decorations for the Cardinal-Infante Ferdinand's Triumphal Entry into Antwerp in 1635. The number and grand scale of commissions Rubens attracted meant that he had great need of competent artists in his studio to whom to delegate work. Cossiers also painted some of the mythological scenes for Philip IV's hunting lodge, Torre de la Parada, near Madrid, between 1635–8, a period when Rubens's health began to decline. When Rubens died in 1640, the market increased for work produced by his erstwhile assistants. Apart from his work in Antwerp, Cossiers was commissioned to paint pictures for churches in Brabant, most notably a grand series for the Béguinage church in Mechelen. His subject-matter became mainly sacred from about 1650, although his work appears to have been in demand with both religious and secular patrons.

D 1660
Black and red chalk (with touches of white); laid down: 28 × 18.2
Signed top left: *Cossiers*
Verso: inscribed: (in ink) *No 84*; (in pencil) 2 / – / 26

The drawings of Cossiers are relatively rare and in the past were often ascribed to Rubens, reflecting the influence that master had upon Cossiers's technique. This drawing relates in style to certain signed drawings by Cossiers of his children by his second wife, Marie van der Willingen. (Each of these drawings *en trois crayons* was inscribed at the upper right.) A portrait of the sixteen-year-old Jan Frans, the eldest of six sons by this marriage, who later took holy orders, was made in 1658 (Lugt Collection, Paris).[2] *Jacobus* is the name which is inscribed on a drawing of 1658 at the British Museum[3] while *Cornelis* (also drawn in 1658) was in the collection of J. Q. van Regteren Altena.[4] Perhaps the youngest son, Guillaume ('*Guilliellemus*') appears on an undated sheet (probably drawn in 1658 as well) at the Pierpont Morgan Library, New York.[5] It is also known that there was a portrait of another son, '*Gerardus*', but this is now lost.[6] It can also be supposed that, if Cossiers drew five of his sons, he may well have drawn the sixth, but no other study with an identifying inscription at the upper right, as found on the rest, is known. A drawing formerly in the collection of the Earl of Leicester, *The Head of a Young Boy looking to the left*,[7] may relate to the drawing of Cornelis but is more sketchy and rapid in handling.

The drawings of Cossiers's sons provide the basis for the attribution of other drawings such as the Edinburgh sheet.[8] There are obvious stylistic similarities in the use of fine cross-hatching to model the form of the face and the strong parallel shading lines. The positioning of the sitter in the picture field is also similar, though the Edinburgh drawing is made from a slightly lower viewpoint. The signature on our drawing, with the linked '*ss*' of '*Cossiers*' written slightly larger than the following letters, is almost identical to the way the artist signs his name on his sons' portraits.

The Edinburgh sheet displays carefully judged strokes of red to accentuate the man's ear, mouth and eyelid and there appear to be similarly considered touches of white heightening on the left tip (and perhaps the right) of the collar, on the bridge of the nose and at the left of the eye. In contrast, Cossiers uses extraordinarily heavy pressure in the shading between the ear and the collar, so much so that five lines are deeply incised into the paper. Other drawings which are very similar in handling are the ex-Hatvany *Head of a Young Girl with Long Hair* (which also uses a low viewpoint)[9] and the delightful *Head of a Child*.[10] Cossiers combined a directness of observation with exceptionally sensitive portrayal, giving these drawings a freshness and immediacy which makes them amongst his best.

JLW

PROVENANCE
David Laing; his bequest to the Royal Scottish Academy, 1879 (L 2188); transferred to the Gallery 1910.

EXHIBITED
Colnaghi 1966, no.63; Edinburgh / London, 1985–6, unnumbered.

Lambert Doomer
34. *Castle Pirmil outside Nantes*

AMSTERDAM 1624–1700 AMSTERDAM

Doomer was a painter and graphic artist whose work included histories, portraits, genre subjects and landscapes, but it was particularly for his topographical scenes, many made on his extensive travels, that he earned his place as one of the most characteristic and appealing of seventeenth-century Dutch draughtsmen. He was baptised on 11 February 1624, son of Harmen Doomer, an ebony carver, frame and cabinet maker from Anrath near Krefeld, whom Rembrandt had painted in 1640, along with a portrait of Harmen's wife, Baertge Martens. (These portraits, now in the Metropolitan Museum of Art, New York, and the Hermitage, St Petersburg, were both later copied by Doomer.) Lambert trained as a joiner with his father. There is some debate about whether he then worked in Rembrandt's studio *c.*1640–44.[1] His work was influenced by this master to an extent. For example, he based one drawing (Royal Collection, Windsor Castle)[2] on Rembrandt's *Resurrection* (Alte Pinakothek, Munich), painted for the Stadholder Frederick Henry and purchased albums of Rembrandt drawings in 1658.[3] However, Doomer's graphic works are generally not easily confused with those of other artists from the Rembrandt school, and retain their individuality in style as well as technique and subject matter. Doomer left for an extended tour of France 1645–6 (see below). He set out from Nantes in July 1646 with the young artist Willem Schellinks (*c.*1627–1678) on a trip along the Loire. He returned to Amsterdam and made sketching forays around the city as well as trips further afield in the Netherlands to Utrecht, Arnhem, Nijmegen and Enkhuizen, recorded in his surviving drawings. In about 1663, Doomer travelled along the Rhine from Cleves to Mönchengladbach, Cologne, Siebengebirge, Boppard and Bacharach to Bingen, making a number of drawings en route.[4] He married Metje Harmens, a widow from Alkmaar, where Doomer lived from 1669–1695, though he still spent occasional periods in Amsterdam. He lived at the *Mannegasthuis* (old men's almshouse) in Alkmaar from 1673–81 and married his second wife Geesje Esdras in 1679. He returned to Amsterdam in 1695, dying there five years later.

D 1082

Pen and brown ink with watercolour: 23.7 × 41.3
Verso: inscribed in ink (in Ploos van Amstel's hand):
Het Casteel van Pilijemi en de Stad Nantes met de Brugh and
(in a different hand): *10 / -'*

Château de Pirmil is now destroyed but lay just outside the city of Nantes beside the bridge of the same name. 'Pilemi' was the sixth of the seven parishes of Nantes. Doomer travelled extensively in western France and made numerous drawings on his journeys. However, many of these no longer survive and the majority are known to us through replicas Doomer made some twenty years later in about 1665 for Laurens van der Hem,[5] and for other patrons about 1671–3.[6]

It is known that Doomer used an account book in which to make some of his sketches, since at Hendrik de Leth's sale of the former Jeronimus Tonneman collection in Amsterdam on 21 October 1754, three albums with more than ninety autograph replicas by Doomer were offered for auction, all of which were made on pages from account books measuring 9 × 16 *duimen* (23.1 × 41.1cm). A panoramic view of Amsterdam on the same paper has been dated to *c.*1671 (on the basis of the buildings portrayed). The trace of red tallying lines of a similar account book can be seen across the upper half in the Edinburgh sheet, which can also be dated to about 1671 on this evidence.[7] (The Gallery owns another such replica on account paper, a *View of the Walls of Nantes with the Church of St Peter*, D 5051.)

Doomer's brothers, Maerten, a merchant, and Hendrik, a broker, lived in Nantes. It was previously thought that the Edinburgh drawing replicated a lost sketch made at Nantes in 1646 (fig.30). This was the year in which the landscape

draughtsman Willem Schellinks described his arrival at the city on 17 May in his meticulous diary (Royal Library, Copenhagen). He left Nantes with Doomer on 3 July as they set off on their trip along the Loire to Angers, Saumur, Tours, Amboise and Orléans.[8] Apparently, the pair argued at Rouen and Doomer continued alone to Le Havre and Dieppe.[9]

Though the original sketch for the Edinburgh drawing was not known to Wolfgang Schulz,[10] it reappeared at an auction in 1986. It is signed in brown ink on the recto: *Doomer: fecit 1645* and also on the verso: *Doomer.f.Ao 1645* and *Pilijemie op de bruck te Nantes.*[11] Schulz knew that some of the original drawings of Nantes were dated 1645 but still believed that Doomer did not travel to Nantes before 1646 (arriving at the city with Schellinks that year). He argued that the artist must have inscribed the wrong date on such drawings many years later, perhaps when making the replicas.[12] However, it would seem strange for Doomer to misdate his work in this way. It is far more likely that he did indeed travel to France in 1645 and that his brothers in Nantes would have provided a base for his travels. The original for the Edinburgh sheet was presumably made by Doomer sketching alone, before Schellink's arrival in the city, as, presumably, was the drawing for *Road to Vetou near Nantes* (Lugt Collection, Paris), and some of the other sketches Doomer made of Nantes and its surroundings.[13]

JLW

PROVENANCE
Ploos van Amstel; J. D. Nijman; David Laing; his bequest to the Royal Scottish Academy, 1879 (L 2188); transferred to the Gallery 1910.

EXHIBITED
Old Master Drawings, Royal Academy, London, 1953, no.323. Colnaghi 1966, no.64; *A Virtuous and Noble Education*, Scottish National Portrait Gallery, Edinburgh, 1971, no.101.

Fig.30 Lambert Doomer, *Castle Pirmil outside Nantes*
Sotheby's London, 1 December 1986, no.63

Hans Baldung (called Grien)
35. *St Martin and the Beggar*

SCHWÄBISCH-GMÜND, C.1484 / 5
–1545 STRASBOURG

Hans Baldung was a painter, draughtsman, engraver, designer of woodcuts and stained glass. His family were of the professional class in Schwäbisch-Gmünd and two relatives, a lawyer and a doctor, are known to have settled in Strasbourg in the 1490s. This learned, moneyed background was somewhat unusual for an artist at that time. Nonetheless, Baldung probably served his artist's apprenticeship in Strasbourg, where the influence of Martin Schongauer (1435 / 50–1491) still held sway, or perhaps in Swabia. He worked in the studio of Albrecht Dürer (1471–1528) in Nuremburg from 1503 to about 1507. When Dürer went to Venice 1505–7, he left the workshop under Baldung's direction, even taking some of the young artist's woodcuts with him to sell on his journey. Baldung moved to Halle where he painted an altarpiece for the Stadtkirche in 1507, his earliest dated painting of *St Sebastian* (which also shows the artist dressed in green, Germanisches Nationalmuseum, Nuremberg). He was in Strasbourg in 1508, becoming a citizen there in 1509, and about this period he gained commissions from the Markgraf Christoph I of Baden. He married Margarethe Herlin in 1509 or 1510, the daughter of a wealthy Strasbourg merchant. From about 1510 he started to use a monogram HBG, the 'G' indicating his nickname 'Grien'. This may have been given to Baldung while in Dürer's studio, referring either to his youth or his liking for the colour green, or may even come from the word *Grienhans* (devil), possibly in relation to the artist's predilection for demonic subjects in his work.[1] Baldung worked in Freiburg-im-Breisgau (where his brother was a university professor) from 1512–17, painting his important *Coronation of the Virgin* in 1516 for the high altar of the cathedral there, where it still remains. Nearby in Isenheim, Baldung may have seen Grünewald's famous altarpiece of *c*.1515, since his work begins to display more drama and pathos at about this time. Baldung also began to produce innovative woodcuts and worked with Lucas Cranach and Dürer on the 1515 Prayer Book commissioned by the Emperor Maximilian. He returned to Strasbourg in 1517 and became a magistrate of the artists' guild *Zur Stelz* from 1533–45. The subject-matter of his work altered with the Reformation as his clients changed, and, though he continued to depict religious scenes, the number of themes from history, classical literature, mythology and allegory increased.

D 4902
Pen and black ink and grey wash: 17.8 diameter

This drawing was once ascribed to Hans Leu II (*c*.1490–1531), the Swiss painter and draughtsman who seems to have worked in Nuremburg with Dürer and with Hans Baldung, perhaps while he was in Strasbourg and certainly in Freiburg-im-Breisgau *c*.1512–13. However, in his catalogue of the Oppenheimer sale, K. T. Parker suggested that instead of being by Baldung's pupil, the drawing might instead be a work by the master himself. Keith Andrews upheld the attribution to Baldung, seeing the weaknesses in the sheet as evidence of a very early drawing by Baldung, rather than a later work by the less accomplished Leu.[2]

The drawing's characteristic hatching is probably influenced by knowledge of the technique of Martin Schongauer. There is a rather tentative attempt to indicate the three-dimensionality of the figures (unconvincing in the 'pantomime horse' stance of the steed's front legs) and certain difficulty was obviously encountered in placing the figures and other elements of the composition into a perspective within the landscape (for example the rocks appear not as if in the distance, but more as a surrealist equine headdress). The details such as the plants, the horse and the *profil perdu* of the beggar are very characteristic of Baldung's early manner.[3]

Comparisons can be made with some of Baldung's earliest known dated drawings of 1503 such as his *Aristotle and Phyllis* (Louvre, Paris) or *Death and the Landsknecht* (Galleria Estense, Modena).[4] However, the penmanship of the Edinburgh sheet is certainly not as accomplished as that found in the *Virgin on the Crescent Moon* (Private Collection, London),[5] and the likelihood must be that it was drawn by Baldung when slightly less experienced. J. E von Borries[6] noted that the closest sylistic parallel with our drawing is a painting rather than a drawing, namely the cabinet piece *Knight wth a Woman and Death* (Louvre, Paris).[7] Baldung based the Louvre picture on Dürer's woodcut of *St George on Horseback* (Bartsch 111) of 1502 or 1503, which is the date suggested for the Edinburgh sheet.

The very careful and precise draughtsmanship, together with the round format,[8] suggest that the design was probably intended for an engraving or perhaps for a stained glass roundel. Two figures are closely related to a woodcut of the same subject which Baldung made in about 1505–7, while directing Dürer's workshop in the master's absence.[9] It is interesting to note that both the Edinburgh drawing and the woodcut above are variants of a composition which first appeared in an anonymous woodcut found in a 1494 prayer book in Basel which was often used as a model by Nuremberg artists.[10] A figure closely resembling the beggar in the Edinburgh sheet can also be found in a Baldung woodcut for a book in 1512.[11]

J L W

PROVENANCE
A. Grahl (L 1199); Henry Oppenheimer, Christie's, London, 14 July 1936, no.355;[12] anonymous collector, Sotheby's, London, 25 March 1965, no.115;[13] P & D. Colnaghi, from whom purchased 1965.

EXHIBITED
Old Master Drawings, exh. cat., Colnaghi, London, 1965, no.70; Colnaghi 1966, no.6; *The Age of Dürer and Holbein German Drawings 1400–1550*, exh. cat., British Museum, London, 1988, no.88, p.199.

Johann König
36. Angels Escorting Lot and his Family from Sodom

NUREMBERG 1586–1642 NUREMBERG

The son of a Nuremberg goldsmith, König is first documented in Rome between 1610 and 1614, but his acquaintance with the work of Hans Rottenhammer the elder suggests that he had already spent some time in Augsburg before travelling to Italy, and may even have completed his training there. By spring 1609 he was almost certainly in Venice, where he is reported to have made a miniature copy (whereabouts unknown) of Veronese's *Marriage at Cana*, now in the Louvre, Paris. In Rome, it is likely that he came into contact with Adam Elsheimer, who died on 11 December 1610. He certainly had detailed knowledge of Elsheimer's small-scale works on copper, which, like the landscapes of Paul Brill and the early paintings of Carlo Saraceni, had considerable influence on his own, especially where the rendering of atmospheric effects was concerned. By 1614 König was back in Augsburg, where he married and was admitted as a master into the guild of painters. In 1622 he was appointed Dean of the Augsburg painters' guild, and in 1623 was elected to the Greater Council of the city. From around 1620 to 1626 he was involved, with Matthäus Gundelach and Johann Mathias Kager, in the decoration of the ducal chamber and courtroom of Elias Holl's new Rathaus. For this he produced a cycle of allegories of various forms of government; a series of idealised portraits of the Roman generals credited with founding the city of Augsburg; and, in collaboration with Gundelach around 1625, a series of virtues and vices clearly inspired by Cesare Ripa's *Iconologia*. In 1626 he executed a monumental *Last Judgment*, still *in situ*, indebted to Venetian art. His other surviving works for the Rathaus are now in the Schaezlerpalais in Augsburg. Sometime in 1631 or 1632, perhaps due to circumstances connected with the Thirty Years' War, he returned to his native Nuremberg, where he remained until his death. In his lifetime, König was best known for his miniatures on parchment and for his small cabinet paintings with historical and mythological themes adopted from Venetian models and executed in faithful emulation of Elsheimer. He was an important pioneer of the Baroque in Germany.

D 5137
Gouache; laid down on panel: 11.4 × 17.4
Signed, bottom left: *Jo: Konig. fe*
Verso: inscribed in ink: *85*

This is an illustration of *Genesis* 19. It is one of a group of four gouaches with Old Testament subjects, including *The Flood* and *The Rainbow after the Flood*, which seem to have been in an English private collection as early as the eighteenth century. The others were also signed, and annotated in an apparently later hand with references to the biblical scenes they represented.[1] These gouaches may have formed part of a larger cycle depicting well-known Old Testament stories planned or produced by the artist. Old and New Testament themes constituted a significant proportion of König's output.

Opinions vary as to when the present gouache was executed. Gode Krämer considered it a 'very early' work, done when König was still in Rome.[2] Despite its obvious affinities with two other gouaches from König's Roman period – *Christ and the Children* (Nationalgalerie, Berlin) and the dated *Orpheus taming the Animals* (Residenz, Munich) of 1613 – Andrews inclined to the view that it was produced between around 1615 and 1620, after his return to Augsburg.[3] He was supported in this by Klaus Dorsch, who proposed a date of 1615/18.[4]

Elsheimer's influence is paramount throughout the gouache, notably in the luminous treatment of the landscape, the detailed description of the foliage and the sympathetic portrayal of the group of figures in the foreground. The impact of Roman architecture on König is also unmistakable. The building in the background appears to have been modelled on the Aqua Claudia or the Palace of Septimus Severus, and the porch on the right based on that of ss. Luca and Martina,[5] though it also closely resembles Etienne Dupérac's reconstruction of the Baths of Diocletian.[6]

C B

PROVENANCE
William Hallsborough Gallery, London; Kate Ganz Ltd, London; from whom purchased 1985, with the assistance of the National Art Collections Fund (Scottish Fund) and contributions from two private donors, to mark the retirement of Keith Andrews as Keeper of Prints and Drawings (1958–1985).

EXHIBITED
Fine Paintings and Drawings of Four Centuries, William Hallsborough Gallery, London, 1958, no. 27; Edinburgh, 1991, no.72.

Anton Raphael Mengs
37. The Adoration of the Shepherds

AUSSIG, BOHEMIA 1728–1779 ROME

The son of Ismael Mengs, court painter to Augustus III of Saxony, Mengs was named after Correggio and Raphael by parents clearly determined that he should become an equally famous artist. Although he did not quite achieve this illustrious status, he was widely regarded as a 'new Raphael', and in eighteenth-century intellectual circles as the greatest living painter. In portraiture, he was close in style to Pompeo Batoni, his principal rival, and, in his history paintings, one of the most important exponents of early Neoclassicism. In 1741 Mengs was taken to Rome, where he made drawings after Raphael and the antique and developed into something of a prodigy, with a precocious talent as a pastellist. In 1744 he returned to Dresden, and the following year was appointed 'painter to the chamber' at the Saxon court. He returned to Rome in 1746 to devote his energies to history painting, and in 1754 was appointed director of the Roman Academy. The turning point in Mengs's career came in 1755, when he met Johann Joachim Winckelmann, one of the founders of Neoclassicism, who provided the theoretical inspiration for much of his work. His first major commission was the fresco Parnassus (Villa Albani, Rome), executed in 1761 for Winckelmann's patron Cardinal Albani and inspired by paintings recently discovered at Herculaneum. For this, as for most of his more ambitious compositions, Mengs adopted an essentially eclectic approach, judiciously admixing stylistic components from Raphael, Correggio and Titian. Though it is judged less charitably today, Parnassus was hailed at the time as a masterpiece, and was the work on which Mengs's enormous reputation as the leader of the Neoclassical reform in painting was based. From 1761 to 1769 and from 1773 to 1777 Mengs was in Spain as court painter to the Bourbon King Charles III. He executed numerous portraits of the royal family and decorated the palaces in Madrid and Aranjuez with dreary frescos which, only because they represented the shift in taste from the Rococo to Neoclassicism, were then widely preferred to those of his rival, Giambattista Tiepolo. In between his two visits to Spain, Mengs returned to Rome, where he was appointed principe of the Academy of St Luke. From 1772 to 1773 he was in the Vatican, painting murals in the Camera dei Papiri for Pope Clement XIV. He was back in Rome, already in ill health, in 1777, and remained there until his death. Mengs was also a fine critic, with a superlative grasp of western pictorial traditions, and an influential, if mediocre, theoretician.

D 4871

Pen and brown ink and wash over indications in black chalk, heightened with white, on thin laid paper. The composition arched at the top and similarly shaped at the bottom. Drawn within a narrow border representing the rabbet of a frame. Pictorial area: 44.3 × 19.5

Because of its format and distinctively arched frame, this highly finished drawing is thought by Steffi Röttgen to be one of three which were under consideration in 1750–1 as possible subjects for the high altar of the Hofkirche (the catholic court church of the Holy Trinity) in Dresden.[1] However, whereas 'modelli' survive for the other two subjects – The Ascension and Pentecost – none for The Adoration is recorded, which may mean that it was rejected as a suitable theme early in the deliberations. The painting of The Ascension, the subject eventually chosen, was begun in 1752 and completed in Rome in 1761. Having survived the allied air raids of 13 and 14 February 1945, it is again in situ in Gaetano Chiaveri's church, on the high altar reconsecrated in 1962.

The present composition exists in a number of versions. In the Louvre,[2] there is an unfinished drawing in black chalk, reinforced with ink and touches of oil in the lower part, which reveals the design at an earlier stage in its evolution, with the arched top already dimly discernible (L 1955). There are minor variations in the composition of the Louvre drawing, and some of the figures, including Joseph and the shepherds, are differently disposed. The arrangement of the figures in the upper register is very different. The Uffizi has what appears to be an autograph replica of our drawing (Santarelli Collection no.9929), in which Mengs concerned himself more with lighting effects[3] and with the kinds of problem that rendering the subject in oils would entail. A copy of the Edinburgh drawing, reworked by the artist or a studio assistant, is in the Philadelphia Museum (formerly collection of Anthony M. Clark), and a counterproof of the Philadelphia drawing, which was damaged in the process, is at Princeton (inv.52–189). A study for the principal group of figures also survives.[4] In the Uffizi are two other drawings in series with the present Adoration: an Ascension (Santarelli 9928) and a Trinity, Virgin and Saint (Santarelli 9925), both of which are squared for transfer and have the same ornate frame, top and bottom, as the Edinburgh sheet. The Uffizi Ascension differs from the

Hofkirche altarpiece in several important respects, notably in the arrangement and disposition of the protagonists. It may, however, have been used for a painting once in the collection of the Marquesa Viudad de la Cenia in Palma.[5]

The style and composition of The Adoration owe much to Correggio's celebrated treatment of the subject in the picture known since the seventeenth century as La Notte (Gemäldegalerie, Dresden). Correggio's most influential work,[6] it was among the 100 pictures sold by Francesco III d'Este to Augustus III of Saxony between 1745 and 1746,[7] so Mengs had ample opportunity to study it. Evidence of the impact of Correggio's painting on Mengs, and of Bolognese derivatives such as Domenichino's Adoration of the Shepherds (National Gallery of Scotland, Edinburgh), can be found elsewhere in the artist's oeuvre, including the late Adoration of the Shepherds in the Prado of 1771/72.

C B

PROVENANCE
Nicolas Rauch, Geneva sale, 13–15 June 1960, no.259; H. M. Calmann, London, by whom presented 1962.

EXHIBITED
German Art 1400–1800 from Collections in Great Britain, City Art Gallery, Manchester, 1961, no.210.

Henry Fuseli (Johann Heinrich Füssli)
38. *Portrait of Mrs Fuseli*

ZÜRICH 1741–1825 LONDON

Fuseli was one of the most spirited and original artists to work in Britain in the late eighteenth and early nineteenth century. Fuseli's father, Johann Caspar Füssli, was a writer, collector and artist who gave his son a full education in poetry, literature and art, teaching him the Neoclassical theories of J. J. Winckelmann and the artist Anton Raphael Mengs. Despite this artistic and literary background, Fuseli became a Zwinglian minister in 1761. He left Zürich in disgrace for publishing an attack on a magistrate there in 1763 and set off to tour Germany with his friend J. K. Lavater. He arrived in London from Berlin the following year, first earning his living as a writer and translator, concentrating on moral philosophy and literature, but later practising drawing again. With the encourage-ment of Sir Joshua Reynolds, whom he met in 1767 or 1768, he decided to become an artist, setting his ambitious sights on history painting and Rome. He travelled to Italy in spring 1770 via Genoa, Milan and Florence, reaching Rome by May that year. Though he made trips to Venice, Naples, Bologna and elsewhere, he lived mostly in Rome, where he became the centre of a group of artists, including George Romney, James Barry, Thomas Banks, Nicolai Abildgaard and Johan Tobias Sergel, as well as John and Alexander Runciman and John Brown.[1] Italy altered his ideas about art. Abandoning the ideas of noble classicism promulgated by Winckelmann and Mengs, he became enthused with the Mannerist art of Rosso, Bandinelli and Parmigianino but, above all, was inspired by the Sistine figures of Michelangelo. He even changed his Germanic name to the more Italianate 'Fuseli'. He spent some time in Zürich before returning to London in 1778. Fuseli's strongly imaginative pictures were grand in manner, usually depicting scenes from Shakespeare, the Greek tragedies, Homer or Dante. However, he was effectively a self-taught painter and the technique of some of his pictures was at first faulted by critics. Fuseli was elected an Associate of the Royal Academy in 1788. His literary tastes found expression in his contribution to Boydell's *Shakespeare Gallery*, started in 1789, and in the pictures he produced for his own *Milton Gallery*, begun in 1790. These projects engrossed him until about 1800, though neither was a financial success. Despite the fact that his art was considered unorthodox by many contemporar-ies (Reynolds tried to prevent his becoming an Academician in 1790), Fuseli was Professor of Painting at the Royal Academy from 1799–1804 and again in 1810–25, being concurrently Keeper there from 1804 until his death. Most of the latter part of his life was involved in writing, teaching and lecturing.

D 5146

Brush and grey wash over traces of black chalk; laid down: 22 × 15.4
Dated (by the artist) in brown ink, lower centre: 31 *May* 1800

Women played a significant part in both Fuseli's actual and imaginative life. Throughout his career, he portrayed women often and obses-sively, from portraits of his wife and other models in their latest finery, to courtesans and predatory sirens, threatening and compelling.[2] The heroines he chose for his history pictures also share this cruel sexual power: Salome, Delilah, Lucrezia Borgia and Lady Macbeth, painted in a mode of stylistic exaggeration once referred to as 'Sado-Mannerism'.[3] Fuseli's own relationships with women were frequently intense. When he returned from Italy to Zürich in 1778, he flirted with the eccentric coquette and earthquake-diviner, Magdalena Hess (married to J. C. Schweizer), and her consumptive sister Martha, prone to religious excess. He was also thrown into emotional turmoil by his love for the niece of his friend Lavater, Anna Landolt. The rejection of Fuseli as a suitor by Anna's father was one of the factors which led him to return to England in 1779, and it is suggested that his first critically acclaimed painting exhibited in the Royal Academy in 1781, *The Nightmare* (Institute of Arts, Detroit), was a psychological attempt to exorcise the pain which Anna had caused him.[4]

The subject of our drawing is Sophia Rawlins, from Batheaston village near Bath, whom Fuseli married in 1788. An amateur artist's model, she was much younger than her husband and both socially and intellectually his inferior. Contem-porary accounts hint at her vulgarity and spiteful argumentativeness but, nonetheless, the marriage proved to be long-lasting. This perhaps owed something to Sophia's tenacity. In 1789 the artist met Mary Wollstonecraft (whose daughter became the poet Shelley's wife). Mary was a friend of William Blake, who possibly introduced her to Fuseli having known him since about 1787. She became infatuated with Fuseli, bizarrely suggesting that she accompany him and his wife to 'experience' the French Revolution in Paris in 1792, but Sophia managed to prevent this jaunt.

Fuseli made numerous drawings and paint-ings of his fashionable wife over a number of years, though the majority date from the 1790s.[5] Hair had a fetishistic fascination for Fuseli. He revelled in drawing complicated coiffure, making

it obsessively elaborate.[6] It is perhaps worth noting that Magdalena Hess claimed that she entered a hypnotic trance whenever her hair was combed.[7] Fuseli made a pencil portrait of Magdalena and her luxuriant tresses in 1779, which anticipates the Edinburgh sheet in its use of a starkly delineated profile looking to the right, offset by the height of heavy hair.[8] Fuseli's highly personal interpretation of such subjects is further emphasised by his drawing of his wife Sophia in 1799 (with her hair arranged in a very similar fashion to the Edinburgh drawing). She is shown sitting in front of a relief medallion of a Gorgon which is inscribed in Greek 'the head of fair-faced Medusa'.[9] It is Sophia's features which also grace Fuseli's Gorgon with the snaking hair of writhing serpents, the sight of whose face turned onlook-ers into stone.

JLW

PROVENANCE
Stewart of Dalguise, near Dunkeld, Scotland; purchased from a Scottish Private Collection by private treaty sale 1987.

EXHIBITED
Edinburgh / London 1994, p.9, no.21.

31 May 1800.

Moritz von Schwind
39. *The Hermit in search of Divine Justice*

VIENNA 1804–1871 NIEDERPÖCKING, NEAR
MUNICH

A painter, graphic artist and designer, Schwind was
essentially a story-teller in the late Romantic /
Biedermeier tradition, preoccupied with fairy tales and
medieval legends. He trained at the Vienna Academy
from 1821 to 1823 under Ludwig Schnorr von Carolsfeld
and Peter Krafft, but his early years were mainly given
over to the production of commercial illustrations. His
close friends included the painters Leopold Kupelwieser
and Ferdinand and Friedrich Olivier; the poets Franz
Grillparzer, Nicolaus Lenau and Eduard von
Bauernfeld; and the composer Franz Schubert, whose
own literary and musical circle provided Schwind with
material that sustained him throughout his career. In
1828 he was persuaded by Peter Cornelius to move to
Munich, where he attended life classes at the Academy.
His first important commission came in 1832 when he
was asked to decorate the Queen's Library in the Royal
Palace (*Residenz*) with scenes from the plays of Ludwig
Tieck. In 1835 he visited Italy, and in Rome was
influenced by Friedrich Overbeck and the other
Nazarenes still working there. On his return to
Germany, he was commissioned to design frescoes for
the castle of Hohenschwangau and assisted Julius
Schnorr von Carolsfeld with his own frescoes in the
Residenz. From 1840 to 1844 Schwind was in Karlsruhe,
where his major achievement was the decoration of the
staircase in the new Kunsthalle. The next three years
were spent in Frankfurt-am-Main, painting *The
Minnesingers' Contest at the Wartburg* for the Städelsches
Kunstinstitut. In 1847 he returned to Munich on his
appointment as a professor at the Academy and, once
settled, started work on a series of forty or more small
oil paintings which he referred to as his *Reisebilder*.
These were done primarily for his own pleasure and
treated genre subjects as well as his favourite themes
from German myth and legend. Several were purchased
by his patron Adolph von Schack, and today they are
considered among his finest works. In Munich,
Schwind regularly contributed illustrations to two
popular periodicals, the *Münchener Bilderbogen* and
Fliegende Blätter. He visited England in 1857 for the
exhibition of Art Treasures in Manchester, and
afterwards designed stained glass for St Michael's,
Paddington and the west window of Glasgow
Cathedral. The last great projects of his life were his
frescoes in the Wartburg near Eisenach and a series of
mural paintings in the foyer of the Vienna opera house.

D 5365
Pen and black ink over pencil on light brown wove
paper: 28.9 × 19.4

This recently discovered, unfinished drawing
illustrates the opening scene of an old German
parable (*Von der Gerechtigkeit Gottes*) in which the
principal protagonists are a hermit searching for
evidence of God's justice on earth and the
archangel Michael, disguised as a youth, who acts
as his companion. The drawing is a reworking
(for what purpose is not known) of an earlier
composition from a cycle of six pen and ink
drawings illustrating scenes from the same story
(Historisches Museum der Stadt Wien, Vienna).
These are datable, on stylistic grounds, to around
1822.[1] The present drawing closely follows the
compositional scheme of the Vienna drawing,
even to the extent of retaining its distinctive
hexagonal format, but stylistically they are very
different. Whereas the flowing contours and
graceful figure types of the earlier drawing reveal
the influence of Schwind's teacher, Ludwig
Schnorr, the conscious archaisms of the Edinburgh drawing recall the works of Ludwig's
brother Julius as much as the medieval German
woodcut.

Drawings made in emulation of Dürer and
other German artists of the *Dürerzeit* such as
Altdorfer, Cranach and Baldung are commonest
in Schwind's oeuvre in the late 1820s and early
1830s, immediately after his removal to Munich.
The present drawing has these characteristics and
is especially close in style to two dated drawings
from Schwind's early Munich period: *Death and
the Woodcutter* (Kunstmuseum, Basel) of 1829 and
Rübezahl (Museum Oskar Reinhart am
Stadtgarten, Winterthur) of 1831. So similar are
the treatment of the spiky branches, the angular-
ity of the draperies, the method of hatching and
the careful description of foreground flora and
funghi that it must have been executed about the
same time.

Schwind again returned to the subject of the
hermit in search of divine justice in 1851, when he
was commissioned by the Munich publishers
Braun & Schneider to produce woodcuts
illustrating the entire story for the sixty-third
issue of the *Münchener Bilderbogen*. His illustrations
were reproduced, in the manner of a modern
strip cartoon, in three bands, each consisting of
three interconnecting scenes. The page on which
they appeared bore the title *Von der Gerechtigkeit
Gottes*, and the narrative text was printed below

the corresponding illustrations.[2] Instead of
designing new compositions for the *Münchener
Bilderbogen*, however, Schwind reverted to the
compositional schemes which he had first
devised in Vienna in the early 1820s. In doing so,
he was observing what had become for him a
common practice. For several other illustrations
for the *Münchener Bilderbogen* and for many of the
oil paintings of his later career, including his
series of *Reisebilder*, he simply resorted to the fund
of drawings which had lain in his portfolio since
the Vienna years.[3]

CB

PROVENANCE
Purchased from Martin Moeller, Hamburg, with funds
from the estates of Keith and Rene Andrews in memory
of Keith Andrews, 1993.

EXHIBITED
Meisterzeichnungen, Martin Moeller, Hamburg, 1993,
no.27.

Heinrich Dreber (Franz-Dreber)
40. *Herdsmen with their Cattle in the Mountains*

DRESDEN 1822–1875 ANTICOLI DI CAMPAGNA

Following the early death of his father, Dreber assumed his stepfather's surname, Franz: hence the compound Franz-Dreber, which he used when signing his drawings. From 1836 to 1841 he studied at the Dresden Academy, where his professors included the landscape painter Ludwig Richter, to whom he remained deeply attached throughout his life. In 1841 he moved to Munich, and spent the next two years travelling and sketching in southern Germany and Austria. Having decided to make Italy his home, in 1843 he settled permanently in Rome, where he led a somewhat solitary existence. His early landscape paintings, such as the *Roman Landscape* (Kunsthalle, Hamburg), reveal the influence of Richter's late Nazarene style but he subsequently converted to the Neoclassical idiom of landscape painting practised by artists of an older generation such as Josef Anton Koch and Johann Christian Reinhart. Inspired by Poussin and Claude, Dreber drew extensively from nature in the Roman Campagna, incorporating the scenes he recorded there into his painted landscapes, which were frequently enlivened with staffage drawn from classical literature and the Bible or from contemporary Italian peasant life. In his mature works, of which *Sappho* (1864–70; Schack-Gallery, Munich) is a prime example, he developed an idiosynchratic combination of Naturalism and Neo-romanticism, which exercised a powerful influence on Symbolist artists such as Arnold Böcklin.

In addition to a very small number of oil paintings, Dreber left a large corpus of drawings, the majority of which are in the print rooms of Berlin, Dresden and Hamburg. He divided his drawn oeuvre into two discrete categories – *Naturstudien* (studies from nature) and *Kompositionszeichnungen* (compositional drawings) – and made a strict distinction between them.[1] Nearly all of his extant drawings date from 1838 to 1852 and, except for the years 1841, 1843, 1847–49, are rarely dated. The drawings of the German period, up to 1843, were executed either in pencil or, more commonly, in pen and ink or sepia. After 1846, pencil became his preferred drawing medium, and from 1847 pen disappeared all but entirely, except in a few compositional drawings. Watercolours, though used but rarely, occur throughout his career, either on their own or as colour washes augmenting drawings in ink or pencil. Between 1842 and 1843 he drew very little in any medium, devoting his time to an assiduous study of oil painting.[2]

D 5366

Pen in black and brown ink, with watercolour washes, over pencil on light brown laid paper: 24.5 × 30.8
Inscribed in pencil, lower right: 7

Although this drawing looks unfinished, partially watercoloured landscape drawings were common among Dreber's German contemporaries, and he may well have left it in this state deliberately. Of the two distinct categories into which he divided his drawings, this belongs to the type he defined as compositional drawings, composed in the studio from motifs recorded directly from nature, with the addition here of figures, cattle, sheep, a dog and a goat. The scene Dreber has represented is what the Germans call the *Almabtrieb*, the annual autumn procedure when cattle are brought from the upper pastures of the Alm to the shelter of a farmhouse or barn to pass the winter. The bells round the cows' necks show that they had previously been roaming free.

In view of its subject matter, this drawing can only have been executed during Dreber's *Wanderjahre*, the two peripatetic years between his departure from Dresden on 10 June 1841 and his arrival in Italy in the summer of 1843. The dates and inscriptions on his drawings of this period, together with other documents, allow us to reconstruct his movements reasonably accurately, and from the available evidence it would appear that the present drawing was most likely made during one of his excursions from Munich to the Bavarian Alps in the autumn of 1841. Stylistically, it is very similar to drawings he made in the Fränkische Schweiz in June and July of the same year, and it is closely linked thematically to *A Village Landscape with Peasants returning Home with their Herds* in Weimar and a dated drawing, also of 1841, formerly in the collection of Friedrich Haniel of Gut Wistinghausen, depicting the return of a herd of cattle through a similar wooded landscape.[3]

Immediately after Dreber died, his son Fortunato systematically marked all of the drawings that had been in his father's possession with a studio stamp embossed *H. Franz-Dreber Roma*.[4] This appears in various sizes, either as a blind stamp or in black ink, on nearly all Dreber's studies from nature and most of his other drawings as well. The absence of a stamp on the Edinburgh sheet suggests that the artist either sold the drawing or presented it to a friend or fellow artist.

CB

PROVENANCE

Dr. M. Andrenyi, Munich; from whom bought by Martin Moeller, Hamburg; from whom purchased 1993.

EXHIBITED

Meisterzeichnungen, Martin Moeller, Hamburg, 1993, no.25.

Adolph von Menzel
41. *Sheet of Studies of Heads*

BRESLAU (NOW WROCŁAW) 1815–1905 BERLIN

A pioneer of Realism, Menzel was the most important artist in Berlin during the second half of the nineteenth century and one of the most accomplished and prolific draughtsmen of the age. Although he studied briefly at the Berlin Academy in 1833, he was almost wholly self-taught apart from what he learned during his apprenticeship in his father's lithographic business, which he inherited in 1832. He achieved early fame as an illustrator, particularly as the chronicler of the life of Frederick the Great, whose career he also charted with comparable success in a series of large oil paintings. By the mid-1840s he had already turned to subjects from modern life including *The Berlin-Potsdam Railway* of 1847 and *The Funeral of the Martyrs of the Berlin Revolution* of 1848 (both Nationalgalerie, Berlin). His early masterpiece, *Le Théâtre du Gymnase* (1856; Nationalgalerie, Berlin), was much admired by Degas. Menzel's gift of precise and detached observation, most evident in his drawings, accounted for the popularity of contemporary subjects such as *William I's Departure for the Army* of 1871 and industrial scenes such as *The Iron-Rolling Mill* of 1872–5 (both Nationalgalerie, Berlin), two supreme examples of his distinctive brand of realism. From the 1850s he travelled extensively in Germany and abroad, and in 1855 he made the first of three visits to Paris which proved important for his stylistic development. By the 1880s he had achieved an international reputation. In 1885 he received an honorary doctorate from the University of Berlin. In 1898 he was elevated to the peerage. He enjoyed the freedom of the city of Breslau, and was an honorary member of the Académie Française and of the Royal Academy in London. Paradoxically, the works for which he is most admired today – the informal landscapes and interiors of the 1840s onwards – were kept hidden from the public during his life-time.

D 5096
Charcoal, stump, and conté-crayon, heightened in seven or eight places with white bodycolour, on buff paper: 32.8 × 19.8
Inscribed in pencil, verso: 4171 and 34 / 80

The sheet consists of four studies of the head of a clean-shaven man with an aquiline nose, wearing a simple three-cornered hat, and four, more detailed studies of a fleshy-faced, older man with side-whiskers and a moustache. The latter is dressed in an open coat and stock and wears a three-cornered hat trimmed with ostrich feathers. The studies of the younger man, which were probably drawn last, are located, two on either side, near the lower edges of the sheet. The others are grouped centrally in an arrangement that testifies to the artist's innate compositional sense. Menzel routinely made multiple studies of this kind, and, typically, both models here are depicted in subtly varied poses. Characteristically, Menzel has partially obliterated with crayon the profile of the head on the left at the top of the sheet, with which he was presumably dissatisfied.

The drawings of the older man (though surely not those of the younger one, as has sometimes been suggested)[1] served as studies for the head of the general standing closest to the viewer in the centre foreground of Menzel's unfinished canvas *Frederick the Great addressing his Generals before the Battle of Leuthen* (fig.31). This was begun in 1858 and abandoned in its present state in 1861. Fifteen sheets of studies for other figures in the same picture, mostly in crayon or pencil, are preserved in the Berlin print room.[2] In the painting, Menzel portrayed Frederick the Great, with his officers gathered round him in a semi-circle, as though observed from a nearby slope, which explains why the models in the present studies were all depicted from above. In its final form, the general's head is tilted even more towards the viewer and his facial expression has been modified to emphasise the seriousness of the occasion.

Menzel's early reputation was established in 1840 with the publication of Franz Kugler's *Life of Frederick the Great*, for which he had provided the 400 illustrations. These were followed by a series of woodcuts for *The Works of Frederick the Great*, which occupied him from 1843 to 1849 and by 436 lithographs for *The Army of Frederick the Great in Uniform*, completed in 1857. Enthused by the subject on which by now he was an authority, he embarked in 1849 on a series of major oil paintings dealing with the most important events in Frederick's reign, for each of which he produced scores of preparatory drawings. *Frederick the Great addressing his Generals before the Battle of Leuthen* (a subject he had already treated before)[3] was the last and largest in the series. It was also, psychologically, by far the most dramatic. The subject was inspired by the valedictory address of Frederick to his staff-officers a few days before the Prussian counter-offensive against the Austrians on 5 December 1757 to recapture the province of Silesia. The king's concluding words acknowledged the possibility of a crushing defeat: 'Prepare the ordinary soldier for the events that will soon ensue and inform him that I consider myself entitled to demand unconditional obedience from him. As for yourselves …, if there is anyone among you who is afraid of sharing all the dangers with me, he may take his leave now without the slightest reproach … Now, gentlemen, farewell! In a short while, we shall either have defeated the enemy or be destined never to see one another again'.[4]

C B

PROVENANCE
Hazlitt, Gooden and Fox, London; from whom purchased 1980.

EXHIBITED
Menzel der Beobachter, Kunsthalle, Hamburg,1982, no.73; Edinburgh, 1984, no.8.

Fig.31 Adolph von Menzel, *Frederick the Great addressing his Generals before the Battle of Leuthen* Nationalgalerie, Berlin

Pierre-Antoine Patel, called Patel the Younger
42, 43. A Pair of Landscapes: Summer and Winter

PARIS 1648–1707 PARIS

Relatively little is known of Patel's life and his surviving oeuvre is not large. He probably trained with his father, the landscape painter Pierre Patel (1605–1676), whose distinguished career included the production of decorative paintings and designs for the Gobelins. Both father and son were independent of the French Academy, and in 1677 Pierre-Antoine was admitted to the Academy of Saint-Luc. His first known painting is the *Landscape with a Mounted Falconer* of 1673 (formerly in the Jacques Petitthory collection, now Musée Bonnat, Bayonne). In 1699 he was commissioned, probably as a result of his being recognised as a specialist in such subjects, to paint a series of twelve landscapes representing the months for the headquarters of the Jesuit order in Paris on the rue Saint-Antoine (Saint-Louis-de-la-Couture, also called Saint-Louis de-la-Culture), now known as Saint Paul-Saint Louis. These were confiscated during the French Revolution and dispersed (nine have since been identified including *January* in the Louvre, Paris, *October* in the Fine Arts Museum, San Francisco[1] and *December* in the Staatliches Museum, Schwerin). Patel's earlier works are often indistinguishable in manner from those of his father,[2] though his later work became freer and more vigorous. He may have collaborated with his father on a group of landscape paintings intended to decorate the apartments of Anne of Austria in the Louvre. Patel *fils* was apparently killed in a duel in 1707.

D 5081 & D 5082

Gouache on vellum: 16.4 × 27.4 and 16.1 × 27.4
Both signed and dated: *AP PATEL* / *1693* (D 5081 lower left, D 5082 lower right).

Unlike his father, who does not appear to have worked extensively in gouache, Pierre-Antoine executed around fifty of these small, highly finished landscapes, doubtless intended for sale to collectors and to adorn their cabinets. All are of roughly the same size and mostly date from the early 1690s. In style and content they represent a combination of sixteenth-century fantastical Flemish landscape, Dutch seventeenth-century snow and winter scenes, and seventeenth-century classicism. Other examples include a *Landscape with a Circular Temple on a Mountain* (Metropolitan Museum of Art, New York),[3] a *Landscape with a Fisherman* (Norton Simon Museum, Pasadena), a *Landscape with the Flight into Egypt* and a *Landscape with Pan and Syrinx* (both Brown University Museum, Providence, Rhode Island), a pair of *Winter Landscapes* exhibited at Colnaghi, New York in 1990 (the second of which is now in the University Art Museum, Princeton),[4] and a *Winter Landscape with Ruins and Figures on a Frozen Lake* with Colnaghi in 1998.[5] Our drawings most probably belong to a series of the Seasons and a candidate for the missing gouache of *Autumn* could be the *Italian Landscape* (a scene of harvesting, signed and dated 1693 and of similar dimensions) sold at auction in 1966.[6] It is also worth noting that the year 1693 may have been one of some significance for Patel with regard to royal patronage: a signed and dated gouache by him of vessels in a port was included as the frontispiece to a bound manuscript inventory of all the vessels and officers in the French royal fleet.[7]

M C

PROVENANCE
Trafalgar Galleries, London, since at least 1968;[8] from whom purchased 1979.

EXHIBITED
Trafalgar Galleries at the Grand Palais, Grand Palais, Paris, 1978, nos 14, 15; *Trafalgar Galleries at the Royal Academy II*, Royal Academy, London, 1979, nos 14, 15; Edinburgh, 1984, nos 4, 5.

François Boucher
44. *The Rape of Europa*

PARIS 1703–1770 PARIS

By the middle of the eighteenth century Boucher had become the dominant figure in French painting. He had originally trained with his father Nicolas, a master painter in the Academy of Saint-Luc, and then studied briefly with François Lemoyne at some time between 1721 and 1723, after which he may also have trained with Louis Galloche. He won the Prix de Rome in 1723 with his *Evilmerodach releasing Joachim from Prison* (location unknown), but there was no room for him at the time at the French Academy there. He finally travelled to Rome at his own expense in 1728 but was back in France by November when he was *agréé* at the Academy, being *reçu* in 1734 with his *Rinaldo and Armida* (Louvre, Paris). From the 1730s onwards he received an increasing number of commissions, not only for paintings but also for tapestry designs for the Beauvais and Gobelins manufactories, porcelain designs for Sèvres and sets and opera designs for the *Opéra* and the *Théâtre la Foire*. His reputation spread rapidly abroad, and in 1748 he declined the position of *premier peintre* to the King of Prussia. With Madame de Pompadour's installation as *maîtresse en titre* to Louis XV in 1745, his commissions for the Crown increased, including work for the royal châteaux at Choisy and Fontainebleau, and for Madame de Pompadour's own château at Bellevue. Boucher was named *premier peintre du roi* in 1765 on the death of Carle Vanloo, prompting the acid observation from Diderot 'Well, my friend, it's at precisely the moment Boucher has ceased to be an artist that he's appointed first painter to the king.'[1] In his later years Boucher mainly painted variations on his favourite theme of the pastoral.

D 5351
Red chalk: 28.3 × 44.1

This drawing was first identified by Alistair Laing[2] as Boucher's *première pensée* for *The Rape of Europa* (fig.32, Louvre, Paris)[3] painted for the special *concours* of 1747 devised by Charles Lenormant de Tournehem, recently appointed *Directeur général des Bâtiments du roi*. This competition was intended to encourage the French school of painting, the quality of which had been perceived to be in decline by many critics at the 1746 Salon. Ten history painters, whose names were supplied by Charles-Antoine Coypel, *premier peintre du roi*, were invited to treat subjects of their choice in 'whichever genre they were inclined by genius and inspiration'. The hope was that history painting would be revived by new subjects chosen from different countries and periods. It was therefore deemed disappointing by some that Boucher should choose a subject well-known in European art and already popular with eighteenth-century painters. The account of the Rape of Europa is taken from the second book of Ovid's *Metamorphoses* and tells how Jupiter, in the guise of a bull, abducted Europa, virginal princess of Tyre. Boucher depicts the beginning of the story in which the courtship takes place on dry land amidst frolicking nymphs strewn with flowers. His rather traditional and decorative choice of subject may be partially explained by the fact that his competition entry was also intended as a tapestry design for the series *Les Amours des Dieux* (Loves of the Gods), commissioned by the Beauvais manufactory in 1747 and completed in 1752.

A number of drawings for the composition have already been identified in the literature on Boucher,[4] a testimony to the care which he exercised in this particular instance. None of them, however, is for the whole composition. In the Edinburgh *première pensée*, unknown until very recently, Boucher would appear to have taken as his initial source of inspiration Veronese's well-known treatment of the same subject (Palazzo Ducale, Venice),[5] there being some similarities in the grouping of the main protagonists, most notably those on the left of the composition. Several features of our drawing recur from Boucher's own earlier 1734 treatments of this theme: the bull turning its head up to gaze at Europa is found in the brown grisaille sketch at Amiens,[6] and the basket of flowers occurs in the Wallace Collection picture.[7] In the final painting, however, Europa has moved to the centre, and Jupiter, in the form of the bull, has adopted a more passive role. The summary, schematic figure style in our drawing can be found in other drawings by Boucher, particularly those of the 1740s.[8] Surviving *premières pensées* by Boucher are rare and Laing has drawn attention to that for the *Death of Adonis* of 1730.[9] Boucher must have executed many such drawings in connection with his paintings, only to discard them once the projects had been completed.

M C

PROVENANCE
Garrigues family, La Rochelle; by descent; Phillips, London, 16 December 1992, no.125 unsold; purchased, through Phillips, 1993.

EXHIBITED
Edinburgh / London 1994, no.11.

Fig.32 François Boucher, *The Rape of Europa*
Musée du Louvre, Paris

Etienne Jeaurat
45. *Family in an Interior*

PARIS 1699–1789 VERSAILLES

The son of a wine merchant from Vermenton (Yonne), Jeaurat was placed by his brother, the engraver Edme Jeaurat, in the Parisian studio of Nicolas Vleughels, whom he accompanied to Italy in 1724 when his master was appointed to the French Academy in Rome. He returned to France in 1728 and was *reçu* into the Royal Academy of Painting and Sculpture in 1733 as a history painter on presentation of his *Pyramus and Thisbe* (Musée, Roanne). He had a long and varied career, exhibiting irregularly at the Salon 1737–69 and producing history paintings, village scenes inspired by northern art, and scenes of Parisian life (for which he is probably best known) such as *The Carnaval of the Streets of Paris* and *Prostitutes being taken to the Hospital (Salpetrière)*, shown at the 1757 Salon and both now in the Musée Carnavalet, Paris. Jeaurat belonged to the literary circle, the *Société du Bout de Banc*, presided over by the actress Mlle Quinaut, which included the writers Piron and Vadé, both of whom shared an interest in the life of the common people. Indeed, Diderot later referred to Jeaurat as 'the Vadé of painting'. Jeaurat's own Parisian street scenes owed much to the influence of Hogarth, who visited Paris in 1743 and whose prints gained wide circulation there. During the reigns of Louis XV and XVI Jeaurat attained almost all available honours, being appointed Rector of the French Academy in 1765, Guardian of the King's pictures at Versailles two years later and Chancellor of the Academy in 1781.

D 5360
Black and red chalk, heightened with white and pink touches of gouache, lightly squared up in graphite: 48 × 64

Jeaurat's graphic masterpiece depicts a well-to-do bourgeois family in the spare but elegant bedroom of the parents, which also functions, for the purposes of this image, as the father's office. The family has been rather improbably gathered together, however, for in real life the father would have conducted his business in a separate office and certainly not in the bedroom. As the father is shown in *profil perdu*, it is reasonable to assume this is not a specific family portrait, but rather a celebration of the virtues of a particular lifestyle and social class.

The room is half panelled, has a tile floor, and is hung with what is probably damask. The clock on the chimneypiece is a Louis XV *pendule de cheminée* in the shape known as *forme violonée*. The time shown would appear to be twenty to eleven in the morning and the maid either sets down or picks up a jug from the hearth. Of the various pictures in the room, the overdoor is reminiscent of Boucher, while to the right there is a possibly Dutch landscape below two portraits. On the right the father works at his *bureau plat*, attended perhaps by a junior partner in the business or practice. The youngest of the three daughters of the family plays with the family dog, while her two elder sisters are engaged in sewing. On the far left sits the mother, possibly making tassel fringes, having temporarily abandoned her other work. In its highly finished state this sheet may have been intended as an exhibition drawing in its own right or as the basis for an engraving. Few of Jeaurat's drawings have been identified, the earliest being a number of delicate wash landscapes dating from 1725 during his stay in Rome.[1] No other grand, multi-figured studies such as ours are known, though there are studies for individual figures in the Nationalmuseum, Stockholm; the Fitzwilliam Museum, Cambridge; and in private collections. A more modest sheet, with three protagonists (*La Convalescente*), was sold in New York in 1996[2] and formerly belonged to Philippe de Chennevières, the art administrator and collector who held the post of *Directeur des Beaux-Arts* 1873–78 in succession to Charles Blanc. De Chennevières described Jeaurat as 'a Chardin with a bourgeois palette'[3] and this disparaging comparison echoed earlier remarks made by those great collectors of the art of the *dix-huitième siècle*, the Goncourt brothers. Comparing the compositions of the two artists they observed 'You look at that of Jeaurat, you enter into that of Chardin.'[4] They themselves owned drawings by Jeaurat, which were misattributed to Chardin at the time, so perhaps their judgement was rather harsh![5]

MC

PROVENANCE
Hôtel Drouot, Paris, 4 December 1992, no.28; bought Moatti, Paris; from whom purchased 1994.

EXHIBITED
Edinburgh / London 1994, no.16.

Hubert Robert
46. *Soldiers Carousing*

PARIS 1733–1808 PARIS

Robert specialised in architectural scenes, set in landscape backgrounds, based on the buildings of ancient and modern Italy and of France. Known as 'Robert des ruines', he was a prolific painter, draughtsman and etcher of decorative landscapes, as well as a landscape designer. The son of a *valet-de-chambre* to the marquis de Stainville, Robert was originally intended for a career in the church. Little is known of his early years, though he certainly received a classical education at the Collège de Navarre, a theological school at the University of Paris. Thereafter, according to Mariette, he took drawing lessons with the sculptor and architectural designer René-Michel Slodtz and exhibited at the *Salon de Jeunesse* in 1752 and 1753. In 1754 he travelled to Rome under the patronage of the comte de Stainville, the future duc de Choiseul, and began to study at the French Academy there. In 1759 he won a pension to the Academy and was deemed by its director, Natoire, to be a promising pupil influenced by the Roman view-painter Panini and the prints of Piranesi. In the company of the engraver Jean-Claude-Richard, Abbé de Saint-Non, he travelled to Naples in 1760 and also visited Pompei and Herculaneum. While in Rome, he met his fellow artist Fragonard and the two of them drew extensively in the gardens of the Villa d'Este. During his eleven years in Italy Robert compiled a vast portfolio of subjects which formed the basis of much of his subsequent production, though he also later chronicled the urban renewal of Paris. Back in France in 1765, he was both *agréé* and *reçu* the following year into the French Academy, his reception piece being the *Port of Ripetta, Rome* of 1765 (Ecole des Beaux-Arts, Paris). Robert exhibited regularly at the Salon 1767–98. His career prospered under the *ancien régime* and in 1778 he was appointed *Dessinateur des Jardins du Roi* and awarded lodgings in the Palais du Louvre (where he lived until 1802). In 1784 he was made *Garde des Tableaux* for the Musée Royal intended for the Louvre and in that connection made a remarkable series of oil-sketches illustrating schemes for the Grande Galerie there. During the Revolution he was imprisoned 1793–4, but on his release he was appointed to the select committee organising the Musée National des Arts, the forerunner of the Musée du Louvre. Active right up to the end of his life, he was criticised in his later work for carelessness and over-production.

D 2261
Brown pen and wash over red chalk; laid down: 29 × 44.5
Signed and dated, lower centre-right: *Robert 1757*

This is probably one of the earliest dated drawings by Robert and therefore provides a fascinating insight into his first years in Rome.[1] The very loose pen and wash style, very different from the refined red chalk landscapes for which he would become well-known, is generically similar to that of Gian Paolo Panini, who taught perspective to the students of the French Academy in Rome. Some of the figure types, especially the soldiers in armour, were certainly inspired by Salvator Rosa, specifically a number of the etchings in his very popular *Figurine* series of *c*.1656–57. Although the drawing is unusual for Robert, it has been pointed out that a similarly untypical, free and spirited early drawing by Fragonard, *Tancred baptising the dying Clorinda*, also dates from 1757. If one accepts the attributions of that drawing to Fragonard[2] and, despite its unusual qualities, of our drawing to Robert, then it becomes apparent that both artists (who would become such close friends during their time together in Rome), underwent a number of dramatic and, as yet, only partly understood changes of style during their early years in the eternal city.

However, it should be noted that as long ago as 1968 Pierre Rosenberg tentatively proposed an attribution for our drawing to Charles-François de La Traverse (1726–*c*.1780), based on comparison with a series of drawings by that artist at Besançon,[3] and that in 1987 he still harboured doubts over the attribution of the *Tancred* drawing to Fragonard.[4] Rosenberg's doubts notwithstanding, the signature and date on our drawing would appear to be genuine: for example, comparison with the signature on the Lehman Collection's drawing by Robert of the

Interior of St Peter's of *c*.1758 shows a similar script,[5] and it was not until *c*.1760 that Robert began to sign his drawings *Roberti*. Perhaps the most plausible explanation of the style and subject-matter of our drawing might be that it reflects Robert's awareness of an artist such as La Traverse, who had arrived in Rome in 1752, was closely associated with the French Academy there, and who has been aptly described as possessing 'a distinctive artistic personality with a dynamic late-Baroque style'.[6]

MC

PROVENANCE
William Findlay Watson; his bequest to the Gallery 1881.

EXHIBITED
Drawings by Old Masters, Royal Academy, London, 1953, no.392; Colnaghi 1966, no.67; *France in the eighteenth century*, Royal Academy, London, 1968, no.595.

Jean-Baptiste (-Henri) Deshays (de Colleville)

47. Apotheosis of a Female Figure

COLLEVILLE, NEAR ROUEN 1729–1765 PARIS

Deshays's early death at the age of thirty-five, probably from tuberculosis, brought to a premature close the brief period in which he had been regarded, not least by Diderot, as the most important religious painter in mid-eighteenth-century France. He had first trained with his father, Jean-Dominique Deshays, and then briefly at Jean-Baptiste Descamps's *Ecole Gratuite de Dessin* in Rouen. Around 1740 he entered the Parisian studio of Hyacinthe Collin de Vermont where he acquired a reputation for the excellence of his drawings. His next master, Jean Restout II, had, like Collin de Vermont, been a pupil of the great *rouennais* history and religious painter, Jean Jouvenet. Deshays won the 1751 Prix de Rome with his *Job on the Dunghill* (untraced) and, prior to travelling to Rome, underwent the obligatory three years at the *Ecole Royale des Elèves Protégés* during which period he received a number of important religious commissions including that for a cycle on the life of St Andrew for the church of that name in Rouen. On his return from his four-year stay in Rome in 1758 he was *agréé* at the Academy and also married Jeanne-Elisabeth-Victoire Boucher, elder daughter of the painter François Boucher. The following year he was *reçu* and enjoyed great critical success at the Salon. His work was seen as continuing the seventeenth-century tradition of painters such as Domenichino, Reni and Poussin. At all the Salons to which he contributed he showed his *Caravanes*, journey scenes very much in the manner of Castiglione and (to Diderot's regret) Boucher. A number of his paintings were shown posthumously at the 1765 Salon, where a decline in his powers was noted.

D 1564
Black chalk, brown pen and wash, heightened with white; laid down: 46.9 × 24.4

A female figure is received in the heavens by two other women and a putto, on the ground below is a vanquished group, one of whom brandishes a torch and could conceivably represent Discord. According to Sandoz,[1] the inspiration of the subject of this drawing may have been literary and perhaps drawn from the theatre, for example the often violent tragedies made popular at that time by Baculard d'Arnaud and others. A drawing by Deshays based on d'Arnaud's *Le comte de Comminges* was among the works exhibited posthumously at the 1765 Salon. Although Cochin, in his memorial essay of 1765, claimed that Deshays's drawings were less well-known than his paintings and small in number,[2] the plentiful evidence of Deshays's posthumous sale catalogue refutes the second part of that statement. The sale,[3] at which Cochin sought the permission of the marquis de Marigny to purchase four drawings for the *cabinet du roi*, consisted for the most part of drawings and provides ample evidence of Deshays's fecundity as a draughtsman. Many of the lots were multiple and unspecified and are described as in Deshays's most frequently used technique, as in the Edinburgh drawing, of pen, wash and white heightening. Today, however, relatively few of Deshays's drawings have been identified, probably because they bear attributions to other artists, notably Deshays's father-in-law, Boucher (of whom Deshays himself owned many examples).[4] Our drawing, though characteristic of Deshays, also shows similarities to Fragonard in the dramatic use of brown pen and wash.

MC

PROVENANCE
Possibly Paignon-Dijonval in 1810;[5] David Laing; Royal Scottish Academy (L 2188); transferred to the Gallery 1910.

EXHIBITED
Colnaghi 1966, no.71; *France in the eighteenth century*, Royal Academy, London, 1968, no.191.

Jean-Laurent Legeay
48. *Landscape with Two Figures*

PARIS C.1710–AFTER 1788, ROME

An architect, draughtsman and teacher, Legeay's reputation rests more on his drawings and projects than on his built work. He studied at the Ecole des Beaux-Arts, Paris and won the Prix de Rome in 1732. While in Rome (1737–42) he would have entered the circle of Piranesi.[1] In 1739 Legeay engraved five plates for the *Nuovo Teatro delle fabriche et edifici in prospettiva in Roma moderna* of G. G. de Rossi and, around 1740, six views of Rome, published by Bouchard with the *Vedute* of Piranesi. On his return to Paris in 1742 he was appointed professor at the *Académie Royale d'Architecture*, where he had a great influence on pupils such as Charles de Wailly and Etienne-Louis Boullée. In 1747 he dispatched from Paris his plans for the church of St Hedwige in Berlin, begun that year but not finished until 1773. His career thereafter took him to Germany where he worked at the court of Mecklenburg-Schwerin 1748–56. In 1756 he went to Potsdam as *premier architecte* to Frederick the Great of Prussia but was discharged in 1763 after profound disagreements with his patron (contemporary accounts attest to Legeay's difficult character). He was in England for most of the rest of the decade where he was in contact with William Chambers and moved in antiquarian circles. In the course of his English sojourn Legeay made four sets of etchings, the *Fontane* (1767), *Rovine* (1768), *Tombeaux* (1768) and the *Vasi* (undated), all of which were published by Mondhare in Paris in 1770. On his return to Paris Legeay failed to re-establish himself there and spent his last years in south-western France (including Toulouse and Marseille) in considerable penury. The last record of him is a letter from Rome, dated 1788, to the widow of Frederick the Great, requesting his unpaid salary of a quarter of a century earlier.[2]

D 5413
Red chalk: 34.3 × 41.5

Legeay's favourite drawing medium was red chalk in which he produced some of the most bizarre and innovative drawings of landscapes and architectural *capricci* of the eighteenth century. Our drawing possibly dates from the mid- to later 1760s, being couched very much in the visual language of the etched *Suites* Legeay produced around that time, in which vegetation and crumbled architecture are combined in a fantastical manner. The style of the two main figures is also typical of Legeay in the later 1750s and 1760s, though their physiognomy and attire, especially of the figure on the left, suggests an oriental influence – hardly surprising given the contemporary vogue for Chinoiserie in the fine and decorative arts.

M C

PROVENANCE

Jean-Pierre Haldi (collector's mark, lower right, not in L);[3] Galerie Louvois Sarl, Paris; from whom purchased 1996.

(Jean-François) Pierre Peyron
49. *Death of Alcestis*

AIX-EN-PROVENCE 1744–1814 PARIS

Peyron, who was regarded for a time as David's great rival, received his first training in Aix, where he was encouraged to take up painting by the *marseillais* artist Michel François Dandré-Bardon. In 1767 he was in Paris and entered the studio of Louis-Jean-François, called Lagrenée the Elder. After three attempts he won the Prix de Rome in 1773 with his *Death of Seneca* (now lost) defeating, amongst others, Jacques-Louis David in the competition. He then studied at the *Ecole Royale des Elèves Protégés* under Dandré-Bardon until leaving for Rome in 1775. With the aid of supporters such as the cardinal de Bernis (French ambassador to Rome) and the comte d'Angiviller (*Surintendant des Bâtiments du roi*), his Roman stay was prolonged until 1782 and he painted some of his most successful works there. After his return to Paris he exhibited his masterpiece, the *Death of Alcestis*, at the 1785 Salon where it had the misfortune to be overshadowed by David's *Oath of the Horatii* (Louvre, Paris). Peyron's subsequent works suffered by comparison with those of David. In delicate health, Peyron painted comparatively little after the 1789 Revolution and his surviving oeuvre is small, much of it suffused with a spirit of tenebrous melancholy derived from Poussin, whose art he revered to excess.[1]

D 3241

Pen, black ink and brown wash, with white heightening, on blue paper: 20.7 × 31
Inscribed by the artist, lower left: *un groupe de la mort d'Alceste par P.Peyron*

Peyron's great painting of the *Death of Alcestis*[2] (Louvre, Paris, fig.33) was commissioned in 1784 on behalf of the king by the comte d'Angiviller for exhibition at the 1785 Salon. The subject is taken from Euripides: Alcestis, daughter of Pelias, wife of Admetus, king of Pherae in Thessaly, offers to die in place of her husband. In the commentary in the 1785 Salon *livret* it is related how the dying Alcestis bids farewell to her children and entrusts them to the grieving Admetus. Peyron drew his inspiration from previous deathbed scenes by Poussin such as the *Death of Germanicus* and the *Testament of Eudamidas*. As Rosenberg and Van de Sandt point out,[3] the story of Alcestis would have been familiar to a late-eighteenth-century audience through the opera by Gluck (*Alceste* 1774) and Quinault's republished drama (*Alceste* 1784). They also suggest that Peyron may have originally contemplated another subject from Euripedes for the 1785 Salon, the *Despair of Hecuba*, Peyron's drawing[4] of which (Metropolitan Museum of Art, New York) forms an exact

pendant to his first surviving drawing[5] for the *Death of Alcestis* (Private Collection, Paris). Both these compositional drawings are dated by Rosenberg and Van de Sandt to 1784 and are of horizontal format, even though the final picture was to be square. Of the three further surviving drawings for *Alcestis*, those in Edinburgh[6] and in the Musée des Beaux-Arts, Rennes[7] are studies of Alcestis herself and the grieving figures round her bed, while the final compositional drawing of square format, matching the painting, is in the collection of Louis-Antoine Prat, Paris.[8] As Van de Sandt has observed, such a detailed working procedure was standard practice for Peyron at that time. Writing to the comte d'Angiviller in 1787 concerning another painting, Peyron explained, 'I am pursuing the same procedure I followed in Rome. There, I used to make a particular study of each group and then make a drawing of the whole … All of which takes much more time, but must one not make sacrifices when it is for the good and well-being of our conscience?'[9]

M C

PROVENANCE
William Findlay Watson; his bequest to the Gallery 1881.

Fig.33 Jean-François-Pierre Peyron, *Death of Alcestis*
Musée du Louvre, Paris

un groupe de la mort d'Alceste par L. Pégron

Pierre-Alexandre Wille
50. *A Tavern Brawl*

PARIS 1748–1837 PARIS[1]

Wille was the son of the German draughtsman and engraver Johann Georg Wille (1715–1808) and his French wife Marie-Louise Desforges (1722–85). From the age of thirteen to fifteen he studied with his father's friend Greuze and then with Vien. He was *agréé* by the French Academy in 1774 as a painter 'dans le genre des sujets familiers', but never *reçu*. He exhibited at all the Salons held 1775–87. His reputation rests primarily on his activities as a draughtsman, however. In his early years he drew sentimental Germanic subjects and pretty interiors, but his major achievement lay in his numerous portrait drawings, including those of the Revolutionary figures of Charlotte Corday and Danton. Wille himself was an ardent Revolutionary, serving in the Garde Nationale 1789–92 and holding the post of *Commandant du Bataillon de la Section du Théâtre Français*. His last years were evidently spent in straitened circumstances and in 1819 he petitioned the duchesse d'Angoulême, daughter of Louis XVI, for assistance towards the maintenance of his wife, confined to a madhouse at Charenton. In 1834 he sold his father's *Journal*,[2] one of the more important sources on artistic life in eighteenth-century France, for forty francs to the Cabinet des Estampes of the Bibliothèque Nationale in Paris.

D 5377
Pen and brown ink; laid down: 34 × 50.2
Signed and dated on the table in the centre: *P.A.Wille filius / del.1784*

This is a typical and fine example of the highly finished pen drawings in the manner of engravings which Wille drew from the 1780s onwards and which were intended for sale or gift. Wille's father recalled in January 1785 'Our son has presented me for my New Year gifts two beautiful drawings, devilishly done in pen. One represents angry drunks; the other, gamblers dressed in ancient costume who are furious with each other.'[3]

Many of them were clever pastiches of Caravaggesque subjects. Our drawing would appear to be most closely based on the example of Valentin de Boulogne (1594–1632), whose work had been avidly collected by Cardinal Mazarin and was therefore well represented in the Royal Collection. The costumes are contemporary, however, and there are Greuzian overtones to many of the figures, for example the face of the small boy on the far side of the table, the awkwardly posed figure of the old woman to the left, or the outstretched arms of the younger male drinker she holds back.

A number of comparable drawings by Wille have appeared on the art market in recent years, of which the closest to ours is the *Cardplayers* of 1784, of identical size and signature, which was with De Bayser in 1975.[4] However, perhaps the greatest of these pastiche drawings is *The Concert* of 1801 in the Polakovits collection, bequeathed to the Ecole des Beaux-Arts, Paris.[5] In his discussion of that drawing Jean-Pierre Cuzin rightly identified three topics worthy of further research in connection with such drawings: the apparent revival of interest in Caravaggism at the end of the eighteenth century;[6] the vogue for drawings which imitate engravings; and the links in the late eighteenth century between Parisian and Germanic art in the fields of painting, drawing and engraving.

MC

PROVENANCE
Galerie de Bayser, Paris;[7] from whom purchased 1994.

EXHIBITED
De Robert à Guérin, Galerie de Bayser, Paris, 1991, no.10.

Pierre-Henri de Valenciennes
51. *Classical Landscape with a Monument*

TOULOUSE 1750–1819 PARIS

A landscape painter who was also a musician and interested in the natural sciences, Valenciennes first trained at the Toulouse Academy, studying with the history painter Jean-Baptiste Despax and the miniaturist Guillaume-Gabriel Bouton. With the support of his patron, Mathias du Bourg, a member of the Toulouse parliament, he travelled to Rome in 1769. He arrived in Paris in 1771 and entered the studio of Gabriel-François Doyen in 1773 on the recommendation of the duc and duchesse de Choiseul. Four years later he was back in Rome, where he remained until 1781, spending much of his time studying perspective with an Italian mathematician. On a brief return to Paris in 1782 he met the landscape painter Claude-Joseph Vernet, who taught him the importance of sky and clouds in landscape. Valenciennes may also have learnt from Vernet the technique of the outdoor landscape oil-sketch, for on his return to Rome that year he began his now celebrated series of landscape sketches in oil on paper, many of which are in the Louvre (presented in 1930 by the princesse Louise de Croÿ). Although he was not the inventor of the oil-sketch *en plein air*, there is little doubt that Valenciennes's advocacy of the practice created widespread interest in the technique. Valenciennes's exact movements during this period are uncertain. In his *Réflexions et conseils à un élève* of 1799 he claims to have visited Asia Minor, Greece, Syria and Egypt, though Geneviève Lacambre has maintained that his travels were confined to France and Italy.[1] After returning to Paris by 1785, he was made a member of the Academy in 1787. In his studio he taught a wide variety of professional and amateur artists, numbering among his pupils Jean-Victor Bertin and Achille-Etna Michallon. Known as the 'David of landscape', he taught perspective at the Ecole des Beaux-Arts 1796–1800 and in 1812 was appointed professor of perspective. He played a prominent role in the foundation of the quadrennial Prix de Rome for *paysage historique*, the first winner of which was Michallon in 1817. Valenciennes's treatise, *Elémens de perspective pratique à l'usage des artistes, suivis de réflexions et conseils à un élève sur la peinture*, was published in 1800. Essentially two books in one, the first part is devoted to perspective, the second is a lengthy essay on the theory and practice of landscape painting. It became the basic manual for a whole generation of Neoclassical landscape painters and was Valenciennes's most lasting legacy until the recent rewakening of interest in his oil-sketches and their importance in the development of open-air landscape painting.[2]

D 5148
Black and white chalk on grey paper: 35 × 51.1
Signed and dated, lower left: *P. Valenciennes an 7* [1798]

Valenciennes appears to have first developed this detailed and highly finished style of chalk landscape drawing in the 1790s;[3] comparable examples include a pair of drawings[4] of 1790 related to the 1793 Salon painting of *Biblis* (Musée des Beaux-Arts, Quimper), *Classical Landscape with Figures near a Lake* of 1796 (Christie's, London, 8 July 1980, no.94), and *Landscape with a Statue of Alexander carved into Mount Athos* of 1799 (Hôtel Drouot, Paris, 5 December 1983, no.155). Our drawing should be considered as a finished work of art in its own right, intended for display or exhibition. In that context it is worth noting that some of Valenciennes's now celebrated *plein air* oil-sketches may have been exhibited at the Paris Salon in the late eighteenth and early nineteenth century. In the artist's posthumous sale catalogue these oil paintings after nature were described as 'having served as models to the pupils of the late M. Valenciennes'. Charles Paillet, the author of the *Notice* at the beginning of the catalogue, described Valenciennes thus: 'One of the restorers of good taste and style among French landscape painters, he trained skilled pupils who, through his advice, have today become the honour of our school; his treatise on perspective is an esteemed work and the dictionary of all the students; this useful monument confirms this principle with regard to its author [Valenciennes]: "Art wins fame through science, science is perpetuated through art."'[5] There were apparently no finished drawings in the sale, from which one can conclude that works such as ours sold well during Valenciennes's lifetime.

MC

PROVENANCE
Hazlitt, Gooden and Fox, London; from whom purchased 1987.

EXHIBITED
French Drawings of the Nineteenth Century, Hazlitt, Gooden and Fox, London, 1980, no.2; *French Drawings*, Hazlitt, Gooden and Fox, London, 1986, no.1; Edinburgh / London 1994, no.19.

Anne-Louis Girodet de Roussy-Trioson
52. *Study for Racine's* Phaedra

MONTARGIS 1767–1824 PARIS

Possessed of a difficult and at times unpleasant personality, Girodet was nevertheless one of the most talented and individual of all David's major pupils. He entered his master's studio in 1784 and tried twice for the Prix de Rome before succeeding in 1789 with *Joseph recognised by his Brothers* (Ecole des Beaux-Arts, Paris), sharing the prize with Charles Meynier. He left for Rome in 1790 and there painted *The sleeping Endymion* (Louvre, Paris), shown to great success both in Rome and at the Paris Salon of 1793. The treatment of the male nude in the *Endymion* is perhaps the most sensuous example of the erotic element often found in Girodet's art and, with its references to the grace of Correggio and the *sfumato* of Leonardo, constituted a deliberate rejection of the strict Neoclassicism advocated by David. Girodet was forced to leave Rome on account of anti-French feeling during the Revolution and spent time in Naples, Venice and Genoa, returning to Paris in 1795. He made his reputation with the *Portrait of Madame Lange as Danaë* (Institute of Arts, Minneapolis) and the *Deluge* (Louvre, Paris), shown at the Salons of 1799 and 1806 respectively. In the latter year he was adopted by Dr Benoît-François Trioson, his tutor and guardian and probably his natural father. At the decennial competition of 1810 his contemporaries judged his *Deluge* superior to David's *Sabine Women* (Louvre, Paris). The fourteen works exhibited by Girodet at the 1814 Salon constituted a virtual retrospective of his career, and the following year he was *reçu* into the Academy. He was also a prolific writer. His collected works appeared in a two-volume posthumous edition published by P.-A.Coupin in Paris in 1829 and consisted of the epic didactic poem *Le Peintre*, its embryonic form *Les Veillées*, and his correspondence and discourses.[1]

Fig.34 Anne-Louis Girodet, *Phaedra, Act IV, Scene 2*
Musée Dobrée, Nantes

D 5395
Pencil: 26 × 34.3

The *Oeuvres de Racine* appeared in Paris in 1801–5 in a three-volume illustrated atlas folio edition published by Pierre Didot (for whom Girodet had worked since 1791).[2] Dedicated to Napoleon, it was sometimes called the *Racine du Louvre* because it was printed on the former Royal Press in the Louvre. A celebration of the master playwright of French classical tragedy, Jean Racine (1639–99),[3] it fitted perfectly into the Consulate's grand design to reaffirm the hegemony of France in cultural and intellectual fields. When the first volume was exhibited in Paris in 1801 it was grandiloquently described as 'the most perfect production in the field of typography in any country or in any age'.[4] The fifty-seven engraved illustrations for the complete work were devised by eight artists chosen by David: Chaudet, Gérard, Girodet, Moitte, Peyron, Prud'hon, Sérangeli and Taunay. Gérard was commissioned to design fifteen in total, Girodet five each for *Andromache* (Volume I) and *Phaedra* (Volume II).[5]

Our drawing is a preparatory nude study for the drawing to illustrate Act IV, Scene 2 of *Phaedra*, in which Oenone has just accused Hippolytus of his passion for Phaedra and Theseus reproaches him, ordering him to leave his presence:

What! Has your anger lost all its restraint?
For the last time, be gone from my sight!
Be off, traitor. Do not wait for an enraged father
To have you torn away from me in disgrace!
(Lines 1154–1156)[6]

Girodet's finished drawing, engraved by R. U. Massard, is now in the Musée Dobrée, Nantes (fig.34).[7] It has been suggested by Osborne[8] that the head of Hippolytus may portray the well-known tragic actor Talma (1763–1826), whom Girodet could have seen in live performances of the play.

So highly did Girodet regard his final drawings for *Racine* that he exhibited them in the paintings sections of the 1800 and 1804 Salons. Those for *Phaedra* were shown at the 1804 Salon, mounted together in one frame (no.212). Apart from the Nantes drawing, four further finished drawings by Girodet for the *Racine* have been identified: *Phaedra rejecting the Embraces of Theseus* (J. Paul Getty Museum, Malibu), *Phaedra confesses her Love for Hippolytus to Oenone* and *Phaedra, having declared her Passion, attempts to kill Herself with the Sword of Hippolytus* (both with Brady / Bellinger

1997);[9] and for *Andromache*, the *Meeting of Hermione and Orestes* (Museum of Art, Cleveland).[10]

The importance Girodet vested in these drawings extended to the preparatory process. Whereas Renaissance masters and, later, David had made nude studies for their paintings, Girodet also followed this procedure for his finished drawings, which he valued as highly as his history paintings: 'I ought to mention here the drawings which I made for the folio editions of Virgil [1798] and Racine printed by M. Didot. It is wrong that drawings should be nothing more than drawings, and yet, when one prides oneself on giving them some style and character, they require the same conception and almost the same preparatory studies as a picture; the only difference is in the method of execution. The artist who succeeds in this sort of drawing can only be a history-painter or sculptor who has the right to expect recognition in his real field.'[11] In addition to our drawing, only three other nude studies for the *Racine* illustrations are known: *The Suicide of Phaedra* (Cabinet des Dessins, Louvre, Paris),[12] *Hermione and Oenone* (Musée Bonnat, Bayonne)[13] and *The Return of Orestes* (Art Institute, Chicago). Interestingly, a rapidly sketched compositional drawing for *The Suicide of Phaedra*, now in the Musée des Beaux-Arts at Rouen,[14] provides the expected evidence that the extraordinarily beautiful and highly finished nude studies and the finished drawings for the engraver would have been preceded by quickly sketched *premières pensées*. Both the *première pensée* and the nude studies are of horizontal format, the normal Neoclassical stage on which to work out visual ideas for multi-figured compositions. The finished drawings are vertical, however, as determined by the shape of Didot's grand publication.

M C

PROVENANCE
Antoine César Becquerel (Girodet's cousin and executor);[15] Henri Becquerel; his wife, Louise Lorieux; her nephew, Pierre Deslandres; then by descent, acquired Richard L. Feigen & Co., New York; from whom purchased 1995.

EXHIBITED
Girodet 1764–1824, Musée de Montargis, Montargis, 1967, no.70; *Neo-Classicism and Romanticism in French Painting 1774–1826*, Richard L. Feigen & Co., New York, 1994, no.18.

Jean-Auguste-Dominique Ingres
53. *Portrait of Mlle Albertine Hayard*

MONTAUBAN 1780–1867 PARIS

Ingres can justly be claimed as the major French painter of the first half of the nineteenth century. Encouraged by his father, who was a painter, sculptor and architect at Montauban, he enrolled at the Toulouse Academy in 1791. He also showed a talent for music, and in 1796 was second violin in the orchestra of the Capitole at Toulouse. In 1797 he travelled to Paris to enter David's studio. He won first prize in the 1801 Prix de Rome for his *Ambassadors of Agamemnon* (Ecole des Beaux-Arts, Paris) but circumstances prevented his travelling to Rome until 1806. In the meantime he was granted a small pension, a studio in the former convent of the Capuchins in Paris, and received official commissions such as those for *Bonaparte at Liège* (Musée des Beaux-Arts, Liège) and *Napoleon Enthroned* (Musée de l'Armée, Paris). He finally travelled to Rome in September 1806 and remained in Italy until 1824. His prolonged stay at the French Academy in Rome was a period of intense activity. There were major paintings for Napoleon such as *Ossian* (Musée Ingres, Montauban), his official *envoi* to the Institut de France of *Jupiter and Thetis* (Musée Granet, Aix-en-Provence), and numerous portraits of the French community in Rome. After the fall of the French Empire in 1814, Ingres suffered a temporary reversal but he soon began to receive official commissions again under the Bourbon monarchy, and in the period 1815–25 produced many works in his troubadour style such as *The Death of Leonardo da Vinci* (Musée du Petit Palais, Paris). In 1824 he returned to France where his *Vow of Louis XIII* (Cathedral, Montauban) was shown to great acclaim at the Salon. He was awarded the Légion d'honneur, made a member of the Institut de France and opened a flourishing studio where he taught many pupils. He returned to Rome as Director of the French Academy 1835–41. Despite various disputes with the critics, the later part of Ingres's career was one of official success, even after he ceased exhibiting at the Salon and reserved his works for specific admirers. In 1853 he was appointed, along with Delacroix, to the imperial commission presided over by Prince Napoleon to direct and supervise the 1855 Exposition Universelle, in which an entire gallery was devoted to his works.

D 5100
Pencil: 21.5 × 15.1
Signed and dated, lower left: *Ingres a Rome / 1812.*

Over 450 portrait drawings by Ingres are known,[1] the majority executed between 1806–24. Some, as may have been the case here, were done out of friendship, others on commission. Albertine (1797–1833) was the eldest of the four daughters of Charles-Roch Hayard (1768–1839), who sold artists'materials from his shop in the Via dei Due Macelli off the Piazza di Spagna, just a short distance from the French Academy in the Villa Medici, Rome.[2] Hayard would therefore have been known by many of the *pensionnaires* at the Academy and Ingres was a faithful client and became a close friend. He drew a total of seven portraits of members of the Hayard family, the first in 1811 and the last in 1843.[3] This portrait of Albertine,[4] aged fourteen or fifteen, was probably made just before her marriage on 17 January 1812 in the church of San Andrea delle Fratte to the landscape painter Pierre-Athanase Chauvin (1774–1832). Naef has suggested that the profile format of this portrait drawing, together with those of others dating from 1810–11, may have been influenced by Ingres's friendship with the medallist Edouard Gatteaux, which began in 1809.[5] Two years later Ingres drew a second portrait of Albertine, heavily pregnant (Musée Bonnat, Bayonne).[6] The Chauvins lived at Piazza Mignatelli, not far from the Via Gregorina, where Ingres had an appartment until his departure for Florence in 1820. Chauvin had been a witness to Ingres's 1813 marriage to Madeleine Chapelle. The Chauvins, who appear to have had four children, did not enjoy good fortune, however, as the painter Granet noted in a letter of 15 January 1830 from Rome to Ingres back in Paris: 'Our friend Chauvin is always ill, as is his wife. This house-hold is not at all happy, without any rapport. They tell you a thousand things.'[7] Two years later Chauvin was dead from a heart attack and his wife died only thirteen months after him.

M C

PROVENANCE
Félix Duban (died 1870, brother-in-law of the sitter); his daughter, Mme Théodore Maillot (died 1898, born Félicie-Charlotte Duban); her cousin, Félix Flachéron (died 1927); Georges Bernheim, Paris, by 1921; purchased probably shortly thereafter by Maria Luisa Caturla, Madrid; Mrs Marianne Feilchenfeldt, Zurich; from whom purchased with the aid of the National Art Collections Fund 1981.

EXHIBITED
Ingres, Ecole des Beaux-Arts, Paris 1867, no.549, lent Duban; *Ingres*, Chambre syndicale de la Curiosité et des Beaux-Arts, Paris, 1921, no.72; Edinburgh 1984, no.19; Edinburgh 1991, no.83; Edinburgh / London 1994, no.15.

Jean-Victor Schnetz
54. *Wounded Officer with two Soldiers and a Drummer*

VERSAILLES 1787–1870 PARIS

Schnetz was a pupil of David and then of Regnault, Gros and Gérard. He exhibited at the Salon 1808–67 and was awarded a first-class medal in 1819 and another at the Exposition Universelle of 1855. In the course of a long career, as yet insufficiently researched, he practised as a painter of history, genre and portraits and as a printmaker. The first of his numerous stays in Rome lasted from 1816 (after a journey made on foot) until 1832. By the mid-1820s he had made an international reputation with his genre paintings with themes from popular Italian life, and he was a friend of both Horace Vernet and Léopold Robert. His studio in the Via del Babuino became a fashionable stop for Grand Tourists and was included by Stendahl in his list of recommended Roman sites in his *Promenades dans Rome* of 1829. Schnetz was made a member of the Institut de France in 1827 and was Director of the Ecole des Beaux-Arts, Paris 1837–41. He was first appointed to the Directorship of the French Academy in Rome 1840–47 and, such was his popularity with the students there, he was reappointed 1852–65. During this latter period he did much to foster a revival of interest in depicting popular Italian life among the students at the Academy.[1] He worked in fresco in the Parisian churches of Notre-Dame de Lorette, Saint-Séverin and Ste-Marie-Madeleine. He was made a member of the Académie des Beaux-Arts in 1837 and of the Légion d'honneur in 1843. His work is widely represented in French museums.[2]

D 5416
Pen and brown ink and brown wash over black chalk, heightened with white gouache, on brown tinted paper: 24.5 × 20.8
Signed, dated and inscribed in pencil, lower left (partially cut through at the corner): *Schnetz 1817 Rome*

The subject-matter of this drawing represents a continuation of the fashion for such military scenes during the Napoleonic era and may well be symptomatic of pro-Republican sympathies on Schnetz's part. His now lost submission to the 1808 Salon had depicted *The Bravery of a French Soldier.*

This belongs to a small group of highly distinctive chiaroscuro drawings with white gouache highlighting by Schnetz which date from his early years in Rome: these include *Homage to the Soldiers of the 45th Column* (Christie's, New York, 22 May 1997, lot 16, illus.);[3] *The Little Drummer* (Private Collection);[4] *Wounded Antique Warrior* (Private Collection, New York)[5] and *The Greek Hero.*[6] Other French artists in Rome at this period, many of them first-generation pupils of David, also employed this technique, indicative of a then widespread interest in drawing as a finished art form.[7]

Our drawing is remarkably similar in style and technique to a number of gouaches produced by Géricault in Rome around this time and Schnetz may have influenced Géricault in this respect. As Wheelock Whitney has pointed out, there is documentary evidence that the two artists knew each other well and were in close touch in Italy,[8] and Géricault is recorded as having a high opinion of Schnetz's work. Indeed, Schnetz was far better known in Rome than Géricault, and his painting *Cain's Remorse* (Accademia di San Luca, Rome) won the Premio dell'Anonimo for painting at the Accademia di San Luca in 1817, the year of our drawing. Géricault complained to his father some years later that he was unable to track down 'les blancs de Schnetz',[9] and he may well have been referring to the passages of pure white gouache found in drawings such as this one.

MC

PROVENANCE
Private Collection, France; from which purchased 1994 by Paul Prouté, Paris;[10] from whom bought by Hazlitt, Gooden & Fox, London; from whom purchased 1996.

EXHIBITED
Nineteenth Century French Drawings and some Sculpture, Hazlitt, Gooden and Fox, London, 1996, no.6.

Louis-Nicolas Cabat
55. *View of the Villa Belvedere, Vatican, Rome*

PARIS 1812–1893 PARIS

First apprenticed 1825–28 as a painter on porcelain at the Gouverneur factory in Paris, Cabat then studied with the landscape painter Camille Flers and, through the dealer Mme Hulin, probably met the landscape painters Bonington and Huet. He worked in the environs of Paris, and then in 1831 in Normandy and in 1832 in the Berry in the company of Jules Dupré (whose style strongly influenced his early work). He was a frequent visitor to the Forest of Fontainebleau but he also travelled to Italy, the first and most important visit lasting from 1836 to 1839. In the mid-1830s he broke away from the naturalistic style of landscape painting, then dominant in France, to develop a highly individual mixture of classicism and religiosity (he was a Catholic convert and at one stage considered becoming a Dominican). Cabat was a regular exhibitor at the Salon from 1830 until his death. In 1847 he married a native of Troyes, Emilie Bazin, through whose paternal grandfather he became particularly attached to the village of Bercenay-en-Othe in the département of the Aube, which he revisited regularly and where he established a studio in the Bazin family house. Cabat was elected to the Institut de France in 1867 and from 1878 to 1885 was Director of the French Academy in Rome. His régime there was criticised for being too lax and he was replaced by the allegedly more rigorous Hébert.[1]

D 5414

Pencil, pen, brown ink and wash, on three pieces of paper, joined together: 43.5 × 77.5

When acquired by the Gallery, this drawing bore the title 'The Villa Medici'. However, the architectural structure depicted here bears no more than a passing similarity to the building that since 1803 has housed the French Academy in Rome. Cabat's directorship of the Villa Medici, 1878–85, may have prompted the mistaken identification. In a recent article Carol Richardson has correctly identified the view as showing the Villa Belvedere, Pope Innocent VIII's late-fifteenth-century retreat from the nearby Vatican palaces.[2] As Richardson demonstrates, the view is taken from just before the Porta Castello, looking along the walls of the Borgo Pio towards the bastion of Belvedere. Such a grand and structured composition, with a bowed figure approaching along a zig-zag road, is broadly reminiscent of Nicolas Poussin's heroic landscapes of the late 1640s. Even before Cabat's first visit to Italy 1836–9 (punctuated by a brief return to France in 1838), contemporary critics had noted his predilection for the work of the seventeenth-century master.[3] Of Cabat's *View of the Gorge-aux-Loups, Forest of Fontainebleau*, exhibited at the 1835 Salon, the critic of *L'Artiste* observed, 'To be sure, he dreams of Poussin as he used to dream formerly of Flemish landscapes; … there are all these great landscapes by the author of Diogenes [ie Poussin, whose painting of *Diogenes* is in the Louvre, Paris] which pass ceaselessly in front of his eyes and which interpose themselves between the real point of view and the painter'.[4] Again, in 1841, W. Tenint in his Salon review referred to Cabat having been 'seduced by the severe school of Poussin to the extent of having sacrificed his own free will to him'.[5] However, around 1834–5 Cabat had deliberately turned towards the art of artists such as Claude and Poussin in his desire to achieve a harmonious idealism in his art, very different from the northern realism of his early work. He was not alone in this idealising tendency, and other French landscape painters who can be mentioned in this context include the Benouville brothers, Caruelle d'Aligny and Paul Flandrin. However, the catalyst in Cabat's case for such an abrupt change in style was provided by his conversion to a devout and liberal Catholicism under the guidance of his spiritual mentor, Père Lacordaire.[6] Richardson has also drawn attention to the possible significance, in this context, of such a papal site.[7] In his drawings Cabat came to adopt a simpler style with greater emphasis on line. The evidence of the landscape drawing now in the Cabinet des Dessins of the Louvre (fig.35), inscribed *Rome 20 Novembre 1836* and bearing a number of stylistic similarities to the Edinburgh drawing, seems to be that the Italian visit of 1836–9 provides a *terminus post quem* for our drawing, though it could date from considerably later (Pierre Miquel has suggested *c.*1850[8]), as Cabat's style remained fairly constant thereafter. Large in size, executed on three pieces of paper joined together, it has to be classed as one of his most ambitious drawings and one intended for display or exhibition.

MC

PROVENANCE

Pierre Miquel, Cannes; from whom bought by Galerie Brame et Lorenceau, Paris; from whom purchased 1996.

Fig.35 Louis-Nicolas Cabat, *Roman Landscape*, 1836
Musée du Louvre, Paris

Jean-Auguste-Dominique Ingres
56. *The Dream of Ossian*

For biography, see cat.no.53.

D 5369

Pencil, black chalk, white and cream heightening and grey wash on green-blue paper: 26 × 20.5
Inscribed in pencil below: *Ingres Pinx rome 1811; Songe d'Ossian* and *Don à son ami et cher confrere hippolite Lebas*

Our drawing is based on Ingres's large oval painting of this subject (fig.36)[1] commissioned by Napoleon in 1811 for the ceiling of his bedroom in the Palazzo di Monte Cavallo on the Quirinal in Rome. After Napoleon's downfall the palace was occupied by Pope Pius VII who removed all trace of Napoleon's decorative scheme. On his return to Rome in 1835 Ingres reclaimed his painting and, with his assistant Raymond Balze, reworked it to a rectangular format (Musée Ingres, Montauban). Eight drawings related to the complete composition have been identified (there are also studies of individual motifs),[2] though scholars have disputed the order in which they were made (at least five, including ours, post-date the initial painting).[3] Nearly all are agreed, however, that the ex-Gilibert watercolour (Private Collection, Montauban)[4] is the first in the sequence and probably predates the painting by a few years. Next, by fairly common consent, come two line drawings on tracing paper (Musée Ingres, Montauban)[5] which were probably done in connection with the painting. These are followed by a pen, ink and wash drawing, signed and dated 1813 (Private Collection, France).[6] Two later watercolours bear erroneous dates by Ingres of 1809 and 1812 (Fogg Art Museum, Cambridge, Mass.; Louvre, Paris).[7] Our drawing has an inscription below stating that it was presented by Ingres to the architect Louis-Hippolyte Lebas (1782–1867). Although it has been suggested that it might have been made and presented to Lebas around 1825,[8] when both he and Ingres were elected to the Institut de France, in certain respects it is closer to the 1851 print by Réveil,[9] from a publication created under Ingres's direction and reproducing his works up to that year, and in style it is also similar to the late signed and dated drawing of 1866 in the Musée Ingres, Montauban (fig.37). In particular, the figure of Ossian's daughter-in-law Malvina has a comparable bound hairstyle. This whole series of drawings, and the later reworking of the original painting, bear fascinating witness to Ingres's continuing fascination with the subject of Ossian, even though the authenticity of the poems had come to be widely, and correctly, doubted.[10]

MC

PROVENANCE
Louis-Hippolyte Lebas; Monsieur Boulot; De Bayser, Paris; Private Collection, Switzerland; Christie's, New York, 11 January 1994, no.343, where purchased.

EXHIBITED
Edinburgh 1994, no.15.

Fig.37 Jean-Auguste-Dominique Ingres,
The Dream of Ossian, drawing
Musée Ingres, Montauban

Fig.36 Jean-Auguste-Dominique Ingres,
The Dream of Ossian, painting
Musée Ingres, Montauban

Songe d'Ossian

Alexandre-Gabriel Decamps
57. Interior of a Buttery in a Farmhouse

PARIS 1803–1860 FONTAINEBLEAU

Decamps spent his childhood years in Picardy, returning to Paris in 1816, where he trained with with Etienne Buhot c.1816–17 and Abel de Pujol c.1818–19. Around this time he formed close friendships with the painters Jadin and Roqueplan. He also studied the collections in the Louvre, particularly the Dutch School. Decamps made his only trip to the Orient in 1828, accompanying Louis Garneray (1783–1857) who had been commissioned to paint the *Battle of Navarino* (Musée national du château, Versailles) and was researching the actual sites of French victories against the Ottoman Empire. The two men soon separated, with Decamps staying on for almost a year in Smyrna (Izmir in modern Turkey) and proceeding on his own to Greece and North Africa (he also visited Italy in 1835). Oriental scenes became very much his stock-in-trade and critics remarked favourably on his *Turkish Patrol* (Wallace Collection, London), exhibited at the 1831 Salon. His moment of triumph came with the *Retreat of the Cimbri* (Louvre, Paris), shown at the 1834 Salon. As a result of his travels Decamps became ardently pro-Turk, in contrast to many of his colleagues who were more fashionably pro-Greek. He continued to show work at the Salon until 1851. The Exposition Universelle of 1855 included 58 of his works. Decamps was made *chevalier* of the Légion d'honneur in 1839 and *officier* in 1851. He retired to Veyrier, near Barbizon, in 1853, moving to Fontainebleau in 1857. Decamps died as the result of a riding accident in the Forest of Fontainebleau.

D 5411

Black chalk, heightened with white chalk, on blue paper: 49.8 × 43.8
Signed on the butter churn, left centre: DC

This belongs to a group of drawings of similar technique and subject-matter which includes *A Farm House Interior with a Table and Baskets* (Art Gallery of Ontario, Toronto, see fig.38).[1] The most closely related to our drawing is the *Interior of a Buttery* (formerly with Houthakker),[2] in which the same table in the same room is sketched from a point to the left of the viewpoint of our drawing and the same scales hang from the ceiling beam, but the butter churn is placed on the table. These drawings may date from after 1853 when Decamps went into semi-retirement at Veyrier, near Fontainebleau.[3]

Throughout his career Decamps produced large, finished genre drawings which were greatly admired by his fellow artists and collectors. The landscape painter Paul Huet recalled how, when he and Decamps both exhibited charcoal drawings at a dealer's in the rue Neuve-Vivienne in Paris, 'I have seen lovers of Decamps's work go into raptures in front of his drawings, in spite of everything, and not look at mine at all'.[4]

M C

PROVENANCE

Decamps sale, Hôtel Drouot, Paris 29 June 1970 (stamp on old mount); Seiferheld & Co., New York; Private Collection; Sotheby's, New York, 19 January 1995, no.346; bought Colnaghi; from whom purchased 1996.

EXHIBITED

Winter Drawings Exhibition, Colnaghi, London, 1995–6, no.40; *Corot, Courbet und die Maler von Barbizon*, Haus der Kunst, Munich, 1996, no.C38.

Fig.38 Alexandre-Gabriel Descamps,
A Farm House Interior with a Table and Baskets
Art Gallery of Ontario, Toronto

Ernest Hébert
58. *Study for* The Women of Cervara (Les Cervarolles)

GRENOBLE 1817–1908 LA TRONCHE (ISÈRE)

After studying with Benjamin Rolland in Grenoble, Hébert left for Paris in 1834 and entered the Ecole des Beaux-Arts where he passed through the studios of Monvoisin, David d'Angers and Delaroche. In 1839 he was awarded the Prix de Rome and stayed in Italy 1840–47 (where he studied under Ingres and Schnetz amongst others). In Florence in 1844 he met and was befriended by Princesse Mathilde, German cousin of the future Napoleon III. He was awarded a first-class medal at the 1850–51 Salon for his painting *Mal'aria* (Musée d'Orsay, Paris) and this really marked the beginning of his official career: throughout the Second Empire and Third Republic his work alternated between scenes of Italian life and fashionable portraits, both suffused with a languid melancholy which was considered highly poetic. He belonged to a generation of late, academically trained, Romantics who anticipated, in certain respects, the Symbolists at the end of the century: Hébert's biographer, Sâr Joséphin Péladan,[1] was an important member of the Symbolist movement. Between 1853 and 1858 Hébert made two long voyages in Italy preparatory to his submissions to the Salons of 1857 and 1859. He was appointed Director of the French Academy in Rome in 1866.

Fig.39 Ernest Hébert, *Les Cervarolles*
Musée d'Orsay, Paris

D 5398
Coloured chalks on beige paper: 48 × 31.3

This is a study for the main figure in the painting *Les Cervarolles (Etats romains)* (fig.39),[2] which Hébert exhibited at the 1859 Salon (1420) where it was well received by most of the critics. It was purchased by the State for 15,000 francs (one of the highest sums ever paid by the Imperial Museums) and placed in the Musée du Luxembourg (it is now in the Musée d'Orsay, Paris). It was essentially a reworking of the theme of Italian peasant women previously explored by Hébert in *The Girls of Alvito* (Musée Hébert, Paris) of 1857 and demonstrates his ambition to make genre painting aspire to the ambition of history painting. Studies of Italian women in costume had been made by French artists since the late eighteenth century and had featured prominently in the Italianate genre scenes of artists such as Léopold Robert. Many of these country models gravitated to Rome, where they were drawn and painted by the artists resident there. Hébert, on the other hand, wished to depict these peasant women at source in their native villages.

His biographer, Sâr Joséphin Péladan, gives a somewhat melodramatic account of the execution of *Les Cervarolles*, claiming that the artist required six months in Cervara di Roma (high up in the Alban hills outside Rome) to persuade these 'fierce beauties'[3] to pose for him and that he was snowbound in dreadful conditions for eighteen months![4] Hébert stayed in Cervara from October 1856 to May 1858 and, such was the size of the canvas he had had delivered from Rome for the painting of *Les Cervarolles*, the roof of his studio had to be raised.

In an article of 1897, Georges Lafenestre speculated that the three figures in the painting might symbolise the three ages of life.[5] A smaller painting by Hébert, *Going to the Well* (Walters Art Gallery, Baltimore),[6] reproduces the central figure of *Les Cervarolles*.

Our drawing was previously unpublished, but a number of other related drawings have been reproduced in the earlier literature. Lafenestre illustrates two studies, one for the head of the central figure, the other showing her full-length, both of which are now in the Musée Hébert, Paris. One bears the date 1854 and the inscription *Adelaide*; in the other the model is referred to as

Adela.[7] Another drawing of her, entitled *L'Orfanella*, is reproduced in a 1906 article by Jules Claretie.[8] A drawing of the entire composition appeared at auction in Paris in 1990.[9]

M C

PROVENANCE
James Mackinnon, London; from whom purchased 1995.

Alexandre-Jean-Baptiste Hesse
59. *A Kneeling Shepherd*

PARIS 1806–1879 PARIS

Initially trained by his father, the painter Henri-Joseph Hesse, Alexandre entered the studio of Jean-Victor Bertin in 1820, enrolling at the Ecole des Beaux-Arts the following year where he frequented the studio of baron Gros, who taught many history painters. He made the first of three trips to Italy in 1830, meeting Horace Vernet in Rome, then continuing on to Venice. He made his début at the Salon in 1833 with his *Funeral Honours rendered to Titian after his Death at Venice during the Plague of 1576* (Louvre, Paris), winning a first-class medal. In the same year he returned to Italy (he made a third trip 1843–7), making copies of Renaissance master-pieces in Florence and Venice. Three years later he was commissioned by the State to paint *Henry IV brought back to the Louvre after his Assassination* (Château, Versailles), destined for the Galerie d'Apollon in the Louvre. Like his uncle, the painter Nicolas-Auguste Hesse, he participated in the 1848 competition to provide an allegorical figure of the Republic. In addition to his Salon paintings (where he continued to exhibit until 1861), he worked on a number of major public commissions for church decorations in Paris,[1] including the chapels of Sainte-Geneviève at Saint-Séverin (1850–2), Saint-François-de-Sales at Saint-Sulpice (1854–60), and that of Saint-Gervais-Saint-Protais (1863–7) in the church of that name. Hesse was elected a member of the Académie des Beaux-Arts, in place of Ingres, in 1867, and was made *officier* of the Légion d'honneur the following year. He was nick-named 'the last Venetian' on account of the strong colouring in his work.[2]

D 5392

Coloured chalks, with white heightening, on tan paper: 47.5 × 35.6
Signed, inscribed and dated, lower left: *Alexandre Hesse / al suo garbatissimo amico / V. Baltard / 1867*

This beautiful drawing is a study for the figure of the kneeling shepherd in the lower right-hand corner of the *Nativity* which Hesse painted for the choir of the country church of Chevry-en-Sereine, near Nemours (see fig.40). Two further studies for the painting, one of a *Standing Infant*, the other of a *Bearded Man*, are in the Ecole des Beaux-Arts, Paris, both forming part of Hesse's bequest of the contents of his studio in 1879.[3]

Hesse was commissioned in May 1861 by Mme Brisson, owner of the Château of Chevry-en-Sereine and whose family were already consider-able patrons of the artist,[4] to decorate the choir and family chapel of the village church there. Of the four murals for the choir, two were in vertical format – *Christ in the Garden of Olives* and *Christ tempted by the Devil*, and two were in horizontal format – *Mary Magdalen in the House of Simon* and *The Nativity*. In order to combat the harmful effects of humidity, the walls of the church were carefully resurfaced with slabs fixed with bronze tenons and were then coated with lead white and wax. The paintings were executed in a mixture of oil and wax. Despite these efforts, it was noted that substantial restoration was necessary only two years after the completion of the scheme in 1863.

Our drawing was dedicated ('to his most kind friend') by Hesse to Victor Baltard (1805–1874), chief architect for the City of Paris and diocesan architect to the département of the Seine. According to the date, it was presented to him four years after the completion of the Chevry-en-Sereine decorations. Baltard was the main dispenser of important contracts to artists for the decoration of public interiors in Paris, both ecclesiastical and secular. Architect of Les Halles and restorer of a number of churches using metal structures, he worked in close collaboration with his friend, the painter Hippolyte Flandrin, on the decoration of a number of churches, most famously Saint-Germain-des-Prés. The presenta-tion of such a drawing as ours to Baltard, with its rather sycophantic inscription, is therefore comprehensible in the circumstances, and also indicates Hesse's own high opinion of this particular sheet. The gift may well have been made in connection with Hesse's work on the decorations for the chapel of Saint-Gervais-Saint-Protais which, as Baltard reported in an official communication of 9 October 1866, were nearing completion:[5] the project was jointly funded by the City of Paris and the State.

MC

PROVENANCE
Victor Baltard; W. M. Brady, New York, from whom purchased 1994.

Fig.40 Alexandre-Jean-Baptiste Hesse, *Nativity*
Church of Chevry-en-Sereine

Georges Seurat
60. *Study for* Une baignade

PARIS 1859–1891 PARIS

For a brief period of five years between 1886, when he exhibited *Un dimanche à la Grande Jatte* (Art Institute, Chicago) and his early death at the age of thirty-one, Seurat dominated avant-garde painting in Paris and forged a new visual language, based on the use of dots of pure colour, which the critic Félix Fénéon dubbed Neo-Impressionism. In 1878 Seurat entered the studio of Henri Lehmann, a former pupil of Ingres. After military service 1879–80, he returned to his artistic career, concentrating particularly on drawing. He exhibited for the first time at the Salon in 1883 and began work later in the year on *Une baignade, Asnières* (National Gallery, London), shown at the Salon des Indépendants the following year. There he made the acquaintance of artists such as Signac, Angrand, Redon and Schuffenecker and with them created the Société des Artistes Indépendants, successor to the Groupe des Artistes Indépendants. In 1885 he was befriended by Camille Pissarro, who was much influenced by his divisionist technique, and in the following year participated in the sixth and last Impressionist exhibition, to which he contributed the *Grande Jatte*. From 1887 he began to turn his attention to the significance of line in painting, believing that certain directions of line could express specific emotions – horizontal lines represented calmness, upward- and downward-sloping lines represented happiness and sadness respectively. Such ideas found expression in paintings such as *Le Chahut* (Rijksmuseum Kröller-Müller, Otterlo) of 1890. Seurat died suddenly in late March the following year, probably of malignant diphtheria.

D 5110

Conté crayon: 32 × 24.5
Verso: inscribed in blue and red crayon respectively:
G Seurat L.Baignade and 368[1]

The study is for the central figure on the bank in *Une baignade, Asnières* ('A bathing place, Asnières) (fig.41).[2] The painting was begun in 1883, submitted in early spring to the 1884 Salon, where it was rejected, and then shown at the newly formed Groupe des Artistes Indépendants, whose exhibition opened in May. Critics compared the monumental, frieze-like, figured design of the painting both to the work of Puvis de Chavannes and to that of the Renaissance masters. It was certainly the result of careful preparation, for no fewer than thirteen related oil-sketches (*croquetons* 'sketchettes')[3] and up to eleven drawings are known.[4] The latter are all drawn on the Michallet brand of 'Ingres' paper which Seurat favoured. It is a heavy-textured, high-quality rag paper which is milky-white when fresh, but creamy off-white after long exposure to light. The black conté crayon which Seurat used was a solid, greasy medium which does not crumble or smudge like charcoal and allows the artist to apply differing degrees of pressure, particularly effective in achieving the penumbral effects Seurat sought. Our study, which would have been made from a studio model (very much in the Beaux-Arts tradition), was translated with only a few alterations into the finished figure in the painting. Relatively well-groomed in the drawing, the boy is less slumped in the painting and has acquired a bathing-suit. He has become the central participant in an allegory of suburban summertime played out by working-class males. Asnières, on the Seine to the west of the centre of Paris, was not a smart area. Some of the earlier oil-sketches, such as that in the National Gallery of Scotland (fig.42), illustrate the plainness of this industrial site, where horses and dogs were bathed: in the final picture the horses have been removed, though the factories of Clichy remain.

M C

PROVENANCE
Georges Lecomte, Paris;[5] Dr Alfred Gold, Berlin, until 1928; sold to Reid and Lefevre, London, in 1928; with Etienne Bignou, Paris; Simon A. Morrison, London; purchased by private treaty through Christie's from a private owner in London 1982.

EXHIBITED
Les dessins de Georges Seurat (1859–1891), Bernheim-Jeune, Paris, 1926, no.148 suppl.; *Seurat: Paintings and Drawings*, David Carritt Limited, London, 1978, no.16; Edinburgh 1984, no.6; *Georges Seurat 1859–1891*, Paris / New York, 1991–2, no.113; *Seurat and the Bathers*, National Gallery, London, 1997, no.7.

Fig.42 Georges Seurat, Study for *Une baignade, Asnières*
National Gallery of Scotland, Edinburgh

Fig.41 Georges Seurat, *Une baignade, Asnières*
National Gallery, London

David Paton

61. *Portrait of Two Gentlemen* (traditionally titled *The Yester Lords*)

FL. FROM C.1660; DIED AFTER 1708 (LONDON?)
Paton was one of the very few Scottish portrait miniaturists active during the seventeenth century. Little is known about his life, which is as yet inadequately researched. Although he is thought to have executed several oil paintings,[1] he is best known for his miniature portraits and copies after Old Master paintings in plumbago, or sometimes pen, on vellum. Existing literature is inconsistent and gives a variety of dates for Paton's career. Andrews and Brotchie propose that he was born about 1650 and that he worked in Edinburgh from 1668.[2] Foskett and Long both suggest that he flourished from around 1660 and that he practised in Scotland until the mid-1690s.[3] Edinburgh's poll tax records for 1694 register one 'David Patton picttor drawer' as a lodger in the house of Robert Mylne, the King's Master Mason (1633–1710), while the city's annuity rolls for 1697–8 twice mention a 'David Paton Limner'.[4] Though he was apparently based chiefly in Edinburgh, correspondence dated 1708 from Jacopo Giraldi, the Tuscan Envoy in London, to Cosmo III de' Medici, Grand Duke of Tuscany, in Florence, records that Paton moved in his old age to London.[5] His widespread reputation is evidenced by the fact that the Grand Duke commissioned a series of miniatures via Giraldi, including portraits of Sir Isaac Newton and of several Scottish gentlemen.[6] One of Giraldi's letters hints that Paton had visited Florence in his early years. Indeed, Paton had accompanied the Hon. William Tollemache (b.1662), youngest son of Elizabeth, Countess of Dysart, on his Grand Tour of Italy in the late 1670s. In 1672 Elizabeth, widow of Sir Lionel Talmash, had married John Maitland, 1st Duke of Lauderdale (1616–1682), one of the most powerful politicians in early Restoration Scotland and a close confidant of Charles II. Manuscripts relating to this tour, which Waterhouse claims took in Florence and Venice,[7] are in Ham House (National Trust), Lauderdale's seat in Richmond, Surrey. Paton may have made an earlier visit to Italy, again under the patronage of the Maitland family; a miniature in plumbago said to be of Richard Maitland (1653–1695), subsequently 4th Earl of Lauderdale and eldest son of the 1st Duke's brother, Lord Hatton, is in the Victoria and Albert Museum and is signed on the reverse 'D. Paton fe. Romae / 1674'.[8] Andrews and Brotchie also note that Paton was known to have been in Turin in 1671.[9] Paton was patronised by many of Scotland's most eminent families. Outstanding examples of his work remain at Ham House, and in the collections of the Duke of Hamilton at Lennoxlove, East Lothian, and of the Duke of Buccleuch and Queensberry.[10]

D 4739
Plumbago on vellum (irregular: corners trimmed): 13.6 × 16.2

This exquisite double portrait is the earliest Scottish drawing in the National Gallery of Scotland. Neither signed nor dated, it is attributed to Paton on the basis of its style and provenance. The drawing was gifted to the Gallery, bearing the traditional title 'The Yester Lords', by a descendent of David Hay of Belton (1656–1726), second son of John Hay, 1st Marquess of Tweeddale (1626–1697). The title derives from Yester House, the Tweeddales' seat in East Lothian, and has hitherto led to the tentative identification of the sitters as either the 1st Marquess of Tweeddale (left) with his stepbrother William Hay of Drummelzier (1649–1726) or as John, 2nd Marquess (1645–1713) with his younger brother David Hay of Belton.[11] For several reasons these identifications now seem impossible.

The drawing can be dated to the early to mid-1660s by the sitters' clothing. Both men wear the latest fashions of the early Restoration period, with bib-style lace cravats tied with ornate tasselled strings and long French wigs, dressed flat on the crown and fuller at the sides, in a style popularised by Charles II (fig.43). The gentleman on the left adopts the vogue for teasing out strands of natural hair to form a fringe. The age of the sitters can only be guessed; however, the fuller face and heavy jowl of the man on the left suggest that he is in his middle years and slightly older than his companion. If one tries to correlate this visual evidence with the Tweeddales' dates, the case for the identification disintegrates. For the sake of argument, if one takes the year 1664 as the date of the drawing, the 1st Marquis (portrayed in other portraits with a cleft chin, which is not shown here)[12] would have been thirty-eight and his step-brother only fifteen. The 2nd Marquess, a few years older than his uncle, would have been nineteen, and his brother David but a child of eight.

If, then, these are not the Yester Lords, who are they? It is conceivable that the portrait shows Paton's great patron, the Duke of Lauderdale (in 1664 still an Earl) with his younger brother Charles Maitland (c.1620–1691), who rose to become an Ordinary Lord of Session in Scotland under the judicial title Lord Hatton and, subsequently, 3rd Earl of Lauderdale. The relative ages of the sitters are feasible (forty-eight versus forty-

four), while comparison with other portraits of the Duke, such as that by Jacob Huysmans in the National Portrait Gallery, London, shows a distinct facial similarity.[13] Furthermore, it is perfectly plausible that the drawing should have passed to the Hay family, for in 1666 John, 2nd Marquess of Tweeddale, married Mary, the only child of the Duke of Lauderdale by his first wife. The wedding took place in Middlesex, where the bride was given away in great splendour by Charles II himself.

Although the style of this drawing can be compared to the work of other contemporary English miniaturists such as David Loggan, William Faithorne and Robert White, the association with Lauderdale makes Paton the most likely candidate. The use of sixteenth-century pictorial conventions – the foreground ledge draped with tapestry, flanking pillars and swagged curtains – imply that this is an ambitious early composition, for which the young artist sought inspiration from traditional portraiture.

K T

PROVENANCE
By descent to Miss J. S. Maxwell, North Berwick, by whom presented to the Gallery 1954.

EXHIBITED
Patrons and Painters: Art in Scotland 1650–1750, Scottish National Portrait Gallery, Edinburgh, 1989, illus. p.22; *The Line of Tradition: Watercolours, Drawings and Prints by Scottish Artists 1700–1900*, National Gallery of Scotland, Edinburgh, 1993.

Fig.43 David Paton after Samuel Cooper, *Charles II (1630–85)*
By courtesy of His Grace The Duke of Buccleuch and Queensberry KT.[14]

Paul Sandby
62. *Horse Fair on Bruntsfield Links, Edinburgh*

NOTTINGHAM 1731–1809 LONDON

Sandby was probably first trained by his older brother Thomas (1721–1798), a skilled topographical draughtsman and architect. Following his brother's footsteps, in c.1746 Paul was employed by the Board of Ordnance at the Tower of London as a military draughtsman. Later that year he was appointed chief draughtsman to the Military Survey in Scotland. He travelled extensively across Scotland with the Survey, which was established in the wake of the Jacobite Rebellion to provide the army with reliable maps, in order to control any future insurrection. Sandby's earliest known drawings date from 1747, shortly after he took up his Scottish post.[1] In 1752 he severed his ties with the Board of Ordnance and took up residence in London and Windsor. Some of his finest works in the decade following his return to England were etchings and engravings, including eight satires attacking Hogarth (1753–4) and *Twelve London Cries* (1760). Actively involved in the creation and promotion of artists' societies, Sandby became a founding member of the Society of Artists in 1761 and of the Royal Academy in 1768. He exhibited regularly at their annual exhibitions, with views of Windsor prominent among his contributions.[2] His appointment from 1768 to 1797 as chief drawing master of the Royal Military College at Woolwich brought a regular income, allowing him to divide his year between summer travel and winter teaching. In 1771 he toured Wales under the patronage of Sir Watkin Williams-Wynn, and again in 1773 with Joseph Banks and the Hon. Charles Greville. These trips resulted in a series of pioneering prints of Welsh views, produced in the recently developed medium of aquatint. Sandby was the first to exploit aquatint's potential for reproducing topographical watercolours, and effectively launched the technique in Britain. In addition to nearly eighty original aquatints, he made copies after drawings by William Pars, Pietro Fabris and David Allan. Sandby painted few oils and, apart from his contribution to printmaking, he is best known for his prodigious output of topographical and picturesque landscapes in watercolour and gouache. Towards the end of his life, his work became increasingly overshadowed by the experimental watercolours of the emerging generation, including J. R. Cozens, Turner and Girtin. His influence and importance were nonetheless acknowledged at his death, earning him the epithet, 'the father of modern landscape painting in watercolours'.[3]

D 5184
Watercolour over pencil: 24.4 × 37.6
Signed and dated in brown ink, lower right corner: *P Sandby Delin 1750*

As chief draughtsman to the Military Survey in Scotland, Sandby was required to conflate information gathered by the surveying parties in the field. Although he accompanied the survey team on several occasions, he was primarily based at the Ordnance Survey Office in Edinburgh. Apart from producing finished copies of maps and topographical views of Edinburgh's principal buildings and prospects, Sandby devoted considerable time to recording the character and lifestyle of the city's inhabitants.[4]

Fairs and markets were integral to the rural economies of many Scottish towns.[5] Originating in the Middle Ages, by the eighteenth century they fulfilled multiple functions, as a stockmarket for horses, cattle and sheep; a hiring ground for farm servants; a mart for food, clothes and other goods; as well as a general social gathering where races were run and much ale was consumed. According to one old statute, fairs attracted 'grit numbers of people of all qualities and ranks, between whom there are quarrels, grudges and miscontentment'.[6] This watercolour is probably an imaginative reconstruction of Edinburgh's All-Hallow fair, which was held annually during the first week of November. Sandby sets his scene around the area of Bruntsfield Links on the Boroughmuir, an expanse of common land to the south-west of the city. The All-Hallow fair never took place on this ground during Sandby's stay in Scotland,[7] and it is likely that he chose the location, one that he had drawn as early as 1747,[8] for its picturesque backdrop of the Castle rock. Comparison with old maps suggests that Sandby manipulated the perspective for artistic effect; however, his documentation of the architecture would appear to be accurate. In the left-hand background is a rare depiction of Wrychtishousis, an important fourteenth-century baronial mansion, demolished in 1800.

Preparatory drawings for the watercolour include a compositional study exploring the disposition of the principal groups (fig.44),[9] as well as a sketch for the gentleman in the foreground holding a basket.[10] Fascinatingly, the dancing couple in the right middle-ground appear to have been borrowed from a drawing by the French engraver and designer, Louis Philippe Boitard (fl.1738–63).[11] Sandby deliberately marginalises the serious trade functions of the fair and delights instead in showing the bawdy behaviour of the drunken crowd. Several town guardsmen, armed with their ancient Lochaber axes, converge on a fight in the middle distance. The tents are probably ale or dram shops, with the names of the respective public houses symbolised by the objects displayed above them. The bough bracing the poles of the tent in the centre might identify an inn called The Green Tree in Edinburgh's Cowgate, while the horns and tail crowning the tent to the left may refer to a tavern called The Black Bull, on the north side of the city's Grassmarket.[12] In the lower left, the soldiers supping whisky by the gingerbread stall and apple barrow serve as a pertinent reminder of the army barracks in the Castle and the politics of post-Rebellion Scotland.

KT

PROVENANCE
Simmonds Family; Mrs R. Hollis; Albemarle Gallery, London; purchased by private treaty 1990.

EXHIBITED
British Watercolours, A Golden Age 1750–1850, J. B. Speed Museum, Louisville, 1977, no.25; *The Discovery of Scotland: The Appreciation of Scottish Scenery through Two Centuries of Painting*, National Gallery of Scotland, Edinburgh, 1978, no.4.19; *Drawings and Watercolours of Edinburgh in the National Gallery of Scotland*, National Gallery of Scotland, Edinburgh, 1990, no.7; *The Great Age of British Watercolours 1750–1880*, Royal Academy, London / Washington, 1993, no.249, exh. London only; Edinburgh / London 1994, no.3.

Fig.44 Paul Sandby, *Study for A Horsefair on Bruntsfield Links*
British Museum, London

Alexander Runciman
63. *Achilles and the River Scamander* (Homer, *Iliad*, Book XXI)

EDINBURGH 1736–1785 EDINBURGH

The son of a builder-cum-architect, Runciman was apprenticed in 1750 to the decorative painter, Robert Norie, son of James Norie, founder of the most successful house-painting firm in eighteenth-century Scotland.[1] Runciman began his career as a landscape artist in the Norie tradition and, after completing his training in c.1755–7, worked independently for a number of years, engaging his own apprentices, including his younger brother, John (1744–1768 / 9). His commissions of the 1760s all came from families already known to the Nories, notably the Clerks of Penicuik in Midlothian.[2] In 1761, Sir James Clerk 3rd Baronet (1709–1782) designed a new house at Penicuik and, in c.1766, he employed Runciman to paint the ceiling of the portico.[3] Sir James subsequently decided to fund both Runciman brothers on a trip to Italy, on the condition that they decorate the great hall and staircases of Penicuik House on their return. Alexander reached Rome in June 1767, proposing to study ornamental painting, and John joined him in the autumn. John's premature death in 1768 / 9, however, prompted Alexander to reassess his career and to take up history painting. Gavin Hamilton, a fellow Scot, was a primary influence in the development of Runciman's new interests. These were realised in his first major history painting, *Ulysses surprising Nausicaa* (untraced), begun in 1769 and exhibited at the Royal Academy in 1772. Runciman stayed mainly in Rome and knew many of the artists and architects resident there, particularly John Brown, James Barry, Johan Tobias Sergel and, latterly, Henry Fuseli.[4] In 1772, having returned to Scotland the previous autumn, he fulfilled his obligation to Sir James at Penicuik House. The ceiling of the great hall was decorated with a monumental narrative depicting themes from the poetry of Ossian, a fictitious third-century Celtic bard. Eulogised as the 'Homer of the North', Ossian enjoyed enormous popularity in the late eighteenth and early nineteenth century through the writings of James Macpherson, published from 1760–5. Purportedly translated from original Gaelic manuscripts, Macpherson's texts generated much controversy and were later proved to be largely his own invention.[5] Runciman decorated the staircase at Penicuik with scenes from the life of St Margaret.[6] The Penicuik paintings were to be his masterpieces. Although he continued to produce and exhibit easel paintings on classical, Ossianic and historical themes, he executed only one other large-scale commission, in 1773, of Biblical scenes for the new Episcopalian Chapel in Edinburgh's Cowgate. In 1772 he was appointed Master of Edinburgh's School of Art, known as the 'Trustees' Academy', a post which he held until his death in 1785.

D 295

Pen and ink and wash over black chalk: 41.5 × 54.7
Signed in black ink, lower left: *ARunciman inv.*
Verso: *Lamentation of Christ*; pen and ink over pencil; signed in pen, lower right: *ARunciman*; inscribed by the artist in pen, left edge: *5–5th day.*

This powerful composition was drawn either towards the end of Runciman's Italian sojourn or shortly after his return to Scotland, and has a fascinating connection with his decoration of Penicuik House. Penicuik's Ossianic scheme was preceded by two very different proposals. The first was of a traditional type, combining a principal panel depicting the *Judgment of Paris*, with subsidiary scenes of bacchanals, bathing nymphs and pastoral landscapes.[7] The second, conceived in Rome, was detailed by Runciman in a letter to Sir James of May 1770.[8] Inspired by antique frescoes in the Golden House of Nero, and by the writings of Homer, Ovid and Catullus, Runciman proposed an ambitious ceiling design comprising a large central oval of the *Marriage of Peleus and Thetis*, surrounded by smaller scenes illustrating the life of Achilles. He mentioned nine Achilles subjects in his letter, to which a number of drawings can be related. At least six further studies, including the present work, have also been connected with this project.[9] Many of these drawings, in varying degrees of finish, are in the National Gallery of Scotland.[10] Runciman's choice of the Achilles theme was undoubtedly influenced by Gavin Hamilton's monumental *Iliad* series, executed in Rome from 1760–75.[11]

Achilles and the River Scamander represents one of the most violent passages in the *Iliad*, when Achilles avenges the death of Patroclus by massacring Trojan soldiers. Enraged at having its waters filled with blood and corpses, the River Scamander assumes human form and demands that he cease. When Achilles refuses, the River raises a seething wave and threatens to engulf him. The intensity of the narrative is paralleled by Runciman's use of dramatic chiaroscuro washes combined with finely-hatched pen lines. In this, the work differs significantly from other drawings in the series, which are executed in a restrained, classicising manner, revealing the influence of James Barry. Indeed, in both spirit and technique, *Achilles and the River Scamander* anticipates Runciman's heroic illustrations to Ossian, drawn after his return from Rome. This similarity led to the work's initial identification as either *Fingal engaging the Spirit of Loda* or *Cormar attacking the Spirit of the Waters* (fig.45), both of which were subjects of the Penicuik cycle. Precisely when Runciman decided to switch Achilles for Ossian is unclear, though it is possible that the idea was germinating before he left Italy. In the early 1770s the authenticity of Macpherson's publications was already the subject of much debate, fuelling the stories' international popularity. Fuseli, who arrived in Rome in May 1770, was exceptionally well-read and may have encouraged Runciman to tap the riches of Scotland's national folk legends.[12] The present drawing has a number of stylistic affinities with the work of Fuseli and his circle. It is probable that they spurred Runciman to abandon his earlier classicising tendencies and embrace the dynamic, unorthodox approach heralded by this drawing and brought to fruition in the Ossianic paintings at Penicuik.

KT

PROVENANCE
David Laing; his bequest to the Royal Scottish Academy 1879 (L 2188); transferred to the Gallery 1910.

EXHIBITED
The Romantic Movement, Tate Gallery and Arts Council Gallery, London, 1959, no.834 (as *Fingal engaging the Spirit of Loda*); *Romantic Art*, Aberdeen Art Gallery, Aberdeen, 1971, no.86; *The Fuseli Circle in Rome*, Yale Center for British Art, New Haven, 1979, no.7.

Fig.45 Alexander Runciman,
Cormar attacking the Spirit of the Waters
The Mackelvie Trust Collection,
Auckland Art Gallery, Toi o Tamaki.[13]

John Brown

64. *The Basilica of Maxentius and Constantine, Rome*

EDINBURGH 1749–1787 LEITH (EDINBURGH)

Although Brown's contemporaries record that he used both oil and watercolour, no paintings by him are known. He is celebrated chiefly as an outstanding and original draughtsman, who excelled in the use of pen and ink, wash, and pencil. Brown may have served an apprenticeship with his father, a goldsmith and watchmaker, before entering the Trustees' Academy in Edinburgh, where he probably studied under the School's first master, William Delacour, and with Delacour's successor, Charles Pavillon. In October 1769, after several months in London, Brown left for Italy with his friend and fellow-artist, David Erskine. Erskine's cousin, Charles (later a Cardinal) held an important post at the Vatican, and introduced Brown to Rome's most cultured circles. He joined the important group of international artists who centred around Henry Fuseli, and which included Alexander Runciman, with whom he maintained a lifelong friendship.[1] While in Rome, Brown developed a proto-romantic and emotionally charged style of drawing, very similar to Fuseli's draughtmanship, and exemplified by such works as *A Roman Lady and her Duenna* (Courtauld Institute of Art, London) and *A Woman Standing among Friars* (Cleveland Museum of Art, Ohio).[2] In 1772 Brown was employed as draughtsman to the antiquarian and collector Charles Townley and William Young, accompanying them on a tour through southern Italy, Sicily and Malta.[3] During his stay in Rome, Brown was made a member of the Accademia di San Luca. From c.1776 to the end of his Italian sojourn in early 1780, he appears to have settled in Florence, where he frequented the Uffizi Gallery. He was a skilled writer of Italian verse and an authority on opera, and his *Letters on the Poetry and Music of the Italian Opera* (1789, 2nd ed. 1791) were published posthumously by his friend and supporter James Burnett, Lord Monboddo. On returning to Edinburgh he became renowned as a portrait and miniature painter. David Steuart Erskine, 11th Earl of Buchan, and founder of the Scottish Society of Antiquaries, commissioned him to produce a series of life-size pencil portraits of many of the Society's most eminent members.[4] His last year was spent in London, where he apparently made portraits of the Royal Family and was again employed by Townley to draw his collection of marbles. He died, probably from malaria contracted in Sicily, following his return journey by sea to Edinburgh.

D 276

Pen and brown ink and red chalk; laid down: 37 × 56.7
Inscribed and signed in brown ink, lower right corner:
Tempe della Pace, Intorno da Roma. Giovanni Brown delinto

This drawing depicts the remains of the imposing Basilica (AD 310–13) which adjoins the north-eastern end of the Roman Forum. Begun by the Emperor Maxentius and finished by his successor Constantine, the building originally consisted of a central nave, crowned by an immense groined vault and flanked by two aisles. Brown's drawing shows the surviving north aisle, comprising three compartments, each seventy-six feet wide and roofed with a great semi-circular, deeply-coffered vault. Vestiges of the huge entablatures, which once stood on monolithic columns and supported the nave cross-vaults, can be seen rising from the spandrels between the arches. In the eighteenth century these ruins were thought to be the remains of Vespasian's Temple of Peace, hence Brown's inscription. The accuracy and sensitivity with which he records the architecture reveal his talents as a topographical draughts-man, and demonstrate the skills for which he was employed by Townley and Young.

This detailed antiquarian view provides an elaborate backdrop for a menacing episode in the foreground where, between gnarled trees, figures flee from, or run to, a violent confrontation. Brown's staging of a murderous encounter before the (supposed) Temple of Peace is deliberately ironic and possesses a drama that may be operatic in inspiration. The dark shadowing and sinister atmosphere accord with the intense and disturbing mood of the figurative compositions most readily associated with his Roman period. The pronounced musculature, elongated limbs and schematic, windswept draperies of Brown's figures recall the mannerist styles of Fuseli and Runciman and reflect a collective admiration for Michelangelo, Parmigianino, and Marcantonio's prints after Raphael and Bandinelli. While the majority of Brown's Roman works are character-ised by a bold tonal pen-and-wash technique, this drawing is purely linear and emulates an etching. Northern European graphic art, in particular the woodcuts and engravings of Dürer, may have influenced Brown in this respect. A more immediate and likely source, however, is Piranesi's famous series of etchings the *Vedute di Roma* (begun c.1748), which includes two views of the Temple of Peace (fig.46). Brown apparently knew Piranesi and drew his portrait in Rome.[5]

The only other surviving drawing of this type by Brown is a view of *Roman Ruins* in the Mildura Arts Centre, Victoria.[6] Dated 1771, this landscape is populated by two lonely figures, one of whom appears in its lunging stance to derive from the *Borghese Gladiator*. In 1774 Brown exhibited *A View of the Coliseum, Rome* at the Royal Academy in London, which may have been conceived as a pendant to the present drawing. Its subject alone suggests that Brown drew such antiquarian 'sets' throughout much of his Roman sojourn. Our drawing may therefore date from anytime between 1771, the date of the Mildura drawing, and Brown's move to Florence in 1776.

KT

PROVENANCE
David Laing; his bequest to the Royal Scottish Academy 1879 (L 2188); transferred to the Gallery 1910.

EXHIBITED
Fuseli, The Arts Council, London, 1950, no.135; *Il Settecento a Roma*, Palazzo delle Esposizioni, Rome, 1959, no.106; *Englishmen in Italy*, Victoria and Albert Museum, London, 1968, no.7; *Romantic Art in Britain: Paintings and Drawings 1760–1860*, Detroit / Philadelphia, 1968, no.78; *British Artists in Rome 1700–1800*, Kenwood House, London, 1974, no.105; Edinburgh 1976, no.13; *The Fuseli Circle in Rome*, Yale Center for British Art, New Haven, 1979, no.55; *Painting in Scotland. The Golden Age*, Edinburgh / London, 1986–7, no.40; *Ecco Roma: European Artists in the Eternal City*, National Gallery of Scotland, Edinburgh, 1992.

Fig.46 Giovanni Battista Piranesi, *Vedute di Roma: View of the Ruins of the Temple of Peace*
British Museum, London

Tempio della Pace, Intime de Roma. Giovanni Bruno delin.

Allan Ramsay
65. *Head of Margaret Lindsay, the Artist's Second Wife, Looking Down*

EDINBURGH 1713–1784 DOVER

Encouraged by his father, the poet Allan Ramsay (1684–1758), Ramsay began to study art at the age of twelve. Raised and educated in Edinburgh, in 1729 he joined the city's newly-founded Academy of St Luke, where he was able to study Old Master drawings and antique casts. In 1732 he is recorded in London as working for the Swedish painter Hans Hysing. Returning to Edinburgh the following year, he helped to design his father's retirement home, 'Guse-pye' house on the Castle Hill, where he established his Edinburgh studio. Ramsay first visited Italy in 1736, when he studied in Rome under the fashionable portrait painter Francesco Imperiali and at the French Academy there, then directed by Nicholas Vleughels. Moving to Naples in 1737, he entered the studio of the aged Francesco Solimena and received numerous commissions for portrait drawings of British residents. On his return to England in 1738, Ramsay set up practice as a portrait painter in London, achieving immediate success. His numerous patrons included such great Scottish families as the Buccleuchs, the Dalrymples of Newhailes and the powerful Argylls, as well as many influential English figures. He returned to Edinburgh regularly, however, and, during an extended stay in 1753–4, painted over forty portraits and founded a debating club with David Hume and Adam Smith, called the Select Society. In 1754 he returned to Rome to resume his studies. He travelled widely and joined the circle of Robert Adam, Clérisseau, Piranesi and Robert Wood. Back in London in 1757, Ramsay won the favour of the Prince of Wales and, following the latter's accession as George III in 1760, he assumed the duties of Principal Painter-in-Ordinary to His Majesty, officially succeeding to the office in 1767. Influenced by contemporary French painters, his mature style of the 1750s-60s is characterised by elegance and delicacy, and a concern for 'naturalism'. A serious injury to his right arm in 1773 precipitated his retirement from painting, although his studio assistants continued to produce replicas of his Royal portraits. An accomplished linguist and writer, throughout his life Ramsay published numerous essays and pamphlets on aesthetic, literary and political subjects, most importantly his *Dialogue on Taste* (1755). After his accident he concentrated on these scholarly pursuits and, during two final visits to Italy in 1775–7 and 1782–4, devoted himself to a treatise (never published) on the site of Horace's Sabine villa. He died on his way home from Italy in 1784.[1]

D 2009

Red chalk, with white heightening, on grey paper: 37 × 27.9

Margaret Lindsay (c.1726–1782) was the eldest daughter of Sir Alexander and Lady Lindsay of Evelick in Perthshire. Her father (d.1762) was related to the Earls of Balcarres, while her mother, born Amelia Murray (d.1774), was the daughter of David Murray, 5th Viscount Stormont, and sister of William Murray, who rose to be Lord Chief Justice and 1st Earl of Mansfield. How Ramsay first met Margaret is unknown, though tradition has it that he was employed to give her drawing lessons, possibly during a stay in Edinburgh in the winter of 1751–52. Margaret's parents, however, deeply disapproved of the match and in March 1752 the couple eloped, marrying in the Canongate Church in Edinburgh's High Street. Thereafter the Lindsays broke off all communication with their daughter, an estrangement that was to be long-lasting and cause Margaret considerable distress. Despite this, their marriage was a happy one. Margaret bore Ramsay six children, three of whom survived to adulthood, and was apparently utterly devoted to her husband whom she 'did love honour and obey … as never a sovereign prince was loved honoured and obeyed'.[2]

Ramsay's most famous portrait of Margaret is the painting now in the National Gallery of Scotland, which portrays her caught in the act of arranging a vase of flowers (fig.47).[3] Acknowledged as one of his finest works, this painting shows that Margaret was an exceptionally beautiful woman, with fair hair and complexion, light brown eyes, narrow nose and sensitive mouth. Robert Adam, who came to know her in Rome in the 1750s, described her as 'a sweet agreeable, chatty body, tho' silent in Company'.[4] Both this painting and the present drawing were originally thought to be associated with the couple's Italian sojourn of 1754–7. It is now accepted, however, that the painting dates to c.1758–60,[5] while the drawing has been identified, on stylistic grounds, as belonging to a group of studies which were produced on the Island of Ischia in 1776, during Ramsay's third trip to Italy.[6] In the Scottish National Portrait Gallery is another drawing of Margaret which would appear to date from the time of this visit.[7] Our drawing displays the delicacy and softness of execution typical of Ramsay's later years. It is an outstanding example of his quest for a more relaxed, informal style of portraiture, and reflects the influence of contemporary French artists such as Maurice-Quentin de La Tour, Jean-Marc Nattier and Charles-Joseph Natoire. Ramsay's advocacy of the 'natural portrait' found intellectual expression in his *Dialogue on Taste* of 1755 and concurred with the philosophical opinions of his friend, David Hume.[8] In this carefully observed study Ramsay reveals Margaret's natural serenity and composure. She is captured in momentary stasis, with her head tilted forward, eyes cast downwards and lips slightly parted, as if reading aloud, or writing. Ramsay's injured arm caused him great discomfort in later life and, when researching Horace's villa, Margaret assumed the role of his amanuensis. This tender and intimate drawing may well record Margaret receiving dictation and is a pose, therefore, which would have been particularly familiar and personal to her husband.

KT

PROVENANCE

General John Ramsay (the artist's son); by descent to his cousin, Lord Murray of Henderland; his wife, Lady Murray of Henderland, her bequest to the Gallery in memory of her husband 1861.[9]

EXHIBITED

Portrait Drawings by Scottish Artists 1750–1850, Scottish National Portrait Gallery, Edinburgh, 1955, no.12; *Allan Ramsay, his Masters and Rivals*, National Gallery of Scotland, Edinburgh, 1963, no.72; *The True Resemblance of Lord Mansfield*, Kenwood House, London, 1971, no.66; *Poet and Painter: Allan Ramsay, Father and Son 1684–1784*, National Library of Scotland, Edinburgh, 1984–5, no.235; *Painting in Scotland. The Golden Age*, Edinburgh / London, 1986–7, no.24; *Allan Ramsay 1713–1784*, Edinburgh / London, 1992, no.107.

Fig.47 Allan Ramsay, *The Artist's Wife, Margaret Lindsay* National Gallery of Scotland, Edinburgh

Robert Adam
66. Cullen Castle, Banffshire

KIRKCALDY 1728–1792 LONDON

Robert Adam was the second son of William Adam (1689–1748), Scotland's foremost architect during the second quarter of the eighteenth century. Raised and educated in Edinburgh, he enjoyed a liberal and intellectual upbringing, surrounded by many of the greatest figures of the Scottish Enlightenment. In 1745–6 he joined his father's architectural practice and, following William's death in 1748, took over the business in partnership with his older brother John. Robert received his earliest lessons in drawing from Paul Sandby, who was stationed in Edinburgh from c.1746–52 as draughtsman to the Military Survey in Scotland. In 1754–7 Adam made a Grand Tour of Italy, during which time he studied antique, Renaissance and Baroque architecture and befriended Charles-Louis Clérisseau, Jean-Baptiste Lallemand and Giovanni Battista Piranesi, among others.[1] This trip greatly influenced the development of his subsequent style – an innovative and international form of neo-classicism, which quickly superseded the prevailing taste in Britain for Palladianism. On returning home, Robert set up practice in London, where he was later joined by his younger brothers James and William. In 1761 he was elected a Fellow of the Royal Society and, along with William Chambers, was appointed Architect of the King's Works. Under Robert's directorship and with the assistance of a large office of highly skilled draughtsmen, including George Richardson, Joseph Bonomi and Giuseppe Mannochi, the Adam practice became one of the most successful and fashionable architectural firms in Britain. Despite his standing, Adam was given few opportunities to build public architecture on a monumental scale, and private commissions for town and country houses constituted the mainstay of his practice. Many of his greatest achievements were in interior design, and involved remodelling or completing projects begun by others. Some of the most magnificent examples of his work include Kedleston Hall in Derbyshire (c.1760–70), Syon House and Osterley Park House in Middlesex (1762–9 and 1763–80 respectively), and Culzean Castle in Ayrshire (1777–92).[2] During the 1770s-80s, Scottish commissions accounted for an increasing proportion of Adam's work and, from about 1775, he re-established an office in Edinburgh to operate the Scottish side of his business. After the deaths of Robert in 1792 and James in 1794, the great Adam practice folded. The bulk of the drawings made by Adam and his office (around 9000 in number) were sold by the family in 1833 to Sir John Soane and now form one of the principal treasures of Sir John Soane's Museum in London.[3]

D 5325

Pen and brown ink and grey wash over black chalk: 35.6 × 51

Signed and inscribed in brown ink, along bottom edge of mount: *Robt Adam Delint View of the Castle of Cullen in the Shire of Bamff.* [sic] *One of the Seats of the Right Honorable The Earl of Findlater & Seafield & c. No. 3.*
Inscribed in pencil, on verso, bottom middle of mount: *R P Adam fecit*

Cullen Castle is situated in Banffshire in north-east Scotland, on the remote coastal shoulder linking Aberdeen and Inverness. Founded in the thirteenth century, the house was developed in a piecemeal fashion by successive generations of the Ogilvy family.[4] It enjoys an idyllic setting, positioned high on a rock overlooking a dramatic woodland bowl and encircled by extensive and densely-planted landscaped gardens.[5] The Adam family had a long association with Cullen, starting with James Ogilvy, 5th Earl of Findlater and 2nd Earl of Seafield, who in 1736 commissioned William Adam to design a new harbour at Cullen and, in 1744, to build a bridge over the gorge-like glen immediately behind Cullen Castle. William's single-span bridge over the Smale Burn, which provided a spectacular axial approach from the west, still stands and features prominently in Robert's watercolour. The succession of the 6th Earl in 1764 marked the beginning of a close relationship with Robert, James and John Adam, whose patronage was continued from 1770 by the 7th Earl. An Ionic entrance screen designed by James in 1767 still exists at Cullen.[6] Surviving drawings related to the Castle include designs for interior decoration and subsidiary buildings,[7] such as a gardener's house,[8] and a banqueting house and gate-lodge.[9] These last two designs may be associated with a grand scheme by Adam and the landscape architect, Thomas White, for a radical remodelling of the estate, which involved removing the old town of Cullen to a site nearer the sea. As part of this proposal, Adam prepared plans for the complete rebuilding of Cullen Castle, the drawings for which are in the Soane Museum.[10] Although Adam's new castle was not executed, other important aspects of the scheme were carried out, including an extensive walled garden.

Another, less finished, version of this watercolour is in the collection of Blair Adam, the Adam family seat, in Fife.[11] It bears the inscription 'From an outline of Mr Clerk's', which suggests that our watercolour originated from a study made by Robert's brother-in-law and sketching companion, John Clerk of Eldin (1728–1812).[12] Although our drawing is probably a reasonably accurate record of Cullen during the 1770s-80s, Adam has romanticised the scene, adopting a low viewpoint and attenuating proportions to stress the grandeur of the surroundings. From the mid-1770s, Adam evinced a renewed enthusiasm for the Picturesque, to which he had been introduced by his early teacher, Paul Sandby. He made hundreds of atmospheric drawings in watercolour and wash, such as this one, which explored the relationship between buildings and their setting. Tait argues that such works played a vital role in the evolution of Adam's designs, helping him to establish mood and composition.[13]

KT

PROVENANCE
Christie's, London, 20 June 1978, no.96; Sotheby's, London, 14 November 1991, no.47, where purchased.

John Robert Cozens

67. *The Euganean Hills from the Walls of Padua*

LONDON 1752–1798 LONDON

Cozens's formative years were spent in London. He was trained by his father, Alexander (1717–1786), a much respected artist and drawing master who devised a system of inventing landscapes using ink blots.[1] The influence of his father's teaching was evident in his early exhibits at the Society of Artists (from 1767 to 1771) and, in 1776, in his first and only exhibit at the Royal Academy, an oil entitled *Landscape with Hannibal in his March over the Alps, showing to his Army the Fertile Plains of Italy* (untraced), which was composed according to the blot method. From 1772 Cozens lived in Bath, before leaving in August 1776 for the Swiss Alps and Italy as draughtsman to the scholar, antiquarian and connoisseur, Richard Payne Knight. Cozens recorded their expedition in a series of fifty-seven drawings, which he began after their arrival in Rome in November 1776. On his return to Bath in 1779, Cozens continued to make finished watercolours from his continental sketches.[2] He worked for various patrons, notably William Beckford of Fonthill (1759–1844), with whom he went back to Italy as one of a large retinue in 1782. This second, brisk tour took Cozens via the Tyrol, to Padua, Venice, Rome and, finally, to Sir William Hamilton's villa in Naples. After Beckford's departure for Geneva that September, Cozens remained in Italy, at Naples and Rome, before returning to England in 1783. Although Beckford later severed relations with Cozens, the artist delivered ninety-four finished watercolours of their trip, many of which are among the most original and beautiful works of his career. Cozens's final years were spent in London. In 1794 he suffered a mental collapse and was placed in the care of Dr Thomas Monro (1759–1833), physician to Bethlehem Hospital (Bedlam). An avid collector of art, in particular contemporary British watercolours, Monro ran an informal evening 'Academy' at his home in Adelphi Terrace, London, where he employed promising young artists to make copies of works in his collection. While caring for Cozens, Monro had access to the artist's drawings, which he made available to his 'pupils', notably the young J. M. W. Turner and Thomas Girtin, on whom they had a powerful formative influence.[3] Financial support for Cozens and his family was raised by the Royal Academy and through a fund organised by several patrons and pupils. He died within four years of being placed in Monro's charge.

D 5023.11
Pen and ink and watercolour over pencil; laid down: 26.7 × 37.7
Inscribed in brown ink in Beckford's hand, on verso of mount: *The Euganeain* [sic] *Hills from the Walls of Padua*

This atmospheric composition is one of the ninety-four finished watercolours which Cozens completed for William Beckford following their tour of 1782.[4] These were based on studies made in a series of seven sketchbooks, which at some undocumented stage passed into Beckford's possession.[5] Cozens's annotated sketches and Beckford's letters allow us to reconstruct their route to Padua in detail.[6] Crossing from Dover to Ostend, they travelled up the Rhine, passed swiftly through Bavaria and the Alps, via Innsbruck, arriving at Verona on 10 June and visiting Venice on the 15th, before doubling back to Padua. Beckford was a temperamental and demanding patron and, soon after arriving in the city, grew intolerant of the fierce heat and impatient to escape to the more temperate climate of the surrounding Euganean Hills. The landscape around Padua inspired some of Cozens's finest finished watercolours. The sketch for our work, inscribed 'June 18–', was the first of two drawings which Cozens made that day from the walls of Padua (fig.48).[7] The other (of which the finished watercolour is in the Tate Gallery, London) depicts the city illuminated by a violent bolt of lightning.[8]

The style of our work, comprising deep, subdued colours and short, deliberate brushstrokes, typifies Cozens's finished watercolours from this journey. Precisely when and how Cozens translated his sketches into finished watercolours is unknown. Some suggest that he began the works in Rome, after Beckford's departure for Geneva; however, it is more likely that they were completed in England following the artist's return in September 1783. Evidence of squaring can be found on a number of the sketches. In the study for our watercolour, a single horizontal pencil line, drawn through the abandoned well-house and above the hills, appears to have provided sufficient guidance for the enlargement. The finished work follows its study quite accurately, with two figures added beneath the ruin to convey a sense of scale.

A tracing from the sketch for our watercolour appears in the 'Beaumont Album', now in the Yale Center for British Art, New Haven.[9] This album, which includes a large number of tracings

from the Beckford sketchbooks, was formerly owned by Sir George Beaumont (1753–1827), a pupil of Alexander Cozens and close friend of John Robert Cozens in Rome in 1783. The purpose of the tracings is unclear, though Christopher White has suggested that they were made by Cozens as a personal record, at the time his sketchbooks passed to Beckford.[10] A copy of *The Euganean Hills from the Walls of Padua*, executed by one of Dr Monro's protégés, is in the Turner Bequest, London.[11] Drawn without figures, this appears to be a copy after the sketchbook study, rather than after our watercolour. This may indicate that Beckford either did not own the original sketchbooks until after the mid-1790s, or, if White's theory is accepted, that he acquired them at an earlier date and lent them to Monro for the use of his 'students'.[12]

KT

PROVENANCE
William Beckford of Fonthill; his sale Christie's, London, 10 April 1805, no.8 (Lugt 6931); purchased Seguier for £7.0.0; Thomas Agnew and Sons; Sir Thomas Barlow Bart.; his daughter, Helen Barlow, 1945; her bequest to the Gallery 1976.

EXHIBITED
Watercolours by John Robert Cozens, Manchester / London, 1971, no.47; *La Peinture Romantique Anglaise et les Préraphaélites*, Petit Palais, Paris, 1972, no.86; Edinburgh 1979, no.11; *Alexander and John Robert Cozens: The Poetry of Landscape*, Art Gallery of Ontario, Toronto, 1986–7, no.167.

Fig.48 J. R. Cozens, *Study for The Euganean Hills from the Walls of Padua*
Whitworth Art Gallery, University of Manchester

David Allan
68. *The Black Stool* (also known as *Presbyterian Penance*)

ALLOA 1744–1796 EDINBURGH

David Allan was the son of a shore-master of Alloa in Clackmannanshire. In 1755, through the support of Charles, 9th Lord Cathcart of Shawpark, he entered the newly-established Foulis Academy of Fine Arts in the College of Glasgow. Through the Cathcarts he was introduced to the Erskines of Mar and other local families. Their collective patronage enabled him to travel to Rome in or about 1767, and subsequently to Naples, where he was befriended by Lady Cathcart's brother, Sir William Hamilton. In Rome, Allan studied at the Accademia di San Luca and with Gavin Hamilton, who encouraged him to take up history painting. In 1773 he won the gold medal of the Concorso Balestra with his painting *The Parting of Hector and Andromache* (Accademia di San Luca, Rome), thus becoming the first British artist to win the prize before 1800. Apart from developing his classical and historical repertoire, Allan also produced numerous studies of contemporary Italian life, including *The Seven Sacraments of the Church of Rome* of 1774 (National Gallery of Scotland, Edinburgh),[1] ten *Roman Carnival* drawings of *c*.1775 (Royal Library, Windsor), and sketches of Italian street characters and rural costumes, drawn between 1770–6 (Art Gallery, Aberdeen).[2] Allan returned to London in 1777. Unsuccessful in establishing a career there, he moved in 1780 to Edinburgh, where he developed a specialism in domestic genre, recording the customs and daily life of the common people. Recurring subjects include his series of Edinburgh street characters, the *Highland Dance* and *Penny Wedding* (all represented in the National Gallery of Scotland). He also prepared book illustrations of the poems and songs of Scottish authors such as Allan Ramsay Senior and Robert Burns, as well as Shakespeare, the Bible and Scottish history.[3] Concurrently, he produced a large corpus of portraits, excelling in cabinet-sized pictures and a 'conversational manner' exemplified by *The Erskine Family* (1780) in the National Gallery of Scotland. In 1786 Allan succeeded Alexander Runciman as Master of the Trustees' Academy in Edinburgh, retaining the post until his death ten years later.[4] Though often compared to William Hogarth, Allan's works contain none of the moralising content of his English predecessor's satires. His paintings and drawings of domestic genre are particularly important as documents of eighteenth-century social history. These established a new direction for art in Scotland, influencing successive generations of Scottish painters, initially via the works of Sir David Wilkie and Wilkie's own followers and imitators.

D 4373
Pen and black ink and watercolour: 39.3 × 51.2
Signed and dated in watercolour, lower left corner: *D. Allan / Oct 1795*. Inscribed in ink, bottom margin: *Black Stool*

Religion pervaded the daily lives and affairs of nearly all Scots during the eighteenth century, most of whom belonged to the Presbyterian Church of Scotland. Presbyterian Ministers, aided by the elders of the Kirk Session, possessed an extraordinary power over their local parishioners and expended great energy in hunting out and castigating sinners. Sins such as fornication, swearing, drunkenness and Sabbath-breaking were punishable by condemnation to the 'Black Stool', known variously as the 'Stool of Repentance', 'Cutty Stool', 'Creepy' or 'Cock Stool'. The stool was commonly placed on a wooden structure, built on two levels, which stood immediately in front of the pulpit. Serious offenders were sentenced to the highest platform, the 'pillar', while the lower tier was used for milder misdemeanours. Following the sermon, the accused were made to confess and repent before the entire congregation, while the Minister thundered a warning of the hellfire and damnation to come.[5]

Here, a young man, mounted on the 'pillar', solemnly receives his public reprimand. The sin is confirmed by a slip of paper, inscribed 'Antinuptial fornication', which has fallen to the floor beside his co-offender, a girl holding a new-born baby, who weeps on a 'cutty stool' in the foreground. Offenders were liable to censure in this way over successive Sundays, the number of appearances being determined by the heinousness of the 'crime'. Allan's humorous inclusion of a dozing couple, seated in the lower left, suggests that this rebuke has been heard many times before. Fear of the merciless humiliation of the 'Black Stool', however, frequently drove perpetrators to desperate and tragic measures. Many fled the country, while women often attempted self-abortion or committed suicide or infanticide. Towards the end of the eighteenth century this puritanical system of discipline began to fold. Public censure came to be regarded as inhumane, or was derided and made the subject of jokes. This changing attitude probably contributed to the popularity of Allan's light-hearted interpretation of the subject, the topicality of which undoubtedly increased with Robert Burns's famous

censure in 1786 at Mauchline Kirk for his affair with Jean Armour.[6]

Allan made a number of copies and variants of *The Black Stool*, of which this drawing, dated 1795, is one of the finest and latest surviving examples. A drawing for a companion piece, entitled *Scottish Catechising*, is in the National Gallery of Scotland (fig.49).[7] *The Black Stool* was first produced as a print for the popular market in 1784.[8] The circulation of these prints prompted individual commissions for watercolour copies, of which one, dated 1792, is in the collection of the Earl of Stair.[9] Two outline drawings, incised and squared for transfer, have also appeared at auction in recent years.[10] Each of these versions incorporates slight variations. In the earlier prints, the officious beadle, wielding the key to the church, beats off a group dogs, two of which Allan shows in the act of mating, thus making a direct reference to the sin of fornication. In the later watercolours, this licentious element is replaced (perhaps at the clients' request) by a less provocative depiction of dogs fighting. Allan's *Black Stool* was etched with variations by Isaac Cruikshank (1756–1811) in the early nineteenth century, testifying to the work's long-lasting appeal.

KT

PROVENANCE
Lt. Col. Dalrymple Hamilton from whom purchased 1946.

EXHIBITED
Prints and Drawings by David Allan 1744–1796, Gladstone's Land, Edinburgh, 1949, no.41; *David Allan 1744–1796: The Scottish Hogarth*, Townhead Institute, Alloa, 1954, no.32; *The Indefatigable Mr Allan*, Scottish Arts Council, Edinburgh / Glasgow / Dundee / Alloa, 1973, no.69; *The Artist and the Kirk*, National Gallery of Scotland, Edinburgh, 1979–80, no.19; *Painting in Scotland. The Golden Age*, Edinburgh / London, 1986–7, no.84; *The Line of Tradition*, National Gallery of Scotland, Edinburgh, 1993.

Fig.49 David Allan, *Scottish Catechising*
On loan to the National Gallery of Scotland, Edinburgh

Joseph Mallord William Turner
69. *Mount Snowdon, Afterglow*

LONDON 1775–1851 LONDON

J. M. W. Turner was perhaps the greatest and most influential of all British landscape painters. He is celebrated as a remarkably inventive and experimental artist who pushed watercolour painting to its technical and expressive limits.[1] The son of a London barber and wigmaker, he received his earliest training under the architectural draughtsman Thomas Malton, before entering the Royal Academy Schools in 1789. From 1794–7 he attended Dr Thomas Monro's private 'Academy', where he collaborated with Thomas Girtin in copying studies made by J. R. Cozens and Edward Dayes. He first exhibited at the Royal Academy, London, in 1790 with a watercolour of the *Archbishop's Palace, Lambeth* (Indianapolis Museum of Art, Indiana). His first exhibited oil painting, *Fisherman at Sea* (Tate Gallery, London), was shown in 1796. In 1799 he was elected an Associate of the Royal Academy, rising to full membership in early 1802. This marked the beginning of a life-long professional relationship with the Royal Academy, of which Turner was a loyal supporter, serving frequently on the Council and Hanging Committee and, from 1807–37, as Professor of Perspective in the Academy's Schools. Turner regarded himself as an heir to the traditions of Claude and Poussin, and to his more immediate predecessor, the distinguished Welsh artist, Richard Wilson. Throughout his career he strove to affirm the status of landscape painting as a serious genre. Tours to Northern England and Wales in the late 1790s effected a rapid advance in his artistic development and provided a rich source of material for his early 'sublime' landscapes. In 1802, following the Peace of Amiens, he made his first trip to the continent, when he studied the paintings in the Louvre. This was followed by frequent trips abroad in subsequent decades, which yielded increasingly abstract paintings in an ever more brilliant palette. His exceptional skills as an illustrative draughtsman were in great demand and many of his European and British tours were made in connection with specific publishing projects. Notable among these were the ambitious *Picturesque Views of England and Wales*, commissioned by Charles Heath in 1826, and a series of illustrations to Robert Cadell's edition of the *Works of Sir Walter Scott*, published in the 1830s. Turner was buried with great pomp in the crypt of St Paul's Cathedral. By a settlement reached several years after his death, the contents of his studio (around 300 oil paintings and over 20,000 drawings) were left to the nation. Known as the 'Turner Bequest' this enormous collection is now housed in the Tate Gallery in London.[2]

D 5284

Watercolour, with some scraping out: 52.7 × 75.6

Turner's tours of North Wales in the summer of 1798 and the autumn of 1799, profoundly affected his approach to landscape. His attraction to the Welsh mountains stemmed, in part, from a deep admiration of the paintings of Richard Wilson (1713 / 14–1782), whose work was particularly influential on Turner during the late 1790s. In old age, Turner was to recall his youthful search for Wilson's birthplace at Penegoes in the Dovey Valley.[3] He filled several sketchbooks during these tours, which in the following years provided material for a series of Welsh views, culminating in his important oil of *Dolbadern Castle* (Royal Academy, London), exhibited at the Royal Academy in 1800 and submitted as his Diploma picture in 1802 (fig.50).

This large and highly finished watercolour of Snowdonia was probably painted in *c.*1799–1800, shortly after Turner's return from Wales. In scale and mood it is comparable to his other Welsh watercolours of this period, especially to a highly worked view of *Cader Idris* of *c.*1799 (Private Collection)[4] and to a group of large Welsh mountain studies in the Turner Bequest.[5] While our work was almost certainly intended for public display alongside, and in competition with, oil paintings, it does not appear to have been exhibited during Turner's lifetime. In common with his other Welsh views, it reveals a preoccupation with the contemporary concept of the 'Sublime'. This term, much used in eighteenth- and early-nineteenth-century aesthetic theory, was commonly applied to denote the profound emotional response, usually fear or astonishment, evoked by the overwhelming grandeur of nature. The imposing majesty of the Welsh mountains is conveyed in this watercolour by Turner's powerful design and by his use of a restricted range of brooding, sombre colours. Drawings of Snowdon appear in several of Turner's sketchbooks, notably the 'North Wales' sketchbook of 1798 and the 'Dolbadern' sketchbook of 1799.[6] Numerous atmospheric studies, together with a long list of descriptive weather effects in the 'Dolbadern' sketchbook,[7] testify to the artist's growing preoccupation with the poetic quality of light. The 'Afterglow' in the title of the present watercolour refers to the gentle light of a fading sunset, which suffuses the heavy mass of the mountainside. A dilute white wash is used to suggest the milky irridescence of the rising moon. The precise location of the site, like a number of Turner's views of Snowdon,[8] has not been firmly established. It is most likely, however, that the work shows the range as viewed from the vicinity of Fachwen, to the north of Llanberis. If this is so, the shimmering expanse of water in the middle ground may be identified as Llyn Padern, with the Llanberis waterfall or the start of the Llanberis path (both of which run very close together) just visible on the hills' lower reaches.[9]

KT

PROVENANCE

Sir Francis Seymour Hayden; Mr Holloway; from whom purchased William Leech, 1864 (as *Moon Rising over Snowdon*); from whom purchased, Revd W. MacGregor, 1887; by whose executors sold, Christie's, London, 23 April 1937, no.8, purchased Frost & Reid Ltd; from whom purchased, B. Figgis, 1941; by descent to Mrs Peggy Parker, 1966, by whom gifted to the Gallery 1991.

EXHIBITED

Winter Exhibition, Royal Academy, London,1886, no.25; *Collection of Pictures and Drawings by J. M. W. Turner, R.A.*, Guildhall, London, 1899, no.107; *Franco-British Exhibition*, Fine Arts Palace, Shepherd's Bush, London, 1908, no.493; *Water-colour Drawings by Joseph Mallord William Turner*, Agnew's, London, 1913, no.17; Edinburgh / London 1994, no.8.

Fig.50 J. M. W. Turner, *Dolbadern Castle*
The Royal Academy of Arts, London

Thomas Girtin
70. *The Village of Jedburgh, Roxburgh*

LONDON 1775–1802 LONDON

Girtin was an exact contemporary of J. M. W. Turner, with whom he led the revolution in the development of watercolour painting, from a second-rate medium reserved for the humble art of topography to one capable of rivalling oils in visual impact and emotional range. In 1788 Girtin, the son of a brushmaker of Huguenot descent, began a seven-year apprenticeship with the topographical artist, Edward Dayes. His earliest works are stylistically indebted to Dayes, who practised a traditional method of watercolour painting, characterised by fine pen outlines tinted with delicate washes. Girtin first exhibited at the Royal Academy in 1796, showing a watercolour copied from a drawing by the antiquarian, James Moore, with whom he toured the Midlands that same year. Between 1794 and *c*.1798, Girtin attended the evening 'Academy' of Dr Thomas Monro at his home in Adelphi Terrace, London. Here he worked with Turner in copying drawings by J. R. Cozens and others. The sketches he made during a tour of Northern England and the Scottish Borders in 1796 marked his departure from eighteenth-century topographical tradition. Tours to Somerset, Dorset and Devon in 1797, were followed in 1798 by trips to North Wales and Yorkshire, at which time Girtin's style was especially close to Turner's. From 1799–1801 he was a prominent member of a select sketching society known as 'The Brothers', who met weekly to compose drawings inspired by literature.[1] His watercolour technique, distinguished by broad washes textured with dots and dashes made with a reed pen, reached new heights in 1800, when he produced some of his most accomplished works, including *White House at Chelsea* (Tate Gallery, London). In 1801 he exhibited an oil painting for the first time at the Royal Academy and began *Eidometropolis*, a 108 × 18ft. panoramic painting of London, which was exhibited in the capital from 1802–3.[2] Though already ill with tuberculosis, in November 1801 Girtin went to Paris and visited the Louvre. On his return in May 1802, he produced twenty soft-ground etchings of Parisian views. His only prints, these were published posthumously in 1803. At his death, aged only twenty-seven, Girtin was acknowledged, alongside Turner, as a leader of the modern British landscape school.

D 5175

Watercolour over pencil: 30.2 × 52.1
Signed and dated in brown watercolour, lower left corner: *Girtin 1800*

Jedburgh and its ruined medieval abbey in the Scottish Borders inspired a series of watercolours by Girtin,[3] of which this work is the last and the greatest. He first tackled the subject in *c*.1793 in a watercolour which was based on a sketch made by James Moore on his Scottish excursion of 1792.[4] Indeed, it may have been Moore's enthusiasm for Scotland which prompted Girtin to include the Border region in his own sketching tour of 1796. Our knowledge of Girtin's route is based principally on the likely dating of his subsequent watercolours. From these, it appears that he travelled from York to Durham, and along the Northumberland coast, before turning inland to Kelso, Dryburgh and Jedburgh.

A panoramic sketch in the British Museum, inscribed '*Jedborough Scot'd T Girtin 1796 X II*', constitutes the only firmly dated evidence of his visit (fig.51).[5] Drawn from the elevated site of the former Jedburgh Castle, this study shows an extensive view of the town looking north, with Jedburgh Abbey to the east, alongside the Jed Water. One contemporary traveller observed that the Abbey 'is seen with the greatest effect from the retired banks of the Jed … The Castle hill commands a view of no less beauty, but of different character, including the vale, with the town, the meandering river, the rising ground of Stewartfield and the distant hills.'[6] The left-hand side of the British Museum sketch formed the basis for our watercolour, painted several years later, in 1800. Girtin may have returned to Scotland in summer 1800. However, if one accepts that the Gallery's watercolour corresponds with the view of *Jedburgh* shown that year in the Royal Academy's spring exhibition, then it

must predate any possible reacquaintance with the area.

The present watercolour of *Jedburgh* was preceded by another of *c*.1796–7, which reproduced the British Museum sketch in its entirety.[7] In this earlier work Girtin deviated from traditional antiquarian topography by subordinating the Abbey (usually the focal element) to a broader study of the landscape and community. His attempt to unify the two distinct halves of the panorama by means of a dark foreground bank was, however, rather awkward. In the Gallery's watercolour, he resolved this issue by omitting the Abbey altogether and concentrating solely on the village. By removing the historical landmark which most readily identified the scene as Jedburgh, Girtin thus broke completely with eighteenth-century topographical convention.

Our view of *Jedburgh* was probably first owned, and may even have been commissioned, by Sir John Ramsden 4th Baronet (1755–1839) of Byram, in the West Riding of Yorkshire. Ramsden has emerged in recent years as one of Girtin's most prominent clients, owning, in addition to this watercolour, at least five major works by the artist. An introduction may have been arranged by the Lascelles family of Harewood in Yorkshire, important patrons of Girtin who moved in Ramsden's social circle.[8]

K T

PROVENANCE
Probably Sir John Ramsden 4th Bart. (1755–1839); by descent to Sir John Frecheville Ramsden 6th Bart.; by whom sold Christie's, London, 27 May 1832, no.21 (as *A View of a Village Street*), acquired by Walker's Galleries; from whom purchased N. N. Dangar, 1932; Mrs Kathleen C. Dangar; Peter Dangar 1971; by whom sold Christie's, London 15 June 1971, no.48; Dr Marc Fitch by 1987; Leger Galleries, London, from whom purchased with the aid of funds from the National Heritage Memorial Fund, the National Art Collections Fund and the Pilgrim Trust 1988.

EXHIBITED
Probably Royal Academy, London, 1800, no.418; *The 28th Annual Exhibition of Early English Water-colours*, Walker's Galleries, London, 1932, no.39; *English Watercolours*, Leger Galleries, London, 1971, no.20; *Watercolours by Thomas Girtin*, Manchester / London, 1975, no.65; *British Watercolours, A Golden Age 1750–1850*, J. B. Speed Art Museum, Louisville, 1977, no.42; *Exhibition of English Watercolours*, Leger Galleries, London, 1980, no.18; *The Fitch Collection*, Leger Galleries, London, 1988, no.34; *The Great Age of British Watercolours 1750–1880*, London / Washington, 1993, no.142; Edinburgh / London 1994, no.2.

Fig.51 Thomas Girtin, *Jedburgh*
British Museum, London

John White Abbott
71. *Chudleigh, Devon*

EXETER 1763 / 4–1851 EXETER

For much of his life Abbott practised as an apothecary and surgeon in Exeter, Devonshire, painting only 'by snatches', though he would have preferred to have devoted all his time to art.[1] He was the nephew of John White (1744 / 5–1825), a prominent lawyer and close friend of the artist Francis Towne, who had moved to Exeter from London in the 1760s. White accompanied Towne on his tours to North Wales in 1777 and to the Lake District in 1786, and it was undoubtedly he who encouraged his nephew to take drawing lessons from Towne, probably from an early age. Abbott assimilated Towne's teaching quickly and thoroughly, and copied many of his works, particularly the sketches from Towne's Continental tour of 1780–81.[2] His drawing style, which barely changed throughout his long life, was deeply indebted to Towne in its use of flat washes and bold pen outlines, and in its decorative simplification of detail. Abbott seems never to have travelled abroad and, judging by his drawings, only ventured out of Devonshire on a very few occasions. Most of his works depict the wooded countryside of Exeter and its environs. In 1791 he toured Scotland and the Lake District, visiting Lancashire, Yorkshire and Derbyshire en route. He recorded the excursion in a series of over seventy sketches.[3] Later trips included Monmouthshire in 1797, and again in 1827, as well as Gloucestershire and Wiltshire. Family tradition claims that in his youth Abbott was taken by his uncle to London, where he met Sir Joshua Reynolds, Sir George Beaumont, Benjamin West and others. This visit must have been brief and unrepeated, however, as Towne commented in 1803 that his pupil had 'much preparation for Painting Landscape – by having studied nature, but that He was not much acquainted with fine works of art'.[4] Indeed, Abbott's knowledge of Old Master paintings seems to have been acquired principally through copying engravings.[5] Although Abbott's reputation now rests entirely upon his drawings, he also painted landscapes in oils. From 1793 to 1805, and again in 1810 and 1822, he was an Honorary Exhibitor at the Royal Academy in London. His early pieces were strongly influenced by Thomas Gainsborough and won praise for their 'repose and harmony'.[6] In 1825, at the age of sixty-two, Abbott inherited the estate of Fordlands in Exeter from his uncle, James White, to which he retired and where he devoted himself fully to painting. In 1831 he was made Deputy-Lieutenant of Devonshire.

D NG 722

Pen and brown ink and watercolour on four sheets of paper, joined; laid down: 49.9 × 50.2
Signed, dated and inscribed in brown ink, on verso of mount: *Chudleigh – Devon / JWA Aug. 29. 1801*. In pencil, below: *Given to Francis Abbott / March 1 1802*.

This striking composition represents one of Abbott's favourite haunts, the picturesque surroundings of Chudleigh, several miles south-west of Exeter. It is very possible that Abbott first sketched this area in the company of his tutor, Francis Towne. In 1773 Towne had been employed by Hugh, 4th Baron Clifford of Chudleigh (1726–1783), to make a series of watercolours and paintings of his local estate, Ugbrooke Park.[7] At Lord Clifford's instigation, the house at Ugbrooke had been rebuilt between 1763 and 1771 by the London-based Scottish architect, Robert Adam. In the mid-1770s the surrounding park was remodelled by the landscape architect, Lancelot 'Capability' Brown. Towne's drawings and paintings for Clifford, which date from 1773–1780, were commissioned both to celebrate the elegant reshaping of the grounds and to record for posterity the estate as it had once been. In later years Towne returned to paint Ugbrooke and its environs, and is said to have given drawing lessons to Lord Clifford's children.

Abbott made several drawings of Ugbrooke Park, dating from the baronetcy of Charles, 6th Lord Clifford (succeeded 1793).[8] He almost certainly knew his teacher's drawings of the estate and, indeed, may have first been introduced to the 4th Baron's son via Towne. The wooded countryside surrounding Ugbrooke and Chudleigh village was sketched by Abbott on numerous occasions over a period of at least thirty years, from 1789 until the early 1820s.[9] It is not possible, on the whole, to trace any real development in his draughtsmanship. His style, well-established by the late eighteenth century, changed little during the subsequent decades, and drawings dated twenty years apart are remarkably similar in handling. This work, dated 1801, is one of his finest drawings, showing a sensitive rendering of trees, with foliage delineated by the frilled lines characteristic of Towne's draughtsmanship. The darkened foreground boulders and overhanging boughs serve as conventional *repoussoirs*, leading the eye to the sunlit rocks at the picture's centre. Although contemporary with the large, experimental watercolours of Turner and Girtin, Abbott's style remains essen-

tially rooted in the traditions of the eighteenth century. A similar, though smaller, study dated 1792 and inscribed 'At Chudleigh Rock' passed through Christie's salerooms in 1972.[10] Abbott's use of several sheets of paper joined together was a method Towne often employed.[11] Hardie suggests that Abbott adopted this approach for ease of manipulation when working outdoors in a breeze. While the pencil underdrawing was probably completed on the spot, the controlled washes of colour and precise pen outlines were applied later in the studio, after the sheets had been pasted onto the mount.[12]

The watercolour was presented to the Gallery by the artist's second son, Francis Abbott (b.1801), the godson of Towne (after whom, it may be supposed, he was named), and until 1868 Secretary to the General Post Office in Scotland.[13] An amateur painter, Francis amassed a considerable collection of Old Master drawings, of which a selection of fifty-five were lent to the National Gallery of Scotland for exhibition in 1886.[14] In this same year he gifted several works to the Gallery, including the present watercolour and two other sketches of cottages by his father.[15]

K T

PROVENANCE
Given by the artist to his son, Francis Abbott, 1802, by whom gifted to the Gallery 1886.

William Blake

72. *Job Confessing his Presumption to God who Answers from the Whirlwind*

LONDON 1757–1827 LONDON

Though celebrated today as one of the greatest imaginative artists of the British School, Blake, a printmaker, painter, poet and mystic philosopher, achieved little commercial success or public recognition during his lifetime. The son of a Soho hosier, he first received drawing lessons from Henry Pars before commencing an apprenticeship in engraving from 1772–9 with James Basire. In 1779 he studied for a short while in the Schools of the Royal Academy, through which he befriended John Flaxman, Thomas Stothard and Henry Fuseli. He first exhibited at the Royal Academy in 1780. Despite his unorthodox attitudes towards art and his distaste for the doctrines of Sir Joshua Reynolds, Blake continued to submit to the Academy's exhibitions for much of his life. Influenced initially by the Swedish scientist and philosopher, Emmanuel Swedenborg, he evolved a radical and highly personal political and religious ideology which he sought to express in his work. *Poetical Sketches*, Blake's first volume of poems, was published in 1783. During the late 1780s, he became preoccupied with finding a way to unify his poetry and painting by combining text and image. Between 1787 and 1789 he developed a unique method of 'relief etching' which enabled him to publish his own works and to perfect what he termed 'illuminated printing'. The first successful essay in this technique, *Songs of Innocence* (1789), was followed by a whole series of volumes, from the prophetic 'Lambeth' books of the 1790s to the later epic poems *Milton* (1804–9) and *Jerusalem* (completed early 1820s). Alongside his printmaking activities, he continued throughout his career to produce works in watercolour and tempera. These included several significant commissions for two of his most loyal patrons, Thomas Butts and John Linnell, notably illustrations to the *Book of Job* and Dante's *Divine Comedy*. In 1818 Linnell introduced Blake to 'The Ancients', a circle of young artists that included Samuel Palmer, George Richmond and Edward Calvert. Devoted supporters of Blake's visionary style, they were among the small group of admirers to mourn his passing in 1827.[1]

Fig.52 William Blake, *The Lord answering Job out of the Whirlwind*, plate 13 from *Illustrations of the Book of Job*
The Pierpont Morgan Library, New York

D NG 1136

Pen and ink and watercolour over pencil: 39.3 × 33
Signed in monogram in watercolour, lower left corner: *WB inv.* Inscribed in pen, lower right of mount: *Job XL c1 to 4v.* Inscribed in pencil, bottom edge of mount: *Moreover the Lord answered Job and said – Shall he that contendeth with the Almighty instruct him? He that reproveth God, let him answer it.* Inscribed on verso: *No.120 page 224.*

This magnificent watercolour was made for Blake's most important patron, Thomas Butts (1757–1845). A clerk in the office of the Commissary General of Musters, Butts's first recorded dealings with Blake date from 1799. His patronage (though greatly reduced after 1816) continued until Blake's death and spurred some of the artist's finest achievements in tempera and watercolour. Our work is one of a group of eighty watercolours of Biblical subjects which were produced for Butts over an extended period from 1800–c.1809.[2] Another watercolour from the set of *God writing upon the Tables of the Covenant* is also in the National Gallery of Scotland.[3] This commission immediately followed another from Butts for fifty small tempera paintings illustrating scenes from the Bible.[4] Despite the open-ended nature of the watercolour commission, and the variations in size and handling between the individual works, it would appear that Blake conceived them as a unified series. Dating the watercolours is problematic. However, as a group, they provide a valuable index to Blake's stylistic development during the first decade of the nineteenth century. This watercolour is tentatively dated to c.1803–5 on the basis of its technique and a comparison with other works in the series.

Blake was particularly fascinated by the Old Testament figure of Job, with whose trials some suggest he equated his own misfortunes. He first tackled the subject in c.1785 in three pen and wash drawings depicting *The Complaint of Job*, and again in c.1799–1800 in a tempera for Butts of *Job and his Daughters*. The Book of Job, which disputes the theory that material misfortunes are punishment for sin, tells the story of a wealthy and God-fearing man, whose faith is put to the ultimate test by subjection to a series of devastating catastrophes and afflictions. In this work, Blake illustrates a climactic passage in the narrative when Job, at the height of his torment and in the presence of his wife and friends, experiences a mystical vision of the Lord, who subsequently grants him redemption.[5]

This scene was recreated on several further occasions by Blake, in the context of a more comprehensive pictorial analysis of the Book of Job.[6] In c.1805–6 Butts commissioned twenty-one watercolours of the Job story.[7] A copy of this set was made in 1821 for John Linnell who, two years later, commissioned Blake to engrave the series.[8] The prints were published with an additional title page and decorative margins in 1826.[9] In these later works, the composition of the scene which shows the Lord answering Job from the whirlwind differs significantly from our earlier watercolour (fig.52). Common to all versions, however, is the motif of the omnipotent deity with outstretched arms. This powerful gesture, which Blake used frequently throughout the Job designs and other works, probably had its source in the ancient depiction of 'Jupiter Pluvius', the rain-bringer, on the Column of Marcus Aurelius in Rome.[10]

KT

PROVENANCE

Thomas Butts; Thomas Butts jun.; Capt. F. J. Butts, offered Sotheby's, 24 June 1903, no.7, £105 bt. in Munning; his widow, sold Carfax Gallery, April 1906; W. Graham Robertson; by whose executors sold Christie's, 22 July 1949, no.18, purchased Robertson's executors for £7,770; presented by the Trustees of Mr Graham Robertson, through the National Art Collections Fund, 1949.

EXHIBITED

Exhibition of the Works of William Blake, Burlington Fine Arts Club, London, 1876, no.95; *Exhibition of Works by William Blake*, Carfax Gallery, London, 1904, no.7; *Exhibition of Works by William Blake*, Carfax Gallery, London, 1906, no.40; *Loan Collection of Works by William Blake*, London, no.11 / Manchester no.9, 1913–14; *Blake Centenary Exhibition*, Burlington Fine Arts Club, London, 1927, no.7; *William Blake* Paris / Antwerp / Zurich / London, 1947, no.8; *Original Works by William Blake from the Graham Robertson Collection*, Bournemouth / Southampton / Brighton, 1949, no.25; *L'Aquarelle Anglaise 1750–1850*, Geneva / Zurich, 1955–6, no.6; Colnaghi 1966, no.92; *Gifts to Galleries. An Exhibition of Works of Art acquired with the Aid of the National Art-Collections Fund for Galleries outside London*, Walker Art Gallery, Liverpool, 1968, no.5; *William Blake: A Loan Exhibition*, National Library of Scotland, Edinburgh, 1969, no.117; *Prints and Drawings Acquired with the Aid of the National Art-Collections Fund*, National Gallery of Scotland, 1983, no.23.

John Sell Cotman
73. *Hell Cauldron* (Traditionally titled *A Shady Pool, where the Greta Joins the Tees*)

NORWICH 1782–1842 LONDON

The son of a barber and haberdasher, Cotman moved to London at the age of sixteen in pursuit of an artistic career. In 1799, after a short term of employment with the publisher Rudolph Ackermann, he followed the example of Turner and Girtin and joined Dr Thomas Monro's private 'Academy'. From *c.*1802–6 Cotman was a prominent member of the sketching society, known as 'The Brothers', of which Girtin had been the leading talent until his death in 1802. His works of this period show the influence of Girtin's graphic style. In 1800 he exhibited for the first time at the Royal Academy, winning the great silver palette of the Society of Arts. Tours to North Wales in 1800 (and possibly again in 1802), and to Yorkshire between 1803 and 1805, made a powerful impression on the young artist, inspiring some of the finest landscape watercolours of his career. These works, however, which were characterised by subdued colours and a flat, semi-abstract quality, found little favour with the buying public of the day, and in 1806 Cotman returned to his native Norwich, where he founded a School for Drawing and Design. He showed regularly in the Norwich exhibitions, in preference to London, and in 1810 was elected Vice-President of the Norwich Society of Artists, becoming President in 1811 (and again in 1833). In the hope of augmenting his meagre income and establishing a reputation, Cotman undertook several illustrative projects for antiquarian publications, of which *Architectural Antiquities of Norfolk* (1812–18) and *Antiquities of Normandy* (1822) were the most ambitious. The latter was the product of three trips to Normandy between 1817 and 1820. Despite his prodigious output in watercolour, oil and etching, Cotman was forced to rely for his livelihood on teaching and on the production of model drawings for copying. In 1823 he opened a school of drawing at his home in Norwich, and in 1834 was appointed drawing master at the recently established Kings College in London. During his middle and later years, in response to the prevailing taste for the works of Turner, Cotman adopted a stronger palette and more varied technique. Although he was elected an Associate of the Old Watercolour Society in 1825, he never achieved commercial success. This failing lead to recurrent bouts of deep and incapacitating depression, which may have contributed to his death at the age of sixty.

D NG 1136

Watercolour over pencil: 45.5 × 35 2

This composition, which dates to *c.*1808, is one of an exceptional group of watercolours resulting from Cotman's memorable visit to Rokeby Park in Yorkshire, in August 1805.[1] Rokeby Hall was at this time the seat of John Bacon Sawrey Morritt (*c.*1772–1843).[2] Cotman was introduced to Morritt by another local family, the Cholmeleys of Brandsby Hall, whom he had, in turn, first met in 1803 through Sir Henry Englefield, Mrs Cholmeley's brother and Vice-President of the Society of Antiquaries. The Cholmeleys welcomed Cotman into their family and social circle, offering him great support and friendship. In later years, he was to recall his time with them as the "happiest and blith[e]somest" of his life.[3] Cotman visited Rokeby with Francis Cholmeley junior during his last sojourn at Brandsby in the summer of 1805. He enjoyed the hospitality of the Morritts for about three weeks, before spending the remainder of the month at the inn at Greta Bridge. While a guest at Rokeby, he was given free access to the grounds, described in 1823 as 'an angular area, of the richest soil and shaded by luxuriant woods, bounded by the Tees and the Greta for the space of about a mile upwards from their confluence'.[4] Forays beyond Rokeby Park provided Cotman with visual material for a series of 'Greta' watercolours, of which about seventeen are known to exist today.[5] Particularly impressive examples include *Greta Bridge* (British Museum, London) and *Devil's Elbow, Rokeby Park* (Norwich Castle Museum, Norwich).

In common with a number of these 'Greta' watercolours, the precise location of the scene shown in our work is still the subject of debate. Though traditionally thought to represent the junction of the Greta and Tees (known locally as 'The Meeting of the Waters'),[6] more recent research has identified it as Hell Cauldron, a spot just above Greta Bridge and beyond Rokeby Park proper, where the river widens after a narrow passage (fig.53).[7] This makes it difficult to trace the early provenance and exhibition history of our work. The problem is compounded by the fact that, in *c.*1806, Cotman produced another, less finished watercolour of the same subject, now in Leeds City Art Galleries.[8] Either version might be identified with the picture of *Hell Cauldron, Rokeby Park*, exhibited by Cotman at the Norwich Society of Artists in 1808.

This Gallery's *Hell Cauldron* demonstrates

Cotman's extraordinary ability to simplify the complex forms of nature into a flat, decorative pattern. Although it was once argued that his finished watercolours were painted 'en plein air', the existence of the Leeds version, and the controlled application of washes, is proof itself that his stylised technique was essentially studio-based.[9] The restrained palette of yellow ochres and limpid blues and greens complements the scene's tranquil and contemplative mood. This was poetically captured by Cotman's biographer, Sydney Kitson, who described the work as possessing the timeless air 'of some dreamland where it is always afternoon'.[10]

KT

PROVENANCE

John Joseph Cotman (the artist's son); pledged by him as part of a large collection to William Steward (pawnbroker, Great Yarmouth); the sale of this collection, Spelman, Norwich, 16 May 1861, no.137, purchased Millar (as *Junction of the Tees at Greta*); W. B. Paterson Gallery, London, from whom purchased (as *The Silent Pool, where the Greta joins the Tees*) 1913.

EXHIBITED

Possibly the Norwich Society of Artists, 1808, no.184 (as *Hell Cauldron, Rokeby Park*); *Loan Collection of Pictures and Drawings by R. P. Bonington and J. S. Cotman*, W. B. Paterson's Gallery, London, 1913, no.17; *John Sell Cotman*, Tate Gallery, London, 1922, no.65; *Exhibition of British Art c.1000–1860*, Royal Academy, London, 1934, no.729; *La Peinture Anglaise XVIII et XIX Siècles*, Louvre, Paris, 1938, no.180; Colnaghi 1966, no.95; *A Loan Exhibition of Drawings and Watercolours by East Anglian Artists of the 18th and 19th Centuries*, Colnaghi's, London, 1970, no.32; *British Watercolours, A Golden Age 1750–1850*, J. B. Speed Museum, Louisville, 1977, no.55; *John Sell Cotman 1782–1842*, London / Manchester / Bristol, 1982–83, no.68; *The Great Age of British Watercolour 1750–1880*, London / Washington, 1993, no.50, exh. Washington only; *Walking the Landscape: With Cotman and Turner in Teesdale*, Bowes Museum, Barnard Castle, 1996.

Fig.53 *Hell Cauldron, River Greta*[11]
Photography by Eddie Ryle-Hodges

Peter De Wint
74. *The Devil's Hole, Lincoln*

HANLEY 1784–1849 LONDON

De Wint was born in Staffordshire. His mother was a Scot and his father a doctor of Dutch extraction. Contrary to his parent's wishes, De Wint chose not to study medicine and, after initial instruction from a local drawing master, Mr Rogers, he moved to London, where he was indentured for seven years to the mezzotint engraver and painter, John Raphael Smith. In 1806 De Wint bought himself out of his apprentice-ship, with a promise to supply Smith with eighteen oil paintings – an indication of his early skills as an artist. He subsequently moved into lodgings at Broad Street, Golden Square, with a fellow pupil of Smith, William Hilton, who from 1823 was Keeper of the Royal Academy, London. Among their neighbours was the watercolourist John Varley, who is said to have given lessons to De Wint free of charge. It was probably through Varley that De Wint entered Dr. Thomas Monro's informal drawing 'Academy' at Adelphi Terrace. There he was able to study the watercolours of Thomas Girtin, whose style made a powerful impres-sion on him. He first exhibited at the Royal Academy in 1807, enrolling at the Royal Academy Schools in 1809 and gaining entry to its Life School in 1811. In 1810 he was made an Associate of the Society of Painters in Watercolours (known subsequently as the Old Watercolour Society and, from 1881, as the Royal Watercolour Society), becoming a full member in 1811. Between 1810 and 1849 he exhibited at least 431 works with this Society.[1] De Wint is celebrated chiefly for his naturalistic views of the English countryside, and travelled abroad only once, in 1828, to Normandy. Many of his summers were spent in Lincoln, and he made frequent sketching excursions to Yorkshire, Cumberland, Westmorland, Gloucestershire and Norfolk, and along the valleys of the Trent and the Thames. Between 1824 and 1835 he also made several trips to Wales. Throughout his life he supported his work by teaching. He supplied topographical illustrations for a number of publications, including W. B. Cooke's *Picturesque Views on the Southern Coast of England* (1849). Although his contemporary reputation was based on his watercolours, he continued to paint (less successfully) in oils, exhibiting them at the Royal Academy between 1807 and 1824. A severe case of bronchitis, contracted in 1843, damaged his health and led to his death six years later.

D 5023.55
Watercolour over pencil: 43.2 × 65.7

The cathedral city of Lincoln provided De Wint with a constant source of inspiration. Writing in *The Art Journal*, his obituarist noted that 'the flat yet picturesque scenery of [Lincoln's] neighbour-hood possessed peculiar attractions for him; for we scarcely remember an exhibition which was not graced by some half dozen views taken from its vicinity, far and near.'[2] De Wint first visited the city in 1806 with William Hilton, who was a native of Lincoln. In 1810 he married Hilton's sister, Harriet, and, after the wedding, set up house with his wife and her brother in London. They returned frequently to Lincoln, however, and in 1814 purchased a house near Lincoln Castle.[3] De Wint's attachment to the city was commemorated after his death by his wife, who erected a monument to her husband and brother in Lincoln Cathedral.[4]

The Gallery's watercolour shows a site known more commonly in Lincoln's historical literature as 'The Glory Hole'. This is situated beneath the High Bridge, one of the city's most famous landmarks, which spans the River Witham in the centre of Lincoln's market district. Begun in the twelfth century, the bridge was later extended to support, on the east side, a chapel to St Thomas Becket and, on the west, a row of half-timbered sixteenth-century shops and houses. These survive today, making this the oldest bridge in Britain still to carry buildings. Contrary to the tranquil mood of De Wint's watercolour, the location bears a rather grim history. The River Witham, which flows from the south of Lincoln-shire, drains a large basin and over the centuries its banks have been widened and deepened to control its volume. As the River passes beneath Lincoln's High Bridge, however, it narrows considerably and here the bed was excavated downwards, making it the deepest section in the Witham's course. The waters beneath the Bridge consequently became notorious as a dumping ground for murder victims, earning the spot its nickname as the place where hapless souls were sent to 'Glory'.[5]

The rich, sombre tones of our work, and of another, smaller version in a Private Collection,[6] are characteristic of De Wint's earliest watercol-ours. Both drawings are of a similar style and period (*c*.1809–12) to De Wint's watercolour of *A Bridge over a Branch of the Witham, Lincoln* in the Tate Gallery, London.[7] According to Gallery

documentation, the old mount (long since discarded) of our watercolour bore an inscription by Thomas Barlow (1845–1945) which alluded to another picture of 'The Devil's Hole' by De Wint in the Victoria and Albert Museum, London. As no work with this title can be identified in that collection, Barlow's note was previously assumed to rest on erroneous information.[8] It seems likely, however, that he was referring either to De Wint's watercolour of *Old Houses on the High Bridge*,[9] or to his oil painting of the same sub-ject,[10] both of which are in the Museum's collection and which show 'The Devil's Hole' or, more correctly, 'The Glory Hole' beneath the bridge, as viewed from the Witham's banks, looking west (fig.54).

KT

PROVENANCE
Sir William Roberts MD; Sir Thomas Barlow Bart.; his daughter, Helen Barlow, 1945; her bequest to the Gallery 1976.

EXHIBITED
An Exhibition of the Works of Peter de Wint, Usher Art Gallery, Lincoln, 1937, no.23; Edinburgh 1979, no.55; *Peter DeWint* (sic) *1784–1849. A Bicentenary Exhibition*, Hanley / Newcastle / Hull / London, 1985, no.29.

Fig.54 Peter De Wint,
Old Houses on the High Bridge, Lincoln
Victoria and Albert Museum, London

Richard Cosway
75. *The Anointing of the Dead Christ*

OAKFORD, DEVON 1742–1821 LONDON

Cosway was almost certainly the son of a Tiverton schoolmaster. Aged twelve he was sent up to London to study with William Shipley at his Drawing School in the Strand, where he won numerous prizes for draughtsmanship between 1755 and 1760. Cosway displayed his paintings, drawings and portrait miniatures at the Society of Artists until 1769. In 1770 he was elected an Associate Royal Academician, with full membership following in the next year. Despite already having established himself as a fashionable miniaturist, Cosway regularly exhibited at the Academy up until 1806. He displayed both his ambitious oil portraiture, including allegorical compositions, and his history paintings, which were comprised of altarpieces and mythological subjects. During the 1770s, Cosway also developed a new and fashionable form of portraiture in small full-length drawings, done in black chalk with the head 'tinted' or 'stained' in watercolour. These proved as popular as the miniatures, with both lucrative forms of portraiture being continued in parallel until c.1810.[1] In 1780 Cosway first portrayed in miniature the eighteen-year-old George, Prince of Wales (later Prince Regent and George IV). Cosway immediately became the Prince's favourite artist, and, in 1785, he began signing his portrait miniatures and drawings with the title, *Primarius Pictor Serenissimi Principis Walliae* [First Painter to the His Royal Highness the Prince of Wales].[2] Over a thirty-year period Cosway executed numerous portrait commissions for the Prince and his circle of mistresses, family and friends. Cosway was a considerable collector of Old Master paintings, drawings and prints, as well as of sculpture, furniture and *objets d'art*. He also acted as an advisor to the Prince, both in the formation of his art collections, and in the decoration of his London palace, Carlton House.[3] In 1781 Cosway married Maria Hadfield (1760–1838), an Anglo-Florentine artist and musician, who had arrived in London during 1779.[4] The first decade of their marriage led to great social and artistic success. This was especially so after the couple moved to Schomberg House in Pall Mall during 1784, which they shared with Thomas Gainsborough and his family. In 1786 the Cosways made a socially triumphant visit to Paris, followed by an art-buying tour through Flanders. Richard Cosway can now be recognised as the most fashionable artist of the Regency period. His highly sensitive portrait miniatures and drawings – many of which were engraved – epitomise both the Prince's image and that of Regency society.[5]

D 5378
Black chalk: 25.5 × 39
Signed in black chalk, lower left, with monogram: CR; Inscribed in black chalk, lower right: 51

This large sheet is one of Cosway's most impressive drawings. It is notable for the delicate handling of the black chalk and the sensual treatment of the religious subject matter. It is almost certainly the 'Companion Drawing of the Pietà', mentioned by the Cosway scholar, George Williamson, as the one he bought at the important sale of drawings by Richard Cosway, held at Christie's, London, in 1896. After the death of the artist in 1821, the drawings had been taken by his widow, Maria, to her girls school at Lodi in Lombardy. A number of these works were acquired by the Milanese dealer Varese. Williamson also owned a second drawing of *The Deposition* (since untraced), executed in a similar technique, and which is very similar in feeling *to The Anointing of the Dead Christ*.[6]

Cosway was profoundly interested in Christianity, Judaism and mysticism, and he assembled a substantial library on these themes. At various points in his career he painted altarpieces and, after 1800, made numerous drawings on religious subjects.[7] He was particularly interested in the Life and Passion of Christ. His treatment of the reclining Christ being assisted by angels or the Magdalen was a recurrent one. In 1791 his composition of *Christ's Passion* or *The Agony in the Garden* (fig.55), was engraved in line by William Sharp and published by Thomas Macklin in his great illustrated Bible.[8] At around the same time, Cosway painted this scene in a small oval oil on panel (fig.56).[9]

More than in most subject drawings by Cosway, our sheet succeeds in demonstrating the results of the artist's study of Old Master draughtsmanship. One might compare this composition to a specific example in his own considerable collection of Old Master drawings, such as the lively copy in black chalk attributed to Sir Peter Paul Rubens of *Studies after Michelangelo's Madonna and Child in the New Sacristy, San Lorenzo, Florence* (National Gallery of Scotland, Edinburgh, D 712). Our drawing may also reveal Cosway's knowledge of Michelangelo's detailed black chalk drawings from the 1530s, such as the *Tityus* (Royal Collection, Windsor Castle), or the so-called '*Warwick*' *Pietà* (British Museum, London), or the *Rest on the Flight to Egypt* (J. Paul Getty Museum, Los Angeles). Cosway was also an avid admirer of the draughtsmanship of Correggio, the Carracci and Rubens.

Our drawing is likely to have been seen by Sir Thomas Lawrence on a visit during 1811 to Cosway's studio in Stratford Place, just off Oxford Street. In a letter written to his close friend, the artist and diarist Joseph Farington, Lawrence described his astonishment at the range and quality of Cosway's Old Master drawings as well his subject drawings. Lawrence praised Cosway for his 'knowledge [and] familiar acquaintance with, study; and often happy appropriation and even liberal imitation of the Old Masters, the fix'd Landmark of Art'.[10]

S L

PROVENANCE
Richard Cosway, London (until his death in 1821); Maria Cosway, Lodi (until her death in 1838); Collegio delle Dame Inglesi, Lodi (until 1896); Signor Varese, Milan; Christie's, London, 1 June 1896, no.129 (sold with no.128 for one guinea); Dr George C. Williamson, London; Christie's, London, 9 November 1993, no.2; W. M. Brady & Co., Inc., New York, from whom purchased 1994.

EXHIBITED
Master Drawings 1760–1890, W. M. Brady & Co., Inc., New York (no. 9) ill.; *Richard & Maria Cosway: Regency Artists of Taste & Fashion*, Edinburgh / London 1995–6, no.175.

left Fig.55 William Sharp after Richard Cosway
Christ's Passion
British Museum, London

right Fig.56 Richard Cosway *The Agony in the Garden*
Fondazione Cosway, Lodi

Sir David Wilkie
76. The Burying of the Scottish Regalia

CULTS 1785–1841 AT SEA, OFF MALTA, BURIED OFF GIBRALTAR

Wilkie achieved international celebrity for his creation and popularisation of an original style of genre painting, inspired by the art of the seventeenth-century Dutch and Flemish masters. The son of a rural minister, he entered the Trustees' Academy in Edinburgh at the age of fifteen. His first major picture, *Pitlessie Fair*, of 1804–5 (National Gallery of Scotland, Edinburgh) anticipated his subsequent development. Drawing on works by David Allan and prints after Teniers and Ostade, it displayed a precocious talent for visual story-telling, and for the examination of emotion as revealed by facial expression and posture. In 1805 Wilkie moved to London (where he settled for the rest of his life), enrolling at the Royal Academy Schools. *The Village Politicians* (The Rt. Hon. the Earl of Mansfield), exhibited at the Royal Academy in 1806, brought instant success and a string of important commissions. He was elected an Associate of the Royal Academy in 1809 and a full member in 1811. Following the end of the Napoleonic Wars, Wilkie travelled to Paris, Belgium and Holland and, in 1817, toured Scotland, visiting Sir Walter Scott at Abbotsford. The triumph of this period was his *Chelsea Pensioners reading the Waterloo Despatch* (Apsley House, London), which required a protective barrier to hold back the crowds when exhibited at the Royal Academy in 1822. The same year Wilkie went to Edinburgh to observe the State visit of George IV, subsequently producing the *Entrance of George IV into Holyrood House*, painted from 1823–30 (Royal Collection, Holyrood House). In 1823, on the death of Sir Henry Raeburn, he was appointed King's Limner for Scotland. Several personal tragedies led to his nervous breakdown in 1824, from which he recuperated by spending the next three years abroad, mainly in Italy, but also in Germany and Spain. This experience deepened his understanding of the grand tradition, in particular the works of Correggio, Velázquez and Titian. His later paintings were larger, broader, darker and more serious than his early work, the most ambitious being the enormous canvas of *Sir David Baird discovering the Body of Sultan Tippoo Sahib* of 1839 (National Gallery of Scotland, Edinburgh). In 1830 Wilkie was appointed Painter in Ordinary to the King, a post which he retained under William IV (by whom he was knighted in 1836) and Queen Victoria. His death, en route home from a trip to the Holy Land, was commemorated by J. M. W. Turner in his famous painting *Peace, Burial at Sea* (Tate Gallery, London).

D 4931

Pen and ink and wash, with watercolour and bodycolour over black chalk, on buff paper: 28.1 × 23.1
Signed and dated in pen, lower middle: *D Wilkie f London 1835 (?1836)*
Verso: Slight sketch in pencil of female head (cropped)

This drawing depicts a scene from one of the most romantic and patriotic tales in Scottish history. In 1651, during the Civil Wars, the Scottish Regalia were transferred for safekeeping from Edinburgh Castle to Dunnotter Castle, near Stonehaven, the remote seat of the Earl Marischal.[1] The defence of Dunnotter was entrusted to George Ogilvy of Barras but, despite his valiant efforts, he was unable to hold off Cromwell's troops and anxiety rose for the Regalia's security. An ingenious plan was hatched by Marischal's mother, the Countess Dowager, together with Mrs Ogilvy and Christian Fletcher, wife of the Reverend James Granger, minister of Kinneff Church. In March 1652, having obtained permission to visit Ogilvy's wife, Mrs Fletcher heroically smuggled the Crown out of Dunnotter in her apron, with the Sword of State and Sceptre concealed in bundles of flax carried on the back of her female servant. The treasures were taken to Kinneff Church where, under the cover of night, they were buried beneath the pavement stone before the pulpit.

Wilkie's interest in the Regalia's history may have first been aroused during his visit to Sir Walter Scott at Abbotsford in 1817. Scott was at this time lobbying the authorities for the recovery of the treasures, returned to Edinburgh after the Restoration, but rumoured to have been removed following the 1707 Act of Union. Through Scott's efforts, a Royal warrant was finally obtained for a search of the Crown-room of Edinburgh Castle, where in February 1818 the Regalia were found intact in a locked oak chest. This momentous occasion was captured by Wilkie in a rapid sketch of 1828.[2] The Regalia's rediscovery led to great rejoicing and, during George IV's state visit to Scotland in 1822, the first by any reigning British monarch since the days of Charles II, they were ceremonially paraded from the Castle to Holyrood House.[3] In preparation for his painting of George IV's entrance at Holyrood, Wilkie made studies of the Honours of Scotland, as well as a drawing of *The Earl of Morton carrying the Scottish Sword of State* (1824).[4]

Although our drawing does not seem to have been worked up into a finished canvas, the existence of several other preparatory studies implies that this was Wilkie's intention. An earlier, less finished, but powerful pen-and-wash study is in the Hunterian Art Gallery of the University of Glasgow (fig.57),[5] while an oil sketch is in a private collection.[6] A detailed study of two of the principal characters (American private collection) is similar in style to Wilkie's contemporary figure drawings for the monumental painting of *Sir David Baird discovering the Body of Sultan Tippoo Sahib*.[7] The dramatic lamplit composition of both this canvas and *The Burial* were clearly influenced by the works of Rembrandt such as his paintings of the *Adoration of the Shepherds* or the *Entombment of Christ*.[8]

KT

PROVENANCE

Probably Wilkie Sale, Christie's, London, 25 April 1842, no.115 (listed under 'Tinted Drawings' as *Burying the Scottish Regalia*), purchased Henry Graves [but possibly also either no.116, listed as 'Ditto, a larger sketch' or, 27 April 1842 (third day of sale) no.376, also listed under 'Tinted Drawings' as *Burying the Scottish Regalia*] (Lugt 16575);[9] probably John Myers, in possession by 1874; by whom sold 7 July 1890, no.224, purchased Heppenstall; by whom sold 31 January 1891, no.80, probably purchased McLellan; his son, Archibald McLellan, 1934; by whom sold at Dowell's, Edinburgh, 31 May 1968, where purchased.[10]

EXHIBITED

Probably *London International Exhibition*, London, 1874, no.218 (lent John Myers); *Romantic Art*, Aberdeen Art Gallery, Aberdeen, 1971, no.99; *La Peinture Romantique Anglaise et les Préraphaélites*, Petit Palais, Paris, 1972, no.334; *Sir David Wilkie: Sketches and Studies*, Aberdeen Art Gallery, Aberdeen, 1985, no.48.

Fig.57 David Wilkie, *The Burial of the Scottish Regalia* Hunterian Art Gallery, University of Glasgow

Sir Joseph Noël Paton
77. *Faust in the Witch's Kitchen*

DUNFERMLINE 1821–1901 EDINBURGH

Noël Paton's artistic leanings were fostered by his father, Joseph Neil Paton, an eminent damask designer.[1] Noël's art was significantly influenced by his upbringing. His father was a keen antiquarian and filled the family home with engravings after Old Masters, antique casts and ancient Scottish weaponry. This enthusiasm was transmitted to Noël, who became a fellow of the Scottish Society of Antiquaries and amassed his own collection, to which he regularly referred in researching his paintings.[2] In religion, Joseph Neil was non-conformist, adopting the Methodist, Quaker and Swedenborgian faiths successively. His views coloured his son's outlook and affected Noël's subsequent interest in, and interpretation of, spiritual, scriptural and historical-religious themes. After an apprenticeship in textile design, and a period as head designer at a Paisley damask factory,[3] Paton enrolled in 1843 at the Royal Academy Schools in London. Around this time he began a life-long friendship with John Everett Millais. Paton's precise relationship to Pre-Raphaelitism remains unclear. He returned to Scotland in 1844, before the formal foundation of the Pre-Raphaelite Brotherhood in London in 1848. In subject matter and technique, however, his paintings show a sympathy with the movement's aims. Subjects from English literature, especially Shakespeare, inspired many of his earlier works on both canvas and paper. He was acquainted with Rossetti and Holman Hunt and was on close terms with Ruskin. *The Bluidie Tryst* of 1857 (Glasgow Art Gallery and Museum, Glasgow), in particular, shows his Pre-Raphaelite affiliation. Paton's first major success came in 1845 when he won a prize for his allegorical cartoon *The Spirit of Religion* in the Westminster Hall Competitions to decorate the Houses of Parliament. Two further submissions in 1847 were also rewarded, of which his celebrated fairy painting *The Reconciliation of Oberon and Titania* (National Gallery of Scotland, Edinburgh) won royal admiration from Prince Albert. This led ultimately to his appointment in 1866 as Queen's Limner for Scotland and to his knighthood in 1867. Apart from painting in oils, Paton was an acclaimed illustrator, producing designs for Shelley's *Prometheus Unbound* (1844) and Coleridge's *The Rime of the Ancient Mariner* (1863), among many other publications. He was also a competent sculptor and prepared ambitious designs for major public projects in Scotland, including monuments to Prince Albert, Robert the Bruce, William Wallace and the Wars of Independence. A highly influential member of the Royal Scottish Academy, he was mourned at his death in 1901 as one of Scotland's most popular artists.[4]

left Fig.58 Moritz Retzsch, *Umrisse zu Goethe's Faust, Plate 6: Faust in the Witch's Kitchen*
National Gallery of Scotland, Edinburgh

right Fig.59 J. N. Paton, *Faust in the Witch's Kitchen*
Courtesy of Perth Museum and Art Gallery, Perth and Kinross Council, Scotland

D 5079

Pen and brown ink and wash over pencil: 24 × 29.9 (image size: arched top)
Signed and dated in brown ink, lower right corner: *J.N.P. 1848*

Paton considered this detailed drawing to be a finished work in its own right. It belongs to the early period, which saw the creation of two of his most accomplished and famous Shakespearean canvases, *The Reconciliation of Oberon and Titania* and its companion, *The Quarrel* (both National Gallery of Scotland, Edinburgh). This composition and *The Quarrel* were among the large group of works which Paton exhibited at the Royal Scottish Academy in 1850 in support of his anticipated nomination to full Academy membership later that year.

The drawing takes its inspiration from a scene in Part One of Goethe's dark and tragic drama, *Faust*, which was begun in Goethe's youth and finished effectively by 1801. The first part of *Faust*, published in 1808, had an immediate impact throughout Europe, inspiring musicians, composers, artists and illustrators alike. Here, as in his contemporaneous fairy paintings, Paton delights in giving shape to the grotesque characters and weird underworld suggested by Goethe's prose. When exhibited, the drawing was accompanied by a lengthy quotation from Hayward's translation of the German text, describing the moment when Faust is lured by 'the loveliest image of a woman' conjured in the magic mirror.[5] Paton's drawing is characteristically packed with detail and faithfully delineates Goethe's script. On a low hearth, a cauldron emits ghoulish fumes. Mephistopheles, the devil incarnate, toys with a whisk as he sprawls on a wooden settle. Reference to earlier dialogue is made by the monkeys in the centre, who play with a large globe, while the two apes to the left, approaching with a crown, anticipate the next

stanza when Mephistopheles pronounces 'Here like a throned king I sit me down, with this my sceptre – but I lack a crown.'[6]

Stylistically, this drawing demonstrates Paton's concern for the primacy of line, which he advocated throughout his life as the basis of all successful design. This inclination was influenced by his initial training as a damask designer and found encouragement through his early contact with Samuel Carter Hall (1800–1889), by whom he was employed to make illustrations for his *Book of British Ballads* (1842–4).[7] Hall was a fervent admirer of contemporary German exponents of outline drawing, in particular Moritz Retzsch (1779–1857) whose etchings to *Faust*, first published in 1816 (English edition, London 1821), were widely known and favoured by Goethe himself. Retzsch's scene of the Witch's Kitchen formed the basis for Paton's drawing (fig.58). Other illustrations to *Faust*, from which Paton may have drawn inspiration, include those by the Nazarene, Peter Cornelius (1811), Delacroix (1825–8) and Theodor Hosemann (1836). An early preparatory sketch for Paton's composition is in the National Gallery of Scotland.[8] A more finished study in the collection of Perth Museum and Art Gallery depicts a later episode in the scene from the Witch's Kitchen, when Faust is coerced into drinking the Witch's potion (fig.59).[9] This may have been intended for a companion piece or as an alternative to the Gallery's drawing, to which it is similar in format.[10]

KT

PROVENANCE
Phillips, Edinburgh, 21 September 1979, no.46, where purchased.

EXHIBITED
Royal Scottish Academy, Edinburgh, 1850, no.566; *Early Victorian Draughtsmen and the Rise and the Scottish Academy*, National Gallery of Scotland, Edinburgh, 1980, no.32; Edinburgh 1984, no.17.

Joseph Nash
78. *Woodsmen Resting under a Tree*

GREAT MARLOW 1808–1878 LONDON

Nash achieved celebrity as a watercolour painter and lithographer of picturesque architectural subjects. He was the son of a clergyman and at the age of twenty-one became a pupil of the French architectural draughtsman, Augustus Charles Pugin. Pugin, who had worked for many years as an assistant to the architect John Nash, was an exceptionally skilled draughtsman of Gothic architecture and produced several volumes which were influential in the development of the Gothic Revival. His passion for medieval buildings was transferred to his son, Augustus Welby Northmore Pugin, famed for his involvement with the building of the Houses of Parliament, and to Joseph Nash. A. C. Pugin regularly took his pupils on sketching excursions to places of architectural interest and Joseph Nash was among the young men who went to Paris, to make drawings for Pugin's *Paris and its Environs* (2 vols., London, 1829 and 1831). The earliest known lithographs by Nash were issued during this same period, in Pugin's *Views Illustrative of the Examples of Gothic Architecture* (3 vols., London, 1831–8). Nash first exhibited at the Old Watercolour Society in 1834, being elected an Associate in the same year, and rising to full membership in 1842. He became one of the Society's longest-standing members and, over a period of forty-five years, submitted a total of 266 works to its summer and winter exhibitions.[1] The majority of his contributions were connected with illustrative projects. Chief among these were his *Architecture of the Middle Ages* (published as a set of twenty-five lithographs in 1838) and his more famous *The Mansions of England in the Olden Time*, a series of views of Tudor and Jacobean houses enlivened with picturesque groupings of figures in period costume (issued in four sets of twenty-five lithographs from 1839–49).[2] During the same period he produced numerous genre pieces, illustrating historical and literary subjects, principally Sir Walter Scott's *Waverley Novels*, Shakespeare and Cervantes's *Don Quixote*. Other notable projects included *Views of the Interior and Exterior of Windsor Castle* (1848), lithographs after Sir David Wilkie's *Spanish and Oriental Sketches* (1846) and illustrations to J. P. Lawson's *Scotland Delineated* (1847–54). Among his most celebrated works were a series of spectacular views of the Great Exhibition of 1851, several of which are now in the Victoria and Albert Museum, London.[3]

D 5023.30

Watercolour and bodycolour over pencil on grey paper: 48.8 × 34
Signed and dated in red watercolour, lower left corner: *J Nash 1857*. Also in brown watercolour, lower right corner: *J Nash 186(o ?)*

This work is unusual in Nash's oeuvre for possessing neither architectural, historical nor literary associations. In common with his more characteristic pieces, however, it employs a liberal use of bodycolour – watercolour rendered opaque by the addition of Chinese White pigment. In contrast to pure watercolour, in which light passages relied for their brilliance on the white paper beneath, bodycolour enabled artists to work in a manner akin to oil painting. The opacity of the pigment allowed for a richer and more powerful tonal range, and for colours to be applied in layers, light over dark. The medium was particularly well-suited for intricate drawing and for the description of surface texture. This quality was evidently especially attractive to Nash, whose architectural and historical illustrations were, in his words, 'made with reference to finish and detail' and designed to be 'seen as closely as possible'.[4]

The sketchy and bravura handling of this work, in which areas of the grey paper ground are left uncovered, contrasts with the fine stipple technique with which bodycolour came to be associated. The woodcutters resting beneath the ancient tree (possibly an oak or beech) recall Nash's habit of populating his historic interiors and architectural views with staffage figures. The two dates on the work suggest that this was a studio piece, sold a number of years after its execution. It is likely that the signature and date in the lower right corner belong to the time of the watercolour's completion. Difficult to read against the brown ground, this inscription may have been overlooked at the later stage when the second, more prominent signature in red watercolour was added. This was perhaps done at the point of sale, with the date guessed from memory.[5]

KT

PROVENANCE
Sir Thomas Barlow Bart.; his daughter, Helen Barlow, 1945, her bequest to the Gallery 1976.

EXHIBITED
Edinburgh 1979, no.32; *Victorian Landscape Watercolours*, New Haven / Ohio / Birmingham, 1992–3, no.35.

Samuel Palmer
79. The Two Pet Lambs

LONDON 1805–1881 REDHILL

Palmer acquired a love of literature at an early age through his father, a bookseller, and his nurse, Mary Ward, who introduced him to the poetry of Milton. Although by 1818 he was studying with the drawing-master William Wate, he received no formal artistic education and developed essentially in isolation. In 1822 he met the painter John Linnell, who encouraged him to look at the works of Dürer and other European Old Masters. Two years later Linnell introduced Palmer to William Blake, whose visionary style (especially his illustrations to Thornton's *Pastorals of Virgil*) made a profound and lifelong impression on the young artist. Around 1824 Palmer paid his first visit to Shoreham in the Darent Valley, Kent, and in 1826 he settled there with his father. Among Palmer's frequent visitors were 'The Ancients', a circle of artist friends which included George Richmond, Edward Calvert and Francis Oliver Finch. Headed by Palmer, this group shared a passion for the ancient poets and painters and looked to Blake as their spiritual leader.[1] The rural seclusion of Shoreham, which Palmer referred to as his 'Valley of Vision', yielded the most imaginative and celebrated works of his career. Characterised by a rich and unconventional mixed-media technique, these included *Valley Rich with Corn*, one of six varnished wash drawings of 1825 (Ashmolean Museum, Oxford) and *The Magic Apple Tree* of 1830 (Fitzwilliam Museum, Cambridge). Palmer returned to London in 1832, and between 1835 and 1836 visited Devon, Somerset and Wales. His works of this period abandoned the visionary fantasy of Shoreham in favour of greater naturalism. Following his marriage in 1837 to Linnell's daughter, Hannah, Palmer spent two years in Italy, which brought about a dramatic change of style incorporating a more brilliant palette. On returning home, financial difficulties forced him to take work as a drawing-master. In 1843 he was elected an Associate of the Old Watercolour Society (with whom he exhibited many works), rising to full membership in 1854. He also became a member of the Etching Club in 1850. Palmer's last twenty years were spent in Surrey, during which period he devoted himself to two major projects which show his mature work at its best: a commission for eight watercolours depicting passages from Milton's poems *L'Allegro* and *Il Pensero* (from which he developed two of his greatest etchings) and a set of illustrations to his own translation of Virgil's *Eclogues*.[2]

D NG 1232

Watercolour and bodycolour, with gum arabic and some scratching out, on card: 20.2 × 43.4

In 1861 Palmer's eldest son died aged only nineteen. This loss, probably the greatest tragedy in Palmer's life, marked the beginning of a prolonged term of deep sadness which profoundly affected the outlook of his later years. In 1862 he moved to Reigate where, aided by his work and an unfailing Christian faith, he slowly came to terms with his grief. The Gallery's watercolour was painted about a year after Palmer's move, and is a particularly fine example from his later period.[3] Spectacular skies, such those shown here, are a common feature in his works of this time and probably reflect Palmer's delight in the sunsets of the Surrey countryside. His son, Alfred, recalled how they would regularly stroll together in the long evenings, when Palmer would point out the beauties of the aerial tints 'with peculiarly well-chosen words'.[4]

The two pet lambs of the picture's title refer to a real lamb, carried by a woman to the right of the group of figures, and to a baby held overhead in the centre. On the distant hillside a shepherd and his flock, illuminated by the setting sun, link the horizon and foreground.[5] Sheep were one of Palmer's favourite subjects and appear continuously in his work from the rustic idylls of his Shoreham years to the Arcadian illustrations to Virgil, left unfinished at his death. Typical of his later period is the panoramic format, of which the artist had two favourite sizes, the 'Little Long' and 'Large Long'. Our work is probably closest to the latter category, which he used less often.[6] The hot, intense colour and varied handling demonstrate Palmer's predilection, following his return from Italy, for creating watercolours which matched the vigour and technical complexity of oils. To some extent he reverted to a method employed in many of his earlier works, whereby the focal areas of the composition are highly finished and detailed, while the foreground (especially to the left) is only roughly indicated. Like many of Palmer's watercolours produced in the years following his son's death, the scene is idealised and highly romantic. The vision is of a blissful, timeless world and suggests nostalgia for happier times. In the pointed metaphor of the child as a lamb, and the imagery of the shepherd elevated above his flock and bathed in radiant light, one can identify an expression of Palmer's religious conviction in his time of mourning.

This work was once owned by Robert Brechin (c.1848–1918), a prosperous Glasgow butcher, who amassed what was described at his death as 'one of the finest private collections in Scotland'.[7] A member of the Glasgow Art Club and of The Royal Glasgow Institute of the Fine Arts, Brechin served frequently on the Institute's hanging committee and played an important role in the organisation of Glasgow's International Exhibition of 1901 and the East-End Industrial Exhibition, to which he was a major lender. His collection, particularly strong in Scottish paintings,[8] included two other watercolours by Palmer, *The Day's Work Done* and *Gleaners* (both c.1880),[9] as well as works by masters such as Constable, Turner, Corot, Fantin-Latour and Boudin, and by the contemporary Hague School.[10]

KT

PROVENANCE
Robert H. Brechin, by 1901; sold Brechin Sale, J. & R. Edmiston, Glasgow, 20 March 1919, no.29, where purchased.

EXHIBITED
Glasgow International Exhibition, 1901, no.951; *East-End Industrial Exhibition*, Glasgow, 1903–4; *British Art c.1000–1860*, Royal Academy, London, 1934, no.824.

Arthur Melville
80. A Moorish Procession, Tangier

LOANHEAD-OF-GUTHRIE 1858–1904 REDLANDS

The son of a grocer, Melville began to study art at the age of fifteen. In 1875 he entered the Royal Scottish Academy Life School in Edinburgh, where he was taught principally by James Campbell Noble, a Scottish 'realist' whose works were influenced by the Hague School of painters. Melville first exhibited at the Royal Academy, London, in 1878 and in the same year travelled to Paris, where he enrolled at the Académie Julian. While in France he began to experiment with watercolour and, inspired by the example of Corot and Millet, made sketching excursions to Brittany and Normandy and to Fontainebleau, Barbizon and Grez-sur-Loing, where he settled in 1879. Shortly after returning to Scotland in 1880, Melville embarked on a two-year trip to the Middle East. He travelled initially to Cairo, where he stayed for a year, before sailing up the Nile to Suez and journeying on to Baghdad and Constantinople. The sketches he made during this tour yielded numerous paintings and watercolours, which he worked up for many years after his return to Britain in 1882. The critical reception of Melville's oil painting *Evie – The Flower Girl* (untraced),[1] exhibited in 1883, brought him to the attention of the so-called 'Glasgow Boys', a progressive and loose-knit group of artists based in the west of Scotland, who shared an enthusiasm for the 'naturalist' subject matter and bold handling of the Dutch and French realists, in particular Jules Bastien-Lepage. Three of the group's leading members were Joseph Crawhall, James Guthrie and Edward Arthur Walton, with whom Melville spent the winter of 1883–4 at Cockburnspath in Berwickshire. While Melville never became a 'Glasgow Boy' proper, they regarded him as a kindred spirit. In subsequent years, he joined various members of the 'Boys' on trips to Orkney, Stirling and France, and exhibited with them in Munich and America in the 1890s.[2] Melville was celebrated chiefly as an innovative watercolourist and during the 1880s his impressionistic technique reached its maturity. He was elected an Associate of the Royal Scottish Academy in 1886 and an Associate of the Royal Watercolour Society in 1888, rising to full membership in 1900. In this year he also became a member of the Royal Scottish Watercolour Society. Melville moved to London in 1889, where he befriended the painter Theodore Roussel (1847–1926), a member of Whistler's circle. In the following year he made the first of several trips to Spain and Tangier, which were to provide him with the colourful and exotic subject matter of his later years, notably his series of Spanish bullfights. He died from typhoid, contracted on his last visit to Spain in 1904. At the memorial exhibition of his works held two years later, he was hailed as 'undoubtedly one of the most brilliantly audacious watercolour painters of his time'.[3]

D NG 947

Watercolour over pencil: 59.3 × 79.8
Signed and dated in watercolour, lower left corner:
Tangiers. / Arthur Melville. 93.

Melville visited Tangier twice, firstly in spring 1890 and secondly in spring 1893. Both trips were combined with a tour of Spain, although it is not clear whether he travelled through Spain first or, like a number of his contemporaries, took the ferry directly from London to Gibraltar, before making the short crossing to the North African coast. It was probably Joseph Crawhall who inspired Melville to travel to Morocco. Crawhall may have visited Tangier as early as 1882 and certainly returned regularly between 1884 and 1893.[4] Regarded as a magical and mysterious place, Tangier attracted many nineteenth-century European artists, notably the great French master Eugène Delacroix. By the 1880s the city supported a thriving community of British expatriates. Among Melville's many contemporaries to visit Tangier were several 'Glasgow Boys', including (in addition to Crawhall) Thomas Millie Dow, John Lavery, Alexander Mann and William Kennedy.

The city's vibrant lifestyle was recorded by Crawhall's friend, R. B. Cunninghame Graham, who recalled that 'Tangier was [then] one of the most fascinating places in the whole world to live in; a miniature Constantinople, it had representatives of every Court in Europe … '[5] This rich cultural mix was matched by the 'picturesque variety' of North Africa's native inhabitants, including, as another contemporary observed, 'men of the desert tribes from Timbuctoo and other remote places, Berbers from the Altas, and from Sûs and Wadnoon; ebony-faced Nubian slaves, negro musicians, Arabs from the country in tattered brown jellabs … mixed in bewildering confusion with the rich town Moors in costly and voluminous garments, and the black-robed Jews … '[6] For many, however, it was the city's dazzling white atmosphere and extraordinary colour which left the deepest impression. Writing in 1897, the painter Norman Garstin described Tangier as a 'city of narrow … lanes that wander hither and thither … all wonderful in the illimitable gradations of white … for the great azure sky above, with the ardent sun and innumerable reflections of the earth are tinting them variously from morn to eve … '[7]

It was precisely these qualities of shifting light and colour, and the city's atmospheric clamour,

which Melville sought to express in this and other watercolours of Tangier. His technique, described in later years by Theodore Roussel, was peculiarly well-adapted for this purpose. After preparing his paper by saturating it in diluted Chinese White pigment, Melville would map out his composition lightly in pencil and then vigorously block in the principal shades in broad, wet masses. Superfluous detail was sponged out, leaving patches of paper, as here, barely stained with colour. Finally, he would lay in the accents in full spots or blots, experimenting with different effects by applying dashes of paint onto a sheet of glass laid over the work, before adding them to the paper. This method was lauded after Melville's death for recreating 'the scintillating splendour and many-coloured movement of the South … with the vividness of dreams … '[8]

KT

PROVENANCE
Mrs Ethel Melville (the artist's wife), from whom purchased 1907.

EXHIBITED
Royal Scottish Academy, Edinburgh, 1894, no.450; *Saint Louis Exposition and Music Hall Association, Twelfth Annual Exhibition*, Saint Louis / Chicago / Cincinnati / New York, 1895, no.360 (as *An Arab Procession – Tangier*); *Autumn Exhibition of Pictures at the Walker Art Gallery*, Walker Art Gallery, Liverpool, 1896, no.760 (offered for sale at £200); *Corporation of Manchester Art Gallery, Fifteenth Autumn Exhibition*, Manchester Art Gallery, Manchester, 1897, no.289 (offered for sale at £200); *The Exhibition of the Collected Works of Arthur Melville RWS, ARSA*, London / Newcastle, 1906, no.99; *The Exhibition of the Works of Arthur Melville RWS, ARSA*, Nottingham / Glasgow, 1907, no.21; *Exhibition of Scottish Art*, Royal Academy, London, 1939, no.634; *The Glasgow Boys*, Glasgow Art Gallery and Museum, Glasgow, 1968, no.91; *Arthur Melville 1855–1904*, Dundee / Edinburgh / Glasgow / Stirling / Sheffield / London, 1977–8, no.43.

Notes and References

1

1. The inscription is tiny and difficult to read, but it is clearly in the same hand as an identical and more legible inscription on Leonardo's drawing of a *Bear's Head* in a private collection, with which the present drawing shares a common history (see A. E. Popham, 'The Drawings at the Burlington Fine Arts Club', *The Burlington Magazine*, LXX, 1937, p.87, pl.B; London, 1989, no.37). The inscription indicates a French provenance for both drawings prior to Lawrence's ownership of them.

2. Popham 1937, p.87.

3. Kenneth Clark and Carlo Pedretti, *The Drawings of Leonardo da Vinci in the Collection of Her Majesty the Queen at Windsor Castle*, revised edition, London, 1968, inv. nos 12372–5. See also Martin Clayton, *Leonardo da Vinci: One Hundred Drawings from the Collection of her Majesty The Queen*, exh. cat., The Queen's Gallery, London, 1997, no.22.

4. I am grateful to Douglas M. Richardson, Keeper of Mammals at London Zoo, and to Daphne Hills of the Department of Zoology at the Natural History Museum, for independently clarifying this issue. Douglas Richardson writes: 'The drawings are most definitely of a domestic dog's paws; the configuration of the hair and the lack of any significant gap between the two middle digits are the deciding factors.' (letter in Gallery files).

5. A. E. Popham, *The Drawings of Leonardo da Vinci*, London, 1946, nos 72, 75–6.

6. Clayton 1997, nos 20 and 21.

7. Martin Clayton has kindly endorsed this proposed earlier dating.

8. See Kenneth Clark, *Leonardo da Vinci*, revised edition, Harmondsworth, 1967, p.79.

9. All four edges of the verso are masked by the mount into which the drawing is inlaid.

10. Anna Forlani Tempesti, *Italian Fifteenth-to Seventeenth-Century Drawings in the Robert Lehman Collection*, New York, 1991, no.80.

11. Popham 1946, nos 63B, 64 and 65.

12. Popham 1946, no.63A.

2

1. For a summary of the arguments, see Philip Rylands, *Palma Vecchio*, English edition, Cambridge, 1992, pp.122–31.

2. Previously incorrectly identified as in the hand of Francesco Maria Niccolò Gabburri (1676–1742), Nicholas Turner has kindly pointed out that this inscription is in the same hand (which has been erroneously identified as that of Carlo Ridolfi) as those on a large group of old master drawings in Lisbon (see the numerous illustrations in *Dessin: La collection du MNAA*, exh. cat., Museu Nacional de Arte Antiga, Lisbon, 1994).

3. For the drawing and the inscription, see John Rowlands, 'Two Unknown Works by Palma Vecchio', *Pantheon*, XXIV, 1966, pp.372–77; Rylands 1992, pp.120–22, 251–2, no.D 4.

4. For the Serina polyptychs, see Rylands 1992, pp.162–3, no.19; and pp.194–6, no.52.

5. In favour of identifying it as a *Self-portrait* were Rowlands 1966, pp.373–4 (with reservations); Keith Andrews (in Edinburgh 1969) and Julien Stock (in Venice 1980); against were Giovanni Mariacher, *Palma il Vecchio*, Milan, 1968, pp.116–17 and Rylands 1992, pp.251–2.

6. For these paintings see Rylands 1992, p.167, no.24 and pp.223–4, no.81.

7. See Francesco Rossi's entry in *Pinacoteca di Brera: Scuola Veneta*, Milan, 1990, pp.444–5. The suggestion that the woodcut portrait of Palma Vecchio in the 1568 edition of Vasari's *Lives* was based on this head seems untenable.

8. I am grateful to Mariolina Olivari for supplying the photograph reproduced here and for confirming that she in no doubt that the painted and drawn heads represent one and the same person.

9. Rylands 1992, pp.173–5, no.32.

10. See, most recently, Rylands 1992, p.251; *Le Siècle de Titien: L'âge d'or de la peinture à Venise*, exh. cat., Grand Palais, Paris, 1993, no.119.

11. For the Rovigo painting, see Rylands 1992, p.150. Rylands pointed our that the Louvre study corresponds most closely to the head of the adulteress in the *Christ and the Adulteress* in St Petersburg (p.197, no.54, where it is dated to 1520–22).

3

1. For the fullest discussion of the drawing, see Edinburgh 1994, no.31 (with previous literature).

2. For the altarpiece and its history, see Jeroen Stumpel, *The Province of Painting: Theories of Italian Renaissance Art*, Utrecht, 1990, pp.27–58; Edinburgh 1994, under no.29. I am grateful to David Franklin for drawing the former publication to my attention.

3. See Edinburgh 1994, p.80, fig.55.

4. Edinburgh 1994, no.30.

5. Stumpel 1990, pp.37–40.

6. *Ibid.*, pp.42–4.

7. See Edinburgh 1994, p.76, fig.53.

8. Bartsch, vol.XVI.54 (61); Edinburgh 1994, no.32.

9. See, for example, Edinburgh 1994, nos 33–5 and figs.13 and 56.

10. See the present writer's appendix in Edinburgh 1994, pp.129–31.

4

1. Cited by Antony Griffiths and Nicholas Turner, 'Drawings from Holkham Hall', *NACF Annual Report*, 1992, p.71.

2. Inv. no.130. See Mario Di Giampaolo, *Disegni Emiliani nelle Gallerie dell'Accademia di Venezia*, Milan, 1993, no.11, as copy after Parmigianino.

3. Barbera Brejon de Lavergnée, *Catalogue des Dessins italiens: Collections du Palais des Beaux-Arts de Lille*, Paris and Lille, 1997, pp.414–15, no.1131, as copy after Parmigianino.

4. Inv. no.E.4012–1919. See Peter Ward-Jackson, *Catalogue of Italian Drawings 14th–16th Century*, London 1979, vol.I, p.51, as copy after Bedoli.

5. Ex-Sagredo Collection, inscribed below *S L no.65*, kindly pointed out to the author by Francis Russell, letter 7 June 1993.

6. Inv. no.1851–3–8–908.

7. Clovis Whitfield, 'A Parmigianino Discovery', *The Burlington Magazine*, CXXIV, 1982, p.287, fig.18.

8. Mario Di Giampaolo, *Girolamo Bedoli 1500–1569*, Florence, 1997, pp.212–13, no.138.

9. Griffiths and Turner 1992, pp.68–71.

10. Hugh Brigstocke, 'Old Master Drawings from Holkham Hall', *Apollo*, CXXXVII, 1993, pp.396–7.

11. A. E. Popham, 'The Drawings of Girolamo Bedoli', *Master Drawings*, II, 1964, pp.257–8 and 262, no.5; idem., 'The Drawings of Girolamo Bedoli', *Aurea Parma*, XLIX, 1965, p.82; A. E. Popham and Christopher Lloyd, *Old Master Drawings at Holkham Hall*, Chicago, 1986, p.280.

12. A. E. Popham, *The Drawings of Parmigianino*, New Haven and London, 1971, vol.I, no.48, vol.III, pl.248.

13. *Ibid.*, vol.I, no.323, vol.III, pl.256.

5

1. Pioneering work was done on Polidoro as a draughtsman by Philip Pouncey and J. A. Gere, *Italian Drawings in the Department of Prints and Drawings in the British Museum: Raphael and his Circle*, London, 1962; see also Alessandro Marabottini, *Polidoro da Caravaggio*, Rome, 1969; Lanfranco Ravelli, *Polidoro Caldara da Caravaggio* (Monumenta Bergomensia XLVIII), Bergamo, 1978; *Polidoro da Caravaggio fra Napoli e Messina*, exh. cat., Museo e Gallerie Nazionali di Capodimonte, Naples, 1988–9, catalogue by Pierluigi Leone de Castris.

2. Letter in Gallery files, 25 February 1965.

3. Pouncey and Gere 1962, vol.I, pp.120–21, nos 208, 209; vol.II, pls.176–7.

4. Oil on panel, 310 × 247. Museo di Capodimonte, Naples, inv.Q.103; Marabottini, 1969, pp.180–192; Naples 1988–9, pp.128–130, cat.X–7.

5. The whole development can be followed admirably in Naples 1988–9, pp.119–31.

6

1. For the Louvre drawing and its relationship to the Edinburgh one, see Catherine Monbeig Goguel in *Francesco Salviati, o la Bella Maniera*, exh. cat., Rome / Paris 1998, no.26.

2. By Catherine Monbeig Goguel in Rome / Paris 1998, no.126. For the frescoes, see Michael Hirst, 'Three Ceiling Decorations by Francesco Salviati', *Zeitschrift für Kunstgeschichte*, XXVI, 1963, pp.146–65, especially fig.15; Francesca Corsi, 'L'appartamento Salviati a Palazzo dei Penitenzieri a Roma', *Antichità Viva*, XXIX, 5, 1990, pp.26–8.

3. For the frontispiece design and related print, see the entries by Pascal Dubourg-Glatigny in Rome / Paris 1998, nos 141–2.

4. See the entries by Candace J. Adelson in Rome / Paris 1998, nos 113–14.

7

1. There is no mention of the drawing in J. A. Gere, *Taddeo Zuccaro: His Development Studied in his Drawings*, London, 1969, nor in the same author's follow-up article, 'Taddeo Zuccaro: Addenda and Corrigenda', published posthumously in *Master Drawings*, XXXIII, 1995, pp.223–323. It was, nevertheless, Gere himself who in 1962 first proposed that the drawing might be by Taddeo rather than by his brother Federico, as indicated in the old inscription (letter in Gallery files). The drawing is accepted as autograph by E. James Mundy in *Renaissance into Baroque: Italian Master Drawings by the Zuccari, 1550–1600*, exh. cat., Milwaukee Art Museum, 1989, under no.3.

2. For stylistically comparable drawings, all of them dated to around 1550, see Gere 1969, nos 69, 72; Milwaukee 1989, nos 3, 7; and Gere 1995, nos 99A, 104L, 264D.

3. See Andrews 1968, vol.I, p.133.

4. Mundy 1989, under no.3, associated the Edinburgh drawing with Taddeo's façade decorations.

5. According to Vasari, Taddeo's three most important façades illustrated scenes from the lives of the Roman hero Furius Camillus (at Palazzo Mattei), of Alexander the Great (at a house near Santa Lucia della Tinta) and from the legend of the messenger god Mercury (at a house in Campo Marzio).

8

1. The most reliable biographical data are supplied by J. A. Gere and Philip Pouncey, *Italian Drawings in the Department of Prints and Drawings of the British Museum, Artists Working in Rome c.1550–c.1640*, London, 1983, pp.80–81; and A. Sacconi in *Dizionario Biografico degli Italiani*, pp.176–80.

2. On this point see *Italian Etchers of the Renaissance and Baroque*, exh. cat., Museum of Fine Arts, Boston, 1989, pp.53–4; Gert Jan van der Smann, 'Il percorso stilistico di Battista Franco incisore: elementi per una ricostruzione', *Arte Documento*, 8, 1994, p.103.

3. Bartsch, vol.XVI.18 (125); Illus. Bartsch, vol.XXXII, 1979, p.174. The reversal of the image resulted in Christ's triumphant gesture being delivered incorrectly with his left hand.

4. I am grateful to Michael Bury for discussing with me the technical issues raised here.

5. A similar pose was used independently for Franco's engraving of *St John the Baptist in the Wilderness*: Bartsch, vol.XVI.35 (130). For the Vatican fresco, see Carlo Pietrangeli (et al.), *Raffaello nell'Appartamento di Giulio II e Leone X*, Milan, 1993, esp. plates between pp.168 and 169.

6. For Salviati's fresco, see Luisa Mortari, *Francesco Salviati*, 1992, p.118. Van der Smann 1994, p.103 suggests some alternative, and additional, sources for Franco's composition.

7. Only seldom did Franco employ pure etching with the freedom of touch evident in the *Resurrection* print (eg Bartsch, vol.XVI.26 (128) and 32 (130), both of which, it has now emerged, were originally etched, with seven other roundels, on a single plate: see Rita Parma Baudille, 'Disegni di Battista Franco per incisioni', *Arte Documento*, 8, 1994, pp.98–9 and fig.21). For the late dating of these prints, see further Boston 1989, no.27; Van der Smann 1994, p.109.

8. For the fresco, see Anna Coliva, 'Battista Franco e Girolamo Muziano nella Cappella Gabrielli in Santa Maria sopra Minerva: una ipotesi di collaborazione', *Arte Documento*, 6, 1992, p.200 and fig.4. For the related drawings, see Rita Parma Baudille, 'L'Ultimo lavoro romano di Battista Franco: la cappella Gabrielli in Santa Maria sopra Minerva', *Arte Documento*, 6, 1992, pp.186–90.

9. For this project, see W. R. Rearick, 'Battista Franco and the Grimani Chapel', *Arte Veneta*, 11, 1959, p.127.

10. When it was in Richard Cosway's collection, the drawing was included in Conrad Martin Metz's *Imitations of Ancient and Modern Drawings …* (1798).

9

1. The attribution to Raffaellino da Reggio was first proposed by Philip Pouncey in 1950.

2. For the arguments for and against connecting the drawing with this chapel, see Andrews 1968, vol.I, p.102. The decorations were evidently complete by the spring of 1576 (see J. A. Gere and Philip Pouncey, *Italian Drawings in the Department of Prints and Drawings in the British Museum: Artists Working in Rome c.1550–c.1640*, London, 1983, p.145).

3. What may be Raffaellino's initial design for this fresco was sold at Sotheby's, New York, 11 January 1990, no.45.

4. Raffaellino's preparatory drawing for the *Dream of St Joseph*, formerly in the Mond Collection, was sold at Sotheby's, London, 4 July 1988, no.17; see also *Correggio and his Legacy*, exh. cat., Washington / Parma, 1984, no.114.

5. This latter fresco in fact appears to be by Gianfrancesco Romanelli or another artist from the circle of Pietro da Cortona, and presumably replaced one by Raffaellino.

6. Gere and Pouncey 1983, p.145, noted that the *Annunciation* was destroyed during a restoration of the church in 1641.

7. The link between the two drawings was first noted by Keith Andrews in Edinburgh 1976; see further Richard-Raymond Alasko in Notre Dame 1983. For Zucchi's design, see Edmund Pillsbury, 'Drawings by Jacopo Zucchi', *Master Drawings*, XII, 1974, pp.21–2 and note 82; idem, 'Jacopo Zucchi in S. Spirito in Sassia', *The Burlington Magazine*, CXVI, 1974, pp.442–3; James Byam Shaw, *Drawings by Old Masters at Christ Church*, Oxford, Oxford, 1976, vol.I, p.86.

8. San Silvestro al Quirinale was given by Paul IV in 1555 to the Theatines, who rebuilt it (consecrated 1584). See Anthony Blunt, *Guide to Baroque Rome*, London, 1982, p.145.

10

1. For biographical details, see Daniele Benati in *The Age of Correggio and the Carracci*, exh. cat., Bologna / Washington / New York, 1986–7, pp.255–62, and the same author's entry for *The Dictionary of Art*, vol.5, pp.856–8. For Agostino as a printmaker, see Diane DeGrazia, *Prints and Related Drawings by the Carracci Family: A Catalogue Raisonné*, Washington, 1979.

2. See Roberto Zapperi, 'The Summons of the Carracci to Rome: some new documentary evidence', *Burlington Magazine*, CXXVIII, 1986, pp.203–5.

3. For the date of Agostino's involvement in the Galleria Farnese, see Giuliano Briganti in *Gli Amori degli Dei*, Rome, 1987, p.35.

4. See the present writer's review of the exhibition 'Drawings by the Carracci from British Collections' (Oxford, Ashmolean Museum, and London, Hazlitt, Gooden and Fox, 1996–7) in *Renaissance Studies*, XI, 4, 1997, p.458.

5. It was engraved by Claude Macé (died 1670), as after Annibale Carracci, for the *Recueil de 283 Estampes … d'après les Dessins des Grands Maîtres que possedoit autrefois M. Jabach et qui depuis ont passé au Cabinet du Roy*, Paris, 1754. See Stephen M. Bailey, *Carracci Landscape Studies: The drawings related to the 'Recueil de 283 Estampes de Jabach'*, doctoral dissertation, University of California, Santa Barbara, 1993, vol.II, pp.423–4, vol.III, figs.109–10, where the attribution to Annibale is supported.

6. Michael Jaffé, *The Devonshire Collection of Italian Drawings: Bolognese and Emilian Schools*, London, 1994, p.72.

7. See Clovis Whitfield, 'The Landscapes of Agostino Carracci' in *Les Carrache et les décors profanes*, Rome, 1988, pp.77–8 and fig.1.

8. Sotheby's, London, 11 July 1972, no.39.

9. Carlo Cesare Malvasia, *Felsina Pittrice*, Bologna, 1841 ed., vol.I, p.308.

10. Two possible exceptions are at Chatsworth (Jaffé 1994, p.75, as attributed to Agostino) and in the Pierpont Morgan Library (Cara D. Denison and Helen B. Mules, *European Drawings 1375–1825*, New York, 1981, no.38, as Annibale Carracci, but possibly by Agostino).

11. As noted by Whitfield 1988, p.77. For Cort's engravings, see Illus. Bartsch, vol.LII, pp.134–40, 150–51, 156–8.

12. In Macé's print (see note 5 above) this is made explicit by the introduction of haloes.

13. For these landscapes, see Whitfield 1988, pp.81–3, figs.3–4.

14. DeGrazia 1979, no.140. Whitfield 1988, p.80 is probably correct in asserting that the print predates the painting by Lodovico Carracci which reproduces part of its landscape.

15. Jabach's paraph (L 2959) does not appear on the drawing, but its inclusion in the *Recueil … Jabach* implies his ownership (see note 5 above).

16. Cordélia Hattori has kindly confirmed that this is a Crozat number, and has pointed out that a portfolio numbered 90 in Crozat's house contained 102 Carracci landscape drawings. The present drawing was almost certainly among the thirty-one of these drawings grouped in lots 510, 511 and 512 of the 1741 Crozat sale, all of which were bought by Mariette.

11

1. For biographical details of Brusasorci, see *Cinquant'anni di Pittura Veronese, 1580–1630*, exh. cat., Palazzo della Gran Guardia, Verona, edited by Licisco Magagnato, 1974, pp.51–5; *Le Dessin à Vérone aux XVIe et XVIIe siècles*, exh. cat., Louvre, Paris, by Hélène Sueur, 1993, p.139.

2. The attribution was first put forward by Philip Pouncey in 1958. See also Andrews 1968, vol.I, p.24.

3. For the painting see Ágnes Czobor and Éva Bodnár, *Musée István Dobó: Guide et Catalogue de la Galerie des Tableaux à Eger*, Budapest, 1960, p.23, no.4. The signature at lower right reads: *Foelix Brusasorci Ver. Pix.* It is possible that this picture may have been derived from another by Brusasorci, now lost, which corresponded more closely to the format of the drawing.

4. For Brusasorci's use of slate and its source, see Verona 1974, pp.67–8, under no.25.

5. For the Budapest painting see Klára Garas (ed.), *The Budapest Museum of Fine Arts*, Budapest, 1985 (English ed. 1988), ill. p.126. For the other two paintings, see Verona 1974, nos 32–3.

6. There are similar treatments of this and related themes by Turchi (Rome, Galleria Borghese and Milan, Castello Sforzesco) and Ottino (Verona, Museo del Castelvecchio). See Verona 1974, nos 91, 92 and 164.

7. Alessandro Ballarin, 'Considerazione su una Mostra di Disegni veronesi del Cinquecento', *Arte Veneta*, XXV, 1971, pp.94, 115; Verona 1974, nos 35–6.

12

1. A good cross-section of these genre scenes, *capricci* and caricatures, together with a perceptive introductory note, was included in *Drawings by Guercino from British Collections*, exh. cat., British Museum, London, 1991, pp.205–29.

2. For Carracci's genre subjects, see Donald Posner, *Annibale Carracci: a Study in the Reform of Italian Painting around 1590*, London, 1971, vol.I, pp.9–24.

13

1. These biographical details are derived from Rudolf Wittkower's chapter on Cortona in *Art and Architecture in Italy 1600–1750*, third edition, Harmondsworth, 1982, pp.231–59, and Jörg Martin Merz's entry in *The Dictionary of Art*, vol.7, pp.905–15.

2. See Andrews 1968, vol.I, p.91; Jörg Martin Merz, *Pietro da Cortona: Der Aufstieg zum führenden Maler im barocken Rom*, Tübingen, 1991, pp.44–6; idem, 'Cortona Giovane' in *Pietro da Cortona 1597–1669*, exh. cat., Rome, Palazzo Venezia, 1997–8, pp.60–61.

3. For examples of such copies, several of which were included in Cassiano dal Pozzo's 'Paper Museum', see Merz 1991, figs.8–13, 52–4, 107–11.

4. Merz 1991, fig.104.

5. This print, of which there are impressions in the Bibliothèque Nationale, Paris, and the Albertina, Vienna, bears the following inscription: *Pietro da Cortona pinx, Ant. Fedi del, Bened.o Eredi sc, 1784 / David placato da Abigail / esiste nel Pal. dell' Ill. Sig.r Michele Grifoni in Via Servi in Firenze* (transcribed by Merz 1991, p.44, n.192). The previous assertion that the print was originally included in a rare volume published in 1779 may be erroneous (Andrews 1968, vol.I, p.91).

14

1. Christel Thiem's attribution of the drawing to Cigoli (note on the mount) has been rejected by Miles Chappell (letter in Gallery files). Among the numerous 'compartmentalised' drawings by Cigoli are three in Vienna (see Veronika Birke and Janine Kertész, *Die italienischen Zeichnungen der Albertina*, vol.IV, 1997, pp.2252–3, 2406–7).

2. Roberto Contini, however, believes that the Edinburgh sheet may be by Salvestrini, on the basis of comparison with a group of the artist's drawings in the Biblioteca Marucellina in Florence. I am grateful to Dott. Contini for offering his opinion of the drawing.

3. Andrews 1968, vol.I, p.109, retained this traditional attribution.

15

1. For biographical details, see Catherine Puglisi's entries in *The Age of Correggio and the Carracci*, exh. cat., Bologna / Washington / New York, 1986–7, p.366 and *The Dictionary of Art*, vol.I, pp.533–7.

2. It was first published by Ann Sutherland Harris, 'Some Chalk Drawings by Francesco Albani', *Master Drawings*, VII, 2, 1969, pp.152–5, and subsequently by A. E. Popham and Christopher Lloyd, *Old Master Drawings at Holkham*, Chicago, 1986, pp.28–9; in the 1991 Christie's auction catalogue; by Daniele Benati, *Disegni Emiliani del Sei-Settecento: Quadri da stanza e da altare*, Milan, 1991, pp.79–80; and by Flavia Ormond in her 1992 catalogue. See also Catherine Puglisi, *A Study of the Bolognese-Roman Painter Francesco Albani*, unpublished doctoral dissertation, New York, Institute of Fine Arts, 1983, pp.334–5 (typescript edition available through UMI, Ann Arbor).

3. See Puglisi 1983, pp.334–5. The Florentine painting has been displayed periodically at both the Pitti and the Uffizi. Sutherland Harris 1969, p.153, suggested a more generic connection with Albani's *Rape of Europa* compositions. She also (p.155, note 20), followed by Puglisi (loc. cit.), detected a possible connection with Albani's painting of the *Penitent Magdalen* in the Pinacoteca Capitolina in Rome.

4. For the various versions, see Puglisi 1983, pp.333–40; Stéphane Loire, *Musée du Louvre, Département des Peintures, École italienne, XVIIe Siècle: 1. Bologne*, Paris, 1996, pp.90–91. Benati 1991, p.79, argued that the drawing must have been made in connection with one of the paintings in which Europa features more prominently than in the Pitti canvas.

5. Scholars are divided over the relative merits of this painting. Eric van Schaack (*Francesco Albani, 1578–1660*, unpublished doctoral dissertation, Columbia University, New York, 1968, no.155), Eduard A. Safarik (*Catalogo Sommario della Galleria Colonna in Roma: Dipinti*, Rome, 1981, p.21), and Benati (1991, p.79) consider it autograph; Puglisi (1983, pp.336–8) on the other hand, deemed it wholly a studio production, preferring instead the version of identical size in the collection of Lord Methuen at Corsham Court.

6. In correspondence dating from 1639–40 it is stated that the painting now in the Pitti was begun 'many years' previously. It may be noted that it is inherently more likely that a small-scale variant of a large canvas would have been produced, rather than vice-versa.

7. See the numerous comparable examples in *Guido Reni: Zeichnungen*, exh. cat., Albertina, Vienna, 1981. An early copy of the Edinburgh sheet in Turin was in the past attributed to Reni himself (see Aldo Bertini, *I Disegni italiani della Biblioteca Reale di Torino*, Rome, 1958, no.594).

16

1. Cited by Elizabeth Cropper in Philadelphia / Cambridge (Mass.), 1988–9, under no.20. Both the canvas and the Edinburgh drawing are discussed at length by Alessandra Ottieri, *Per una revisione del catalogo di Pietro Testa*, unpublished 'Tesi di specializzazione', Università di Roma, 1986, pp.105–23 (I am grateful to Elizabeth Cropper for this reference).

2. Philadelphia / Cambridge (Mass.) 1988–9, fig.20a.

3. *Disegni dell'Europa Occidentale dall'Ermitage di Leningrado*, exh. cat., Uffizi, Florence, 1982, no.33.

4. Philadelphia / Cambridge (Mass.) 1988–9, no.19.

5. See Elizabeth Cropper in Philadelphia / Cambridge (Mass.) 1988–9, nos 15–17.

6. This detail recurs in the personification of the River Serchio in a Testa etching of 1637: see Philadelphia / Cambridge (Mass.) 1988–9, no.36.

7. This provenance is given in previous publications, but Howard's paraph (L 2957) is not present on the drawing. It may have been inscribed on the old mount, which unfortunately appears to have been discarded when the sheet was remounted.

17

1. See Andrews 1968, vol.I, pp.92–3; *idem* in Edinburgh 1976; Hugh Brigstocke, 'A Pietro da Cortona Landscape for Edinburgh', *The Burlington Magazine*, CXXII, 1980, pp.342–5; Jörg Martin Merz, *Pietro da Cortona: Der Aufstieg zum führenden Maler im barocken Rom*, Tübingen, 1991, pp.187–8, figs.200, 202. The other two drawings are inv. nos RSA 118 (autograph) and D 1836 (studio). The most directly comparable drawing by Cortona is the *Wooded River Landscape with Cascades and Fishermen* formerly at Holkham Hall (sale Christie's, London, 2 July 1991, no.27) and now jointly owned by Birmingham Museum and Art Gallery and the Barber Institute of Fine Arts.

2. Churches also feature in several other painted and drawn landscapes by Cortona and were probably intended to allude to the triumph of Christianity over pagan antiquity. See Louise Rice, 'A newly discovered landscape by Pietro da Cortona', *The Burlington Magazine*, CXXIX, 1987, pp.76–7.

3. As noted by Rice 1987, p.77.

4. For Cortona as a landscapist, see Giuliano Briganti, *Pietro da Cortona, o della Pittura barocca*, 2nd revised edition, Florence, 1982, pp.177–82, 348–9, figs.65–75, 92, 95–100, 295–6; Rice 1987, pp.73–7; Merz 1991, pp.183–9, 303–5, figs.112, 115–16, 199–201, 266–72; *Pietro da Cortona 1597–1669*, exh. cat., Palazzo Venezia, Rome, 1997–8, nos 26–31.

5. Giulio Mancini, *Considerazioni sulla Pittura*, edited by Adriana Marucchi and Luigi Salerno, Rome, 1956, vol.I, pp.262–3.

6. Rice 1987, pp.73–7.

7. The drawings are the study for *St Ivo Intervening on Behalf of the Poor* in the National Gallery of Scotland (see *Effigies and Ecstasies: Roman Baroque Sculpture and Design in the Age of Bernini*, exh. cat., National Gallery of Scotland, Edinburgh, 1998, no.88) and *Architects Submitting a Plan to Pope Alexander VII, with Mount Athos Behind* in the British Museum (see Richard Krautheimer, *The Rome of Alexander VII, 1655–67*, Princeton, 1985, p.10, fig.5)

8. Letter of 17 July 1666 from Cortona in Rome to Cardinal Leopoldo de' Medici in Florence, published by Wolfram Prinz, *Geschichte der Sammlung der Selbstbildnisse in den Uffizien*, Berlin, 1971, p.166, doc. no.4 (cited by Nicholas Turner, *Italian Drawings in the Department of Prints and Drawings in the British Museum: Roman Baroque Drawings c.1620–c.1700*, 1999, vol.I, p.54).

18

1. See London 1977, no.66; A. E. Popham and Christopher Lloyd, *Old Master Drawings from Holkham Hall*, Chicago, 1986, no.129. The picture is discussed by Robert Enggass, *The Paintings of Baciccio: Giovanni Battista Gaulli 1639–1709*, University Park and London, 1964, p.121.

2. Published by Maurizio Fagiolo dell'Arco and Rossella Pantanella, *Museo Baciccio: in margine a quattro inventari inediti*, Rome, 1996, p.91, fig.53. Dott. Fagiolo dell'Arco kindly supplied a photograph of this drawing.

3. Dieter Graf, *Die Handzeichnungen von Guglielmo Cortese und Giovanni Battista Gaulli*, Düsseldorf, 1976, vol.I, p.124, no.367, and vol.II, fig.470.

4. Fagiolo dell'Arco and Pantanella 1996, pp.20–21, 115 (no.107).

5. *Ibid.*, p.118.

19

1. For biographical details, see Amalia Barigozzi Brini and Klára Garas, *Carlo Innocenzo Carloni*, Milan, 1967; *Carlo Carlone 1686–1775: Der Ansbacher Auftrag*, exh. cat., Residenz, Ansbach, 1990; *The Dictionary of Art*, vol.5, pp.774–5.

2. See Andrews 1968, vol.I, p.30.

3. They appear in this conventional manner in Carlone's own *Deposition* altarpieces in Weingarten and Calvisano, and in *bozzetti* for them in Munich and Budapest. See Ansbach 1990, pp.153–8, no.11.

4. See Marco Bona Castellotti (ed.), *La pittura lombarda del '700*, Milan, 1986, plate 145.

5. This combination would admittedly have been iconographically rare, but there is an *Immaculate Conception with St Joachim and St Anne* by Francisco de Zurbarán in the National Gallery of Scotland's own collection (see Hugh Brigstocke, *Italian and Spanish Paintings in the National Gallery of Scotland*, 2nd edition, Edinburgh, 1993, pp.207–9).

20

1. The attribution to Lusieri was made in 1988 by the present 11th Earl of Elgin. I am most grateful to Lord Elgin for supplying transcripts of letters from Lusieri preserved in his family archive, and for his permission to quote extracts from them here.

2. The inscription indicates that the watercolour was copied by Lady Ruthven after an original by Lusieri. For *The South-east Corner of the Parthenon* (inv. no.D 710) see William St Clair, *Lord Elgin and the Marbles*, 2nd edition, Oxford, 1983, pl.III(a).

3. In a letter to Lord Elgin dated Athens, 7 May 1819 (in French), Lusieri reported that 'Milord and Miladi Ruthven with her brother have been here for several months', adding that 'this Lady draws like an artist'.

4. By the terms of his contract with Lord Elgin, dated Messina, 18 October 1799. See also C. I. M. Williams, 'Lusieri's surviving works', *The Burlington Magazine*, CXXIV, 1982, p.495.

5. Letters of 16 August 1819 from Lusieri to Hamilton, and of 30 August 1819 from Lusieri to Lord Elgin.

6. The others are the *Monument of Philipappos*, which was finished in August 1805, and a *Study of an Owl* which roosted in the pediment of the Parthenon and watched Lusieri at work, both still in the Elgin Collection at Broomhall (see *Turner and Byron*, exh. cat., Tate Gallery, London, 1992, nos 21 and 22). The lower right portion of *The South-east Corner of the Parthenon*, mentioned above, is unfinished.

7. Quoted and discussed by A. H. Smith, 'Lord Elgin and his Collection', *Journal of Hellenic Studies*, XXXVI, 1916, p.258.

8. An initial, unsuccessful investigation of the tumulus, which later came to be called erroneously the 'Tomb of Aspasia', was undertaken in 1802–3 by other members of Lord Elgin's team. See A. H. Smith, 'The 'Tomb of Aspasia'', *Journal of Hellenic Studies*, XXXVI, 1926, p.253.

9. See *The British Museum: Elgin and Phigaleian Marbles*, The Library of Entertaining Knowledge [no author], London, 1833, vol.I, p.3.

10. In his letter of 15 October 1820 to William Richard Hamilton, Elgin expressed his exasperation at not having obtained from Lusieri objects that had been collected for him, 'especially the golden wreath of myrtle, found in the vase, in Aspasia's Tumulus' (Smith 1916, p.288). The myrtle spray was eventually recovered by Elgin from Lusieri's estate by an agreement of 10 February 1824 (*ibid.*, pp.289–90).

11. The fundamental study of the objects found in the tomb remains Smith's 1926 article cited in note 8 above. I am most grateful to Zahra Newby and Dyfri Williams of the Department of Greek and Roman Antiquities at the British Museum for allowing me to examine these objects and consult the files on them, and for supplying photographs and other information.

12. See Smith 1926, p.254.

13. Edward Hawkins, *Description of the Ancient Marbles in the British Museum; with Engravings*, Part IX, London, 1842, title-page and verso of title-page; A. H. Smith, *Department of Greek and Roman Antiquities, Catalogue of Greek Sculpture*, III.2, 1904, no.2415 (marble urn).

14. See Smith 1916, pp.352–3; *idem*, 1926, pp.254–5; Ian Jenkins, *Archaeologists and Aesthetes in the Sculpture Galleries of the British Museum 1800–1939*, London, 1992, pp.37–8, and pl.II.

15. See R. A. Higgins, 'The Elgin Jewellery', *British Museum Quarterly*, XXIII, 1961, p.106; *Greek Gold: Jewelry of the Classical World*, exh. cat., British Museum, London, 1994, pp.58–9, no.10.

16. The inscription was first published and discussed by Smith 1926, pp.256–7.

17. *Ibid.*, 1926, p.257.

21

1. See H. Miedema ed. *Karel van Mander. The Lives of the Illustrious Netherlandish and German Painters*, Doornspijk, 1996, vol.III, pp.100–06 and G. Denhaene's entry on Lombard in *The Dictionary of Art*, vol.19, pp.547–8.

2. Miedema, *op. cit.*, p.106.

3. First recognised by A. E. Popham, note on mount. Andrews 1985, vol.I, p.48 and G. Denhaene, *Lambert Lombard, Renaissance et Humanisme à Liège*, Antwerp, 1990, no.15. For the prints of Lombard's designs see Hollstein, vol.XI, p.94, nos 53–65.

4. K. Boon, *The Netherlandish and German Drawings of the XVth and XVIth centuries of the Frits Lugt Collection*, Paris, 1992, vol.I, p.247–250.

5. *Ibid.*, p.248. Boon suggests that the Lugt drawing may have been used by one of Lombard's pupils for the print engraved in the Van Sichem edition, probably before 1568 when Van Sichem left Antwerp.

6. C. Dittrich, *Van Eyck, Bruegel, Rembrandt*, exh. cat., Vienna / Dresden, 1997, no.17, pp.52–3.

7. Denhaene 1990, no.18.

8. *Ibid.*, no.8, engraved by Hans Collaert the Elder (Hollstein, vol.IV, p.190, no.465).

9. *Ibid.*, no.48.

10. *Ibid.*, no.17.

11. 20.9 × 10.1cm, photograph in Gallery file, information from G. Gordon, 1987.

12. Boon, *op. cit.*, p.248 and note 13.

13. *Ibid.*, p.248 and note 10.

14. Andrews 1985 had the forename as Richard. The collection of Robert Udney (1722–1802) was sold in two auctions before his death; 25 April 1800 and 28 May, 1802, and after his decease, 18–19 May 1804, all held at Christie's, London. The drawings were sold under the direction of Philipe and Scott, 4–10 May 1803 (see Supplement to L 2248, p.329).

22

1. *Printmaking in the Age of Rembrandt*, exh. cat., Boston / St Louis, 1981, no.6, pp.9–11, *Mannerist Prints, International Style in the Sixteenth Century*, exh. cat., Los Angeles / Toledo / Sarasota / Austin / Baltimore, 1989, no.103, pp.238–9, and Illus. Bartsch, vol.55, 1991.

2. H. Miedema ed. *Karel Van Mander. The Lives of the Illustrious Netherlandish and German Painters, Commentary*, Doornspijk, 1997, vol.IV, 67–94 and I. M. Veldman entry on Heemskerck, *The Dictionary of Art*, vol.14, pp.291–4.

3. Andrews 1985, vol.I, p.36 and New Hollstein, *Maarten van Heemskerck*. Part I, 1993, nos 161–8, pp.140–5.

4. RSA 26. Andrews 1985, vol.I, p.36 and Washington / Fort Worth 1990–1, no.48, p.116. A contemporary inscription in black chalk on the verso of this sheet, 'no 30 misdoen[sin]van job / van heemskerk / 8 stuks't / stuk 6 gl-s / 48' is in the same hand as that found on another work by the artist in the Rijksprentenkabinet, Amsterdam (Boon 306). This means that the eight drawings were offered for 6 guilders each. I am grateful to Ger Luijten for confirming this.

5. Inventory no.11260.

6. Inventory nos MB 1959 / T21; MB 1959 / T22; MB 1959 / T23.

7. J. F. McCrindle collection, Princeton.

8. New Hollstein, op. cit., p.11.

9. New Hollstein, Maarten van Heemskerck. Part II, 1994, p.11.

10. Albertina, Vienna, no.7626.

11. New Hollstein, Maarten van Heemskerck. Part I, 1993, no.159, p.138. See, too, no.160, p.139, for Heemskerck's other earlier design for an engraving from the book of Job; Job on the Dunghill with his Wife and Three Friends.

23

1. H. Miedema, ed., Karel van Mander. The Lives of the Illustrious Netherlandish and German Painters. Commentary, Doornspijk, 1998, vol.v, pp.68–69 and notes 31, 32. There is some doubt about the date of Stradanus's arrival in Florence, which could be as late as 1550.

2. Ibid. p.69. The series of black chalk drawings (now at the Uffizi, Florence, F17325–32) after Michelangelo's Sistine Chapel Last Judgement were presumably made in Rome at this period.

3. Baldinucci Notizie de professori del disegno … parte seconda del secolo quarto, Florence, 1688, p.142.

4. K. van Mander, Het Schilderboek, Haarlem, 1604, fol.267 v.

5. Illus. Bartsch, vol.56, no.043, p.137.

6. Van Mander, op. cit., fol.267 v. Stradanus's autograph copy of the Crucifixion, signed and dated 1581, was in the hospital of Santa Maria Nuova, Florence (now Museo Casa Vasari, Arezzo).

7. A. B. Vannucci, Jan van der Straet, detto Giovanni Stradano: flandrus pictor et inventor, Milan, 1997, p.392,. illus.

8. Hollstein, vol.vII, p.76, nos 108–145. For more information about this series, see Vannucci, no.694, p.389–92.

9. '& il sesto et ultimo farà vedere tutti I misteri della Passsione del Saluador [sic] del mondo in 40 pezzi'. See R. Borghini, Il Riposo, Florence, 1584 (reprint, ed. M. Rosci, Milan, 1967, pp.583–4, and Vannucci, no.375, p.294.

10. Vannucci, nos 374–411, pp.263–271.

11. Vannucci no.373, p.263 and K. Boon, The Netherlandish and German Drawings of the XVth and XVIth Centuries of the Frits Lugt Collection, Paris, 1992, vol.1, no.198, p.345–7. This was the likeness on which Hendrick Goltzius based his engraved portrait of Stradanus. Goltzius later drew Stradanus from the life in 1591 in a drawing also in the Lugt Collection, Boon no.103, pp.191–3.

12. W. T. Kloek, Beknopte Catalogus van de Nederlandse Tekeningen in het Prentenkabinet van de Uffizi te Forence, Utrecht, 1975, no.230 (7781F), and Vannucci, no.404, p.269. Kloek titles the Uffizi drawing 'John with five Women under the Cross' but there are only five figures in total at the foot of the Cross. This scene, which has no biblical basis, was much depicted by artists. The Virgin was usually shown with St John, but the evangelists conflict on the names and number of other holy women who accompanied them (sometimes called 'the Three Maries'). Amongst those mentioned are Mary Magdalen, Mary mother of James and Joseph, Mary wife of Clopas (who may be the same person as the mother of James and Joseph), and Salome (possibly the same as the mother of Zebedee's children mentioned in Matthew). See J. Hall, Dictionary of Subjects and Symbols in Art, London, 1974 (1979 edition), p.84, p.155.

13. Andrews 1985, vol.1, pp.83–4. Vannucci, no.421, p.272.

14. Vannucci, nos 411–20, pp. 270–2. See, too, C. Kruyfhooft et al. 'Catalogue of the Stichting Jean van Caloen, Loppem, Belgium' in Delineavit et Sculpsit, Tijdschrift voor Nederlandse prent-en tekenkunst tot omstreeks 1850, 18, November 1997, nos 3, 4, 5, pp.11–12.

15. Hollstein, vol.xvI, pp.13–4, nos 23–4, Miedema, op. cit., p.72, note 66 and Vannucci, no.695, pp.393–395.

16. Sadly few of these survive: see D. van Sasse van Ijsselt, 'Johannes Stradanus: de decoraties voor intochten en uitvaarten aan het hof van de Medici te Florence,' Oud Holland, CIV, 1990, pp.149–79. I am grateful to Dr van Sasse van Ijsselt for help in connection with this entry.

24

1. For Goltzius's printmaking, see 'Print Publishers in the Netherlands 1580–1620', in Dawn of the Golden Age. Northern Netherlandish Art 1580–1620, exh. cat., Rijksmuseum, Amsterdam, 1993–4, pp.177–183.

2. K. van Mander De grondt der edel vryschilder-const, Haarlem, 1604, fol.274 r. For Van Mander's writing on Goltzius, see H. Miedema, ed., Karel van Mander. The Lives of the Illustrious Netherlandish and German Painters. Commentary, Doornspijk, 1998, vol.v, pp.174–225.

3. Amsterdam 1993–4, nos 1, 2, pp.329–331.

4. 'Without Ceres and Bacchus, Venus would freeze', No.1990–100–1: L. Nicholls, 'The "Pen Works" of Hendrick Goltzius', Philadelphia Museum of Art Bulletin, Winter 1992, p.4 and p.19. The picture was probably later with Queen Christina of Sweden and then King Charles II in London.

5. K. van Mander, Het Schilderboek, Haarlem, 1604, fol.285 r. and v., quoted by L. Nicholls, op.cit., pp.4–5 and Appendix, p.54.

6. E. K. J. Reznicek, Hendrick Goltzius. Drawings Rediscovered 1962–1992, Lunenburg, Vermont, 1993 (first published in Master Drawings, XXXI, 3, 1993), p.6. (Supplement to E. K. J. Reznicek, Die Zeichnungen von Hendrick Goltzius, Utrecht, 1961.)

7. W. Kloek, 'Northern Netherlandish Art 1580–1620', in Amsterdam 1993–4, p.70, fig.113.

8. Andrews 1985, vol.1, p.32.

9. Reznicek 1961, vol.1, K424, K425. pp.449–50, vol.2, figs.332–3.

10. Ibid., K439, pp.454–5, K164, pp.304–5, vol.2, fig.227 and fig.256.

11. Illus. Bartsch, Hendrick Goltzius, vol.3, 1984, no.226, p242. It is suggested (p.241) that Goltzius did not develop such woodcuts until his return from Italy after being inspired by blocks by N. Boldini and A. Andreani, though the Hercules and Cacus key block dated 1588 may prove that he started on them earlier.

12. Reznicek 1993, no.K430a, p.78, fig.67.

13. Illus. Bartsch, op. cit., no.021, pp.24–30. The fourth state of the print was dated 1615. This may have been Goltzius's last engraved plate, left unfinished at his death in 1617.

14. Ibid., no.160k, p.161–2. Though dated 1597 in the second state, the style of this plate clearly points to an earlier date.

25

1. C. C. Malvasia, Felsina Pittrice. Vite dei Pittori Bolognesi, 1678, (Bologna, 1971 ed. by M. Brascaglia), p.165. A copy of Michelangelo's Last Judgement, now in the British Museum, London, was made by Calvaert in Rome in 1574 (Inv. no.1935–9–11–6).

2. Malvasia recorded that Calvaert's practice of painting on copper had a lasting effect on Reni, who painted many works on this support while in Calvaert's studio. He also noted that both Reni and Albani had completed works on copper which were then signed by Calvaert. See G. Finaldi and M. Kitson, Discovering the Italian Baroque. The Denis Mahon Collection, exh. cat., National Gallery, London, 1997, p.24 and p.132.

3. Andrews 1985, vol.1, pp.16–17. Andrews lists three figures on verso.

4. K. Andrews, 'The Marriage at Cana – a trio by Denys Calvaert', The Burlington Magazine, CXXVII, 1985, p.757.

5. 25.6 × 20.1cm, Inv.A1895.9.15.1014, A. E. Popham, Catalogue of Drawings by Dutch and Flemish Artists in the British Museum, vol.v, London, 1932, p.148, no.1.

6. Hollstein, vol.IV, p.85, no.12. K. Andrews managed to trace copies of this rare print only in the Albertina, Vienna and the Bibliothèque Nationale, Paris.

7. Black chalk, heightened with white, 40.2 × 29.8cm. See E. Llewellyn and C. Romalli, Drawing in Bologna 1500–1600, exh. cat., Courtauld Institute, University of London, 1992, no.6, reproduced.

8. For example, two drawn versions of The Adoration of the Shepherds (see Old Master Drawings, Colnaghi, New York, May 1987, no.17) or painted versions of The Holy Family with St John in a Landscape (National Gallery of Scotland N.G.2447 and National Gallery Warsaw, Inv. no.231090). A related sketch is in the Albertina, Vienna, no.17662, Budapest Museum, no.67.442 and a drawing which links elements of the Edinburgh and Warsaw paintings was sold Sotheby's, London, 30 October 1980, no.76, not illustrated (Witt Library photograph).

9. T. Pugliatti, Giulio Mazzoni e la Decorazione a Roma nella cercha di Daniele da Volterra, Rome, 1984, illus. fig.435.

10. Arnold and Seena Davies, Scarsdale, New York, 1986: Witt Library photograph. The drawing is in black ink with blue wash, 27.9 × 20.3cm.

26

1. Andrews 1985, vol.1, p.122 (Addenda) and K. Andrews, 'An early Rubens drawing', The Burlington Magazine, CXXVII, 1985, pp.526–531.

2. A hunter's horn within a shield: Heawood 2647.

3. F. Lugt, 'Rubens and Stimmer', Art Quarterly, VI, 1943, pp.99–100, p.114 note 2.

4. Ibid., p.99–106 for list of works Lugt identified as copies by Rubens and see Creative Copies. Interpretative Drawings from Michelangelo to Picasso, exh. cat., The Drawing Center, New York, 1988, p.71, no.16, for a more recently discovered Rubens copy after Stimmer (Nationalmuseum, Stockholm, Inv. no.572 / 1972).

5. New York, 1988, p.71.

6. K. Belkin, 'Rubens und Stimmer', in Tobias Stimmer 1539–84, Späterenaissance am Oberrhein, exh. cat., Kunstmuseum, Basel, 1984, p.203.

7. Illus. Bartsch, Hendrick Goltzius, vol.3, 1980, p.43, no.36. See Andrews, August 1985, p.531 and figs 38 and 39 for other possible sources.

8. Plate 7 in the series Mediceae Familiae Rerum Feliciter Gestarum Victoriae et Triumphi …, published by Philips Galle in Antwerp in 1583.

9. Illus. Bartsch, op.cit., 1980, p.311, no.288, see also no.285, pp.310–11.

10. Andrews, 'An early Rubens drawing', op.cit., p.526, note 4, and p.531, note 10.

11. Anabel Squire Sprigge was a professional sculptress, and the drawing was apparently bequeathed to her by a friend, Henry, whose surname is now unknown. Letter in Gallery files from Giles Robertson, Edinburgh, 7 January 1985.

27

1. Savery's birth is often given as 1574 but 1578 is the date established by S. A. C. Dudok van Heel and M. J. Bok in 'De familie van Roelant Roghman', in W. T. Kloek (with the assistance of J. W. Niemeijer), De Kasteeltekeningen van Roelant Roghman, vol.II, Alphen aan den Rijn, 1990, p.14, note 2.

2. This included works by Abraham Bloemaert, Joachim Wtewael and Cornelis van Haarlem.

3. Dawn of the Golden Age. Northern Netherlandish Art 1580–1620, exh. cat., Rijksmuseum Amsterdam, 1993–4, p.316.

4. Statens Museum, Copenhagen, Inv. no.Tu86 / 4.

5. Andrews 1985, vol.1, p.77–8. D 1707 has the incription M.N 9, tallying with the inscription M.N 8 on the verso of D 1706. David Laing owned all of these sheets along with three other drawings by the artist.

6. The watermark of D 1707 (near Heawood 1185. Crozier, Basle early 17th-century) is consistent with this dating.

7. J. Spicer et al. Prag um 1600, Kunst und Kultur am Hofe Rudolfs II., exh. cat., Essen / Vienna, 1988, pp.383–5, nos 250–4 and Master Drawings from the National Gallery of Canada, exh. cat., Vancouver / Ottawa / Washington, 1988–9, no.36, pp.117–9.

28

1. Andrews 1985, vol.1, p.71.

2. For a discussion of Raphael's design, see M. Winner, 'Progetti ed Esecuzione nella Stanza della Segnatura' in C. Pietrangeli et al., Raffaello nell'appartamento di Giulio II e Leone X, Milan 1993, pp.247–93; illustrated p.259, p.285 detail.

3. Letter in Gallery files to Professor Michael Jaffé, 7 December 1959. Jaffé's reply of three days later noted 'There is no doubt that you are correct in your attribution'.

4. G. B. Pezzini, S. Massari, S. P. V. Rodinò, *Raphael Invenit. Stampe da Raffaello nelle collezioni dell'istituto nazionale per la Grafica*, Rome, 1985, p.41.

5. E. Haverkamp-Begemann, 'Rubens' Three Caryatids', in *Boymans Bijdragen*, Museum Boijmans Van Beuningen, Rotterdam, 1978, p.46.

6. *Ibid.*, p.44.

7. J. S. Held, *Rubens. Selected Drawings*, 2nd ed., New Haven and Oxford, 1986, p.8. Held intentionally increased the number of Rubens's copies in the second edition of this book.

8. *Creative Copies. Interpretative Drawings from Michelangelo to Picasso*, exh. cat., The Drawing Center, New York, 1988, pp.87–9, no.21.

9. For example, *Kneeling Man seen from behind*, Boijmans Van Beuningen Museum, Rotterdam.

10. Lugt, no.142. See too 'P. H. Lankrink's Collection', Editorial in *The Burlington Magazine*, LXXXVI, 1945, pp.29–35 and entry on Lankrink by R. Jeffree in *The Dictionary of Art*, vol.18, p.748.

29

1. *Dawn of the Golden Age. Northern Netherlandish Art 1580–1620*, exh. cat., Rijksmuseum Amsterdam, 1993–4, no.5, p.335.

2. W. Kloek, 'Northern Netherlandish Art 1580–1620', in Amsterdam 1993–4, p.19, and no.7, p.337.

3. P. J. J. van Thiel, 'Cornelis Cornelisz. van Haarlem as a Draughtsman', *Master Drawings*, III, 1965, pp.123–54 and Amsterdam 1993–4, no.10, p.333.

4. Van Thiel, p.123.

5. Amsterdam 1993–4, p.338, and note 8.

6. L. McGee, *Cornelis Corneliszoon van Haarlem: Patrons, Friends and Dutch Humanists*, Nieuwkoop, 1991, p.347, note 11.

7. Oil on panel, 20 × 28.5cm, Private Collection. Information from P. J. J. van Thiel, letter in Gallery files, 11 September 1992. I am grateful to Dr van Thiel for helpful comments on the Edinburgh sheet.

8. K. G. Boon, *Netherlandish Drawings of the Fifteenth and Sixteenth Centuries from the Rijksprentenkabinet, Amsterdam*, The Hague, 1978, vol.1, no.142, p.52.

9. With Jean-Max Tassel, Paris, 1997.

10. See sale catalogue, Christie's Amsterdam, 11 November 1996, no.19, p.23.

11. I am grateful to George Keyes for this suggestion. See G. S. Keyes, 'Pieter Mulier the Elder', *Oud Holland*, 90, 1976, p.230–61. Fig.3, p.232, provides a close comparison.

30

1. *The Age of Rubens*, exh cat., Boston / Toledo, 1993–4, p.345 and R.-A. d'Hulst's entry on Jordaens in *The Dictionary of Art*, vol.17, pp.648–54.

2. The sketch on the verso does not appear to relate directly to the *Zodiac* series but the fact that the figure is foreshortened may imply it could have been intended for one of the ceiling paintings in Jordaens's house. See note 3 below.

3. For the Zodiac series, see A. Hustin, 'Les Jordaens du Sénat. Les signes du Zodiaque', *L'Art*, LXIII, 1904, pp.35–42; U. Moussalli, 'Un chef-d'oeuvre inconnu. Les douze signes du zodiaque de Jacques Jordaens', *Le Jardin des Arts*, 1956, p.667; R. J. Tijs, *P. P. Rubens en J.Jordaens, Barok in eigen huis. Een architectuurhistorische studie over groei, verval en restauratie van twee 17de-eeuwse kunstenaarswoningen te Antwerpen*, Antwerp, 1984, p.336. ill. pp.337–45, 348–9, p.369, note 39; *Jacob Jordaens (1593–1678)*, exh. cat., Koninklijke Museum voor Schone Kunsten, Antwerp, 1993, *Paintings and Tapestries*, vol 1, p.258, and notes 3–6.

4. The earlier sale was held at the Kolveniershof, Antwerp, see Antwerp 1993, vol 1, p.258, note 5.

5. *Ibid.*, p.258, note 6.

6. Antwerp 1993, vol.II, no.B19.

7. He had originally published it as such in *De Tekeningen van Jacob Jordaens, Bijdrage tot de geschiedenis van de XVIIe-eeuwse kunst in de Zuidelijke Nederlanden*, Brussels, 1956, no.228, but published it as authentic in his catalogue entry in Antwerp 1993.

8. Similar use of red chalk as corrective outline can be seen in *Two Crouching Nudes*, National Gallery of Art, Washington, Inv.B.7643, while a more integrated use of the *trois crayons* technique can be seen in a sheet of *Three Heads* in the Louvre, Paris, Inv.20.037. Both were exhibited at Antwerp 1993, nos B.50 and B.49.

31

1. K. Nelson, *Jacob Jordaens: Design for Tapestry*, Pictura Nova V, Brepols, 1998, p.5.

2. *Ibid.*, the contract is quoted in full, Appendix III, pp.192–3.

3. *Ibid.*, pp.7–8.

4. *Ibid.*, p.104.

5. *Ibid.*, p.33 and p.103. The Archduke apparently owned another set woven with gold threads (lost) and a third set is in the Museo Diocesano in Tarragona, Spain.

6. *The Age of Rubens*, exh. cat., Boston / Toledo, 1993–4, no.46, p.353. Elsewhere Cats rendered the proverb as 'Siet alderhande jongen die pijpen even soo gelijk de moeders songen' (Look around you at the young, pipe they will as their mothers sung).

7. *Ibid.*, pp.353–4, for a discussion of the nuances of meaning of the proverb illustrated in Jordaens's different designs of the subject.

8. *Jacob Jordaens (1593–1678)*, exh. cat., Koninklijke Museum voor Schone Kunsten, Antwerp, 1993, vol.I, A.55, pp.178–181 and vol.II, B.69, p.110.

32

1. The documents relating to Roghman's baptism and burial were found by S. A. C. Dudok Van Heel, Gemeentearchief, Amsterdam, and were cited by W. Kloek in 'Een berglandschap door Roelant Roghman', *Bulletin van het Rijksmuseum*, Amsterdam, 1975, no.2, p.100.

2. A. Houbraken, *De Groote Schouburgh der Nederlantsche Konstschilders en Schilderessen*, Amsterdam, 1718–21, vol.I, p.174.

3. Like Roghman, Rembrandt also valued Roelant Savery's work highly, owning a book of his Tyrolean views, at least some of which were probably bought by Lambert Doomer at Rembrandt's sale of *Papier Kunst* on 20 December 1658 (*Een dito [boekje] groot met teeckenige in 't Tirol van Roelant Saverij nae 't leven geteeckent*). Doomer, interestingly in view of the stylistic links with Roghman, then also copied some of these Savery drawings: for examples, see M. van Berge-Gerbaud, *Rembrandt et son école. Dessins de la collection Frits Lugt*, Paris, 1997, nos 48 & 49, pp.112–5.

4. W. Kloek (with the assistance of J. W. Niemeijer), *De Kasteeltekeningen van Roelant Roghman*, vol.II, Alphen aan den Rijn, 1990, p.115, p.131 note 7, p.132. See too H. W. M. van der Wyck (with the assistance of J. W. Niemeijer), *De Kasteeltekeningen van Roelant Roghman*, vol.I, Alphen aan den Rijn, 1989, no.218, p.237. I am grateful to Wouter Kloek for his comments on this drawing.

5. S. J. Fockema Andreae, J. G. N. Regnaud, E. Pelinck, *Kastelen, Riddershofsteden en Buitenplaatsen in Rijnland*, Leiden, 1952 (1974 Arnhem reprint), p.56. For the Edinburgh sheet see p.95, pl.99.

6. M. C. Plomp, *The Dutch Drawings in the Teyler Museum*, Haarlem / Ghent / Doornspijk, 1997, vol.II, p.322. Plomp also notes (p.323, note.1) that only 241 drawings were listed at the Ploos van Amstel sale in 1800. The largest groups of surviving drawings from this series are in the Rijksprentenkabinet, Amsterdam and the Teyler Museum, Haarlem.

7. *Seventeenth Century Dutch Drawings from American Collections*, exh. cat., Washington / Denver / Fort Worth, 1977, no.26, p.29.

8. Plomp, *op. cit.*, p.322–3.

9. Kloek 1990, p.130.

10. See *Seventeenth Century Dutch Drawings from American Collections*, exh. cat., Washington / Denver / Fort Worth, 1977, no.26.

11. MS Inventory, Rijksprentenkabinet, Amsterdam no.228.

12. The drawings are listed in the possesion of Van Hoeck in L. Smids, *Schatkamer der Nederlandsse Oudheden*, Amsterdam, 1711, see Plomp *op.cit.*, p.322.

13. Plomp, *op. cit.*, p.323.

14. *Ibid.* Roos was a dealer who bought the whole series which was subsequently dispersed.

33

1. See *The Age of Rubens*, exh. cat., Boston / Toledo, 1993–4, p.402 and H. Vlieghe's entry on Cossiers in *The Dictionary of Art*, vol.8, pp.1–2.

2. Inv. no.1367. C. von Hasselt, *Flemish Drawings of the Seventeenth Century from the Collection of Frits Lugt*, exh. cat., London / Paris / Bern / Brussels, 1972, no.20, pp.26–8.

3. A. M. Hind, *Catalogue of Drawings by Dutch and Flemish Artists in the British Museum*, 1923, vol.II, no.1, p.98, pl.49.

4. *Kabinet van tekeningen: 16e en 17e eeuwse Hollandse en Vlaamse tekeningen uit Amsterdamse verzameling*, exh. cat., Rotterdam / Paris / Brussels, 1976–7, no.43, pl.106.

5. F. Stampfle, *Netherlandish Drawings of the Fifteenth and Sixteenth Centuries and Flemish Drawings of the Seventeeth and Eighteenth Centuries in the Pierpont Morgan Library*, Princeton, 1991, no.264, p.118. A repetition of this drawing is in the Louvre, Paris (Inv. no.21.918).

6. Listed as in the Paignon-Dijonval collection in 1810, together with the British Museum drawing. Five such portraits were at the same time in the collection of Viscount Palmerston (so could not have included the two Paignon-Dijonval sheets). See Stampfle, p.118, who suggests that repetitions, such as that in the Louvre, may explain this discrepancy.

7. Christie's, London, 2 July 1991, no.65.

8. M. Jaffé, 'Figure Drawings attributed to Rubens, Jordaens and Cossiers in the Hamburg Kunsthalle' in *Jahrbuch der Hamburger Kunstsammlungen*, XVI, 1971, pp.39–50.

9. Thomas Le Claire, *Women Observed. Twenty Master Drawings*, at W. M. Brady, New York, 1996, no.7 (inscribed *P.P Rubens*).

10. Thomas Le Claire, *Master Drawings 1500–1900*, at W. M. Brady, New York, 1998, no.12.

34

1. W. Sumowski, *Drawings of the Rembrandt School*, vol.2, New York, 1979, p.783.

2. C. White and C. Crawley, *The Dutch and Flemish Drawings at Windsor Castle*, Cambridge, 1994, no.349, p.231.

3. P. Schatborn, Review of W. Schulz's book (see note 4) in *Simiolus*, 9, 1977, no.1, p.48ff. Schatborn argues that the influence of Rembrandt on Doomer cannot be seen in the drawings of the 1640s and dates instead from about the time of the purchase of albums at Rembrandt's *Papier Kunst* sale of 20 December 1658, when Doomer could have made copies after his newly acquired Rembrandt drawings. While Doomer copies after Rembrandt are known (eg. Lugt Collection Inv.8236), this does not necessarily prove his apprenticeship to this master as he also copied work by Roelant Savery (possibly also bought in 1658–see Roghman catalogue entry no.32, note 3) and Jan Hackert (eg. Sumowski, *op. cit.*, no.435, p.934).

4. W. Schultz, *Lambert Doomer. Sämtliche Zeichnungen*, Berlin, 1974, pp.22–25.

5. M. van Berge-Gerbaud, *Rembrandt et son école. Dessins de la collection Frits Lugt*, Paris, 1987, no.44, p.104–5. Van der Hem (1621–78) was a rich lawyer with a passion for collecting who commissioned a number of topographical views to add to the pages for his copy of the *Atlas Maior*, published in eleven volumes in 1662 by Dr Joan Blaeu (now Nationalbibliothek, Vienna). He commissioned various artists to provide views of places in the Atlas including Willem Schellinks, Jacob Esselens, Jan Hackaert and others, as well as eleven drawings from Doomer, one a view of Nantes dated 1665. See, too, P. H. Hulton, 'Drawings of England in the Seventeenth Century from the Van der Hem Atlas … ' in *The Walpole Society*, XXXV, 1954–6, Part 1, pp.xiv-xvii.

6. See Schulz, *op. cit.*, nos 139–40, pp.71–2.

7 H. M. van der Berg, 'Willem Schellinks en Lambert Doomer in Frankrijk', *Oudheidkundige Jaarboek*, XI, 1942, p.7.

8. *Ibid.*, p.ii.

9. Sumowski, *op. cit.*, p.814.

10. Schulz, *op. cit.*, no.81, p.57.

11. 23.4 × 35cm: Sotheby's, London, 1 Décember 1986, no.63, repr.

12. C. Brown in his review of Schulz, *op. cit.*, in *The Burlington Magazine*, CXXI, 1979, p.325–6, points out that we have no reason to doubt Doomer's annotation of dates. Schulz insisted that Schellinks and Doomer travelled together by sea to Nantes via the Isle of Wight, but Doomer could equally well have gone to the Isle of Wight on his return journey alone.

13. M. van Berge-Gerbaud, *op. cit.*, no.35, pp.85–6 and *Master Drawings from the National Gallery Canada*, exh. cat., Vancouver / Ottawa / Washington, no.44, pp.144–6.

35

1. G. von der Osten, *Hans Baldung Grien, Gemälde und Dokumente*, Berlin, 1983, p.301.

2. Andrews 1991, p.2.

3. J. E. von Borries, review of Von der Osten in *The Burlington Magazine*, CXXVII, 1985, p.98.

4. C. Koch, *Die Zeichnungen Hans Baldung Griens*, Berlin, 1941, nos 1, 2, p.69.

5. *The Age of Dürer and Holbein. German Drawings 1400–1550*, exh. cat., British Museum, London, 1988, no.89, p.119.

6. J. E. von Borries, *op. cit.*, p.98.

7. Inv. no.RF2467, Von Osten 1983, pl.1.

8. For other related roundels, see Andrews 1991, p.2 and London 1988, no.91a, p.121.

9. Hollstein G, vol.II, no.124, p.114. Andrews refers to this in his review of London 1988 in *The Burlington Magazine*, CXXX, 1988, p.787.

10. L. Oehler, *Mitteilungen des Oberhessischen Geschichtsvereins*, N.F.44 (1960), pp.133ff., quoted by J. E. von Borries, p.98. The 1494 prototype is reproduced in W. L. Strauss, *The Complete Drawings of Albrecht Dürer*, New York, 1974, vol.1, p.172.

11. M. Mende, *Hans Baldung Grien. Das Graphische Werk. Vollständiger Bildkatalog der Einzelholzschitte, Buchillustrationen und Kupferstiche*, Unterschneidheim, 1978, no.338.

12. Bought by Smith for 32 guineas.

13. Bought by Betts for £200.

36

1. Letter from Klaus Dorsch of 18 December 1985. See also *European Drawings: Recent Acquisitions*, Hazlitt, Gooden & Fox, London, 1988, nos 47 and 48.

2. Letter of 10 April 1986.

3. Andrews 1991, p.10.

4. Letter of 18 December 1985.

5. Andrews, p.10.

6. H. Ost, 'Studien zu Pietro da Cortonas Umbau von Santa Maria della Pace', *Römisches Jahrbuch*, XIII, 1971, p.231.

37

1. Notes from her unpublished catalogue raisonné.

2. L. Demonts, *Musée du Louvre: Inventaire général des Dessins des Écoles du Nord*, vol.II, 1938, p.114, no.618, pl.CLVII.

3. Andrews 1991, p.12.

4. *European Master Drawings*, exh. cat., Thomas Williams and Lutz Riester, New York and London, 1991, no.32; repr. in colour, p.73.

5. *German Art 1400–1800 from Collections in Great Britain*, exh. cat., City Art Gallery, Manchester, 1961, p.74.

6. D. Ekserdjian, *Correggio*, New Haven and London, 1997, p.205.

7. C. Gould, *The Paintings of Correggio*, London, 1976, p.205.

38

1. See J. Ingamells, *A Dictionary of British and Irish Travellers in Italy 1701–1800*, London, 1997, pp.385–6. He also travelled to Turin in 1776 with the Scottish portrait painter Allan Ramsay.

2. *Master Drawings from the National Gallery of Canada*, exh. cat., Vancouver / Ottawa / Washington, 1988–9, no.77, pp.242–5.

3. J. Daniels, 'Sado-Mannerism', *Art & Artists*, no.9, February 1975, pp.22–29.

4. *Henry Fuseli 1741–1825*, exh. cat., Tate Gallery, London, 1975, no.159, pp.122–3.

5. G. Schiff, *Johann Heinrich Füssli 1741–1825*, Zurich / Munich, 1973, vol.1, pp.229ff; vol.2, figs 1106–1119. Schiff did not know the Edinburgh drawing, which is not catalogued by him.

6. Fuseli may have been influenced in depicting these elaborate hairstyles by drawings done by John Brown in Rome (e.g. D 4875, National Gallery of Scotland) which have an air of sexual menace. See *The Fuseli Circle in Rome*, exh. cat., Yale Center for British Art, New Haven, 1979, nos 49, 58, 60, and *The Poetical Circle. Fuseli and the British*, exh. cat., Sydney / Auckland, 1979, p.27.

7. *Henry Fuseli 1741–1825*, exh. cat., Tate Gallery, London, 1975, no.4.

8. *Ibid.*, no.176.

9. *Ibid.*, no.182.

39

1. P. Halm, 'Moritz von Schwind: Jugendgedanken und reifes Werk', *Festschrift Eberhard Hanfstaengl zum 75. Geburtstag*, Munich, 1961, pp.136 and 145.

2. F. Haack, *Moritz von Schwind*, Bielefeld and Leipzig, 1913, p.63 and Halm, p.164. The text reads as follows: Ein Einsiedler, den Zweifel überkamen über die Gerechtigkeit Gottes, wollte ausziehen sie zu suchen. Er verließ die Hütte und den stillen Wald und zog der Straße zu. Da gesellte sich ein Jüngling zu ihm und sie reisten selbander. Gegen Nacht kamen sie an ein Schloß, wo sie freundliche Aufnahme fanden. Als sie des Morgens weiter wanderten, brachte der Jüngling einen Becher hervor, den er im Schlosse entwendet. Die zweite Nacht brachten sie bei einem Geizhals zu, dem Morgens beim Abschied der Jüngling den Becher schenkte. Sie gingen durch das Dorf und der unheimliche Jüngling trat in ein ärmliches Haus und er forderte Einlass zu trinken. Kaum hatten sie das Dorf hinter sich, ging das Haus in Flammen auf und brannte nieder. Darauf eilten sie dem Gebirge zu, und aus einer einsamen Hütte tönte Jammer und Wehklage. Sie fanden die klagenden Eltern bei einem kranken Kind. Sogleich bereitete der Jüngling einen Trank, gab ihn dem Kinde und es verschied augenblicklich. Da erschrack der Einsiedler und er zauderte, dem Verdächtigen weiter zu folgen, der den Vater des Kindes zum Wegweiser genommen. Der Zorn übermannte ihn aber, als der entsetzliche Gefährte den Wegweiser von der nächsten Brücke in den Abgrund stürzte und verwandelte sich in den Erzengel Michael. "Du spürtest," sprach er, "der Gerechtigkeit Gottes nach, und Du hast ein Stück davon gesehen. Der Becher, den ich den guten Menschen nahm, war vergiftet, und der Geizhals wird seiner Sünden Lohn darin finden. Die armen Leute, deren Haus ich ansteckte, werden es wieder aufbauen und einen Schatz im Schutte finden. Das Kind, das ich von der Welt nahm, wäre zum Verbrecher und Sünder herangewachsen, denn der Vater, den ich in den Abgrund stieß, war ein Mörder und Räuber. So ist gut vor Gott gerecht, was vor Menschenaugen ungerecht ist." Da ging der Einsiedler in seine Klause zurück und war von allen Zweifeln geheilt.

3. Halm, pp.135–169.

40

1. R. Schöne, *Heinrich Dreber*, Berlin, 1940, p.194.

2. Schöne, pp.197–8.

3. C. G. Boerner, Leipzig, 16.5.1934, no.59 (repr.).

4. Schöne, p.195.

41

1. *Menzel der Beobachter*, exh. cat., Hamburg, 1982, p.134 and Andrews 1991, p.12.

2. *Adolph Menzel*, exh. cat., Berlin, 1980, pp.364–369, nos 230–244.

3. As a rather indifferent woodcut in Kugler's *Geschichte Friedrichs des Großen* (1840) and as a lithograph for his own *Denkwürdigkeiten aus der brandenburgisch-preußischen Geschichte* (1834–36).

4. Compiled and translated from H. von Tschudi, *Adolph von Menzel: Abbildungen seiner Gemälde und Studien*, Munich, 1905, no.121 and *Adolph Menzel*, exh. cat., Nationalgalerie, Berlin, 1980, p.306.

42, 43

1. P. Rosenberg, M. C. Stewart *French Paintings 1500–1825: The Fine Arts Museums of San Francisco*, San Francisco, 1987, pp.74–5.

2. The distinguished collector and connoisseur P.-J. Mariette noted of the son, rather disparagingly, 'Il eut un fils qui peignit aussi le paysage et qui voulut suivre la manière de son père, mais qui demeura toujours dans la médiocrité, et, comme ces ouvrages ont du rapport et que tout le monde n'est pas en estat de faire la distinction, on attribue quelquefois au père ce qui appartient au fils, en quoy l'on fait beaucoup de tort au premier.', *Abecedario* (compiled 1740–50), Paris, 1851–3, 1966 ed., IV, p.89.

3. J. Bean and L. Turčič, *15th–18th Century French Drawings in the Metropolitan Museum of Art*, New York, 1986, no.231, signed and dated 1693.

4. *Claude to Corot: The Development of Landscape Painting in France*, exh. cat., Colnaghi, New York, 1990, nos 17A, B, signed and dated 168(8?) and 1693.

5. Colnaghi, New York and London, 1998, no.27.

6. Mrs G. A. M. Rice, her sale, Christie's, London, 22 November 1966, no.135 (illus.), bought by Herbert Bier.

7. *Abrégé de la Marine du Roy au premier janvier 1693*, sold Hôtel Drouot, Paris (Laurin-Guilloux-Buffetaud-Tailleur), 29 March 1985, no.1.

8. Noted on photographs in the Witt Library, Courtauld Institute, London.

44

1. 'Salon de 1765' in *Diderot Salons* (ed. Seznec and Adhémar), Oxford, 1960, vol.II, p.77.

2. As noted in the Phillips sale catalogue, see provenance.

3 A. Ananoff and D. Wildenstein, *François Boucher*, Lausanne / Paris, 1976, vol.II, no.350. For a full discussion of the painting see C. Bailey, *The Loves of the Gods. Mythological Painting from Watteau to David*, exh. cat., Paris / Philadelphia / Fort Worth, 1991–2, no.47.

4. Ananoff and Wildenstein, vol.II, p.51, nos 2–7; *François Boucher* exh. cat., New York / Detroit / Paris, 1986–7, pp.238–9, nos 1–6.

5. T. Pignatti, *Veronese*, Venice, 1976, vol.I, no.216, II, figs.522–5.

6. Ananoff and Wildenstein, I, no.103.

7. *Ibid.*, no.104.

8. For example, Paul Prouté, Paris,1987, nos 30–1, and the *Bacchus and Ariadne: Design for a Fan Leaf* in the National Gallery of Canada, Ottawa (A. E. Popham and K. M. Fenwick, *European Drawings in the Collection of the National Gallery of Canada*, Toronto, 1965, no.223).

9. Phillips catalogue entry: the drawing was exhibited by Patrick Perrin, Paris, 1988, no.3.

45

1. For example, see *Maîtres Français 1550–1800: dessins de la donation Mathias Polakovits à l'Ecole des Beaux-Arts*, Paris, 1989, no.80, *View of the Banks of the Tiber*.

2. Christie's, London, 10 January 1996, no.202.

3. P. de Chennevières, *Une collection de dessins d'artistes français*, Paris, 1893, p.183.

4. E. and J. de Goncourt, *Chardin, étude contenant quatre dessins gravés à l'eau-forte*, Paris, 1864, p.20.

5. E. Launay, *Les frères Goncourt collectionneurs de dessins*, Paris, 1991, pp.335–6.

46

1. See the full entry on our drawing in *J. H. Fragonard e H. Robert a Roma*, exh. cat.,Villa Medici, Rome, 1990–91 no.4 (not exhibited). The earliest dated drawings by Robert are two imaginary views of 1756 inspired by the arch of Septimus Severus and the Arch of Constantine respectively, both in the Musée des Beaux-Arts, Valence.

2. The attribution is upheld by J.-P. Cuzin, *Jean-Honoré Fragonard, Vie et oeuvre*, Fribourg, 1987, pp.45–7, fig.51.

3. Noted in the 1968 *France in the eighteenth century* catalogue entry. On La Traverse's drawings at Besançon, see M. I. Cornillot, *Collection Pierre-Adrien Pâris*, Besançon, 1957, nos 96–105, and J.-F. Méjanes, 'Un album de dessins de La Traverse', *La Revue du Louvre*, 1972, pp.381–86. There is a further group of his drawings in the National Library, Madrid.

4. *Fragonard*, exh. cat., Paris / New York, 1987–8, p.65, fig.19.

5. Robert Lehman Collection, Metropolitan Museum of Art, New York, exh. and illus. *Hubert Robert Drawings and Watercolors*, National Gallery of Art, Washington, 1978, no.3.

6. H. Guichard, entry on La Traverse in *The Dictionary of Art*, vol.18, p.843.

47

1. M. Sandoz, *Jean-Baptiste Deshays 1729–1765*, Paris, 1977, no.110, fig.26.

2. 'His drawings were less well known than his paintings. Those which have been found at his home, although very small in number, have created a very great impression.' C.-N. Cochin, *Essay sur la vie de M. Deshays*, 1765, reprinted in Sandoz, pp.13–16.

3. 26 May 1765 and following days, Paris (Lugt 1440), also reproduced in Sandoz, pp.149–54.

4. Nos 121–149 in the posthumous sale catalogue were 'esquisses et ebauches' by Boucher.

5. *Catalogue de la collection de dessins et d'estampes de M. Morel de Vende, vicomte de Paignon-Dijonval*, Paris, 1810, no.3601 (lav. de b. et d'e ch., reh. de bl.'; 18 p. × 9p.), as identified by Sandoz.

48

1. Piranesi first arrived in Rome in the autumn of 1740 and Legeay left Rome for Paris 9 January 1742. Piranesi evidently owned a number of drawings by Legeay which were inherited by his two sons (J. Scott, *Piranesi*, London and New York, 1975, p.320, note 2).

2. Legeay's biography has been the subject of widely differing interpretations concerning the known facts of his life. I have essentially followed the most recent findings of Gilbert Erouart, first published in *Piranèse et les français 1740–1790*, exh. cat., Rome / Dijon / Paris, 1976, pp.179–200, elaborated on in 'Jean-Laurent Legeay. Recherches', *Piranèse et les Français: Colloque tenu à la Villa Médicis*, Rome, vol.II, 1978, pp.199–212, and summarised in Erouart's monograph, *L'architecture au pinceau. Jean-Laurent Legeay: Un Piranésien français dans l'Europe des Lumières*, Paris, 1982, of which a penetrating and informative review by Robin Middleton, neatly summarising the problems of Legeay chronology, was published in *The Burlington Magazine*, CXXV, 1983 pp.766–7. See also Mary L. Myers, *French Architectural and Ornament Drawings of the Eighteenth Century*, Metropolitan Museum of Art, New York, 1991, pp.96–101.

3. Jean-Pierre Haldi (b.1937), Director, Musée des PTT Suisses, Berne. His collector's mark will be included in the next Supplément to Lugt. I am most grateful to Mària van Berge-Gerbaud for this information.

49

1. P. Rosenberg and U. van de Sandt, *Pierre Peyron 1744–1814*, Neuilly-sur-Seine, 1983.

2. *Ibid.*, no.103, fig.97, pl.VI; a now lost painting of this subject was exhibited by Peyron at the 1791 Salon, and a further version, signed and dated 1794, came to light at Sotheby's, Monaco, 16 June 1989, no.398, acquired by Colnaghi and published by them in their exh. cat. *1789: French Art During the Revolution*, Colnaghi, New York, 1989, no.41, entry by Ugo van de Sandt.

3. *Loc. cit.*

4. *Ibid.*, no.109, fig.92.

5. *Ibid.*, no.105, fig.93.

6. *Ibid.*, no.107, fig.95.

7. *Ibid.*, no.106, fig.94.

8. *Ibid.*, no.108, fig.96.

9. Peyron to d'Angiviller, Paris, 17 November 1787 (Musée Paul-Arbaud, Aix-en-Provence, file 3144 A1). Quoted in Colnaghi, New York, 1989, pp.262, 265.

50

1. Older sources give Wille's date of death as 1821 or after. The correct date of 1837 was discovered by Colin Clark, 'Pierre-Alexandre Wille: The Later Years', *Master Drawings*, XVIII, 1980, pp.268–9.

2. G. Duplessis, *Mémoires et journal de J.-G.Wille graveur du roi publiés d'après les manuscrits autographes de la Bibliothèque impériale avec une préface par Edmond et Jules de Goncourt*, Paris, 1857.

3. Duplessis, vol.II, p.109. I am grateful to my colleague Helen Smailes for drawing my attention to this intriguing reference.

4. De Bayser catalogue, 1975, no.40, pen and brown ink, 34 × 50.5, signed and dated: *P. A. Wille Filius / del.1784.*

5. *Maîtres Français 1550–1800: Dessins de la donation Mathias Polakovits à l'Ecole des Beaux-Arts*, exh. cat., Paris, 1989, no.118.

6. The young J.-L. David, in Rome 1775–80, had expressed his admiration for the 'brutal', though 'excellent', work of Caravaggio, Ribera and Valentin (whose *Last Supper* he copied). See E. J. Delécluze, *Louis David son école et son temps*, Paris, 1855 (1983 ed), pp.112–14.

7. By whom advertised in *The Burlington Magazine*, CXXXIII, 1991, illus.

51

1. G. Lacambre, 'Pierre-Henri de Valenciennes en Italie: un journal de voyage inedit', *Bulletin de la Société de l'Histoire de l'Art français*, 1978, pp.139–72.

2. P. Conisbee, 'Pre-Romantic Plein-Air Painting', *Art History*, 2, no.4, 1979, pp.413–28; P. R. Radisch, 'Eighteenth-Century Plein-Air Painting and the Sketches of Pierre Henri de Valenciennes', *Art Bulletin*, LXIV, 1982, pp.98–104.

3. Comparable examples include *Paysage classique avec une femme puisant de l'eau à une fontaine et une lavandière*, 1796, Paul Prouté, Paris, exh. cat., 1983, no.33; *A Classical Landscape with Figures near a Lake*, 1796, Christie's, London, 8 July 1980, no.94.

4. Christie's, London, 25 March 1969, no.170. For further discussion see *De David à Delacroix, la peinture française de 1774 à 1830*, exh. cat., Grand Palais, Paris, 1974–5, p.629.

5. Valenciennes's posthumous sale catalogue (Lugt 9578), Paris, 26 April 1819 and following days, p.4. Valenciennes himself was deeply interested in natural history and the second part of his sale included sections devoted to shells, reptiles, insects and minerals.

52

1. P.-A. Coupin, *Oeuvres posthumes d'Anne-Louis Girodet-Trioson peintre d'histoire, suivies par sa correspondance …* , Paris, 1829.

2. C. M. Osborne, *Pierre Didot the Elder and French book illustration 1789–1822*, New York, 1985, in particular 'Didot's Racine', pp.113–40.

3. On the late-eighteenth-century revival of interest in Racine, see J. H. Rubin, 'Guérin's Painting of Phèdre and the Post-Revolutionary Revival of Racine', *The Art Bulletin*, LVIII, 1977, pp.601–18.

4. *Second Exposition publique des produits de l'industrie française*, Paris, 13 Ventose, An IX.

5. Prud'hon was the original choice for *Andromache*, but in the end he only produced the illustration for the frontispiece to the three-volume *Racine*.

6. Coupin, vol.II, p.343.

7. *French Painting: The Revolutionary Decades 1760–1830*, exh. cat., Sydney / Melbourne, 1980–81, no.62. The original drawings for *Racine* were mounted in the vellum copy of the *Oeuvres* which Pierre presented to his brother Firmin in appreciation of his work. It was put up for auction in 1810 at the sale of Firmin Didot's library but withdrawn because it failed to fetch the reserve of 3200 francs. Around 1814 the drawings were bought by the Marquis de Château Géron who immediately sold them to the dealer Schrot, with the exception of Prud'hon's frontispiece and Gérard's drawing for *Bajazet* Act 2 Scene 1, which he kept for himself.

8. Osborne, pp.128–9.

9. Bellinger / Brady catalogue, 1997, nos 32, 33.

10. On the Cleveland drawing, see *Visions of Antiquity: Neoclassical Figure Drawings*, exh. cat., Los Angeles / Philadelphia / Minneapolis, 1993–4, no.55.

11. Coupin, vol.II, p.243.

12. *Le beau idéal ou l'art du concept*, exh. cat., Louvre, Paris, 1989, no.55.

13. *Dessins français du XIXe siècle du Musée Bonnat à Bayonne*, exh. cat., Louvre, Paris, 1979, no.80.

14. *La donation Baderou au musée de Rouen, Peintures et dessins de l'Ecole Française: Etudes de la revue du Louvre et des Musées de France*, 1980, vol.I, p.115, fig.11.

15. The son of a cousin of Girodet's, Becquerel (1788–1878) was a distinguished soldier and scientist. He was given the task by his family of ensuring the posthumous publication of Girodet's literary works. His grandson, Henri, gave the family name to the unit by which radioactivity is measured.

53

1. H. Naef, Die *Bildniszeichnungen von J.-A.-D. Ingres*, Berne, 1977–80.

2. At some point Mme Hayard took over the running of the shop, and her husband was appointed *inspecteur des Poudres et poudrières* to the Holy See (Naef, vol.I, p.460, letter of 11 November 1837 from Rome of the *liègois* painter Edmond Duvivier to his mother. Duvivier married the youngest Hayard daughter, Caroline).

3. Naef, vol.I, pp.451–69.

4. Naef, vol.IV, no.81.

5. Naef, 'Eighteen Portrait Drawings by Ingres', *Master Drawings*, IV, 1966, p.258.

6. Naef, vol.IV, no.112.

7. Naef, vol.I, p.455.

54

1. See L. Bénédite, *Gazette des Beaux-Arts*, 1908, pp.49–50.

2. See *Les années romantiques: La peinture française de 1815 à 1850*, exh. cat., Nantes / Paris / Plaisance, 1995–6, p.482.

3. G. Bazin, *Théodore Géricault*, Paris, 1992, vol.V, no.1641, illus. The episode referred to was the execution of four Republican sergeants at La Rochelle, whose heroism is commemorated in the stele depicted in the countryside.

4. Bazin, no.1642, illus. Bazin p.63 discusses nos 1641–2 and also 'Une autre gouache dont j'ai vu la photographie – non reproduite ici – s'apparente aux deux précédentes. On y voit un lancier se pencher sur un jeune soldat blessé, en présence d'un grenadier embrassant un soldat nu-tête'.

5. Wheelock Whitney, *Gericault in Italy*, New Haven and London, 1997, p.21, fig.16.

6. *Dessins Anciens*, Galerie de Bayser, Paris, 1984, no.44.

7. See Victor Carlson's entry for Henri-Joseph de Forestier's drawing *The Wrath of Saul against David c.1817* (Baltimore Museum of Fine Art) in *Visions of Antiquity: Neoclassical Figure Drawings*, exh. cat., Los Angeles / Philadelphia / Minneapolis, 1993–4, no.76.

8. Whitney, p.20.

9. C. Clément, *Géricault*, Paris, 1973 ed., pp.198–9.

10. Prouté catalogue, no.106, December 1995, no.55 illus.

55

1. The most detailed published biography of Cabat is to be found in P. Miquel, *Le paysage français au XIXe siècle 1824–1874*, Maures-la-Jolie, 1975, vol.III, pp.482–531. The most recent exhibition of his work was *Louis Cabat (1812–1893)*, Musée des Beaux-Arts, Troyes, 1987.

2. C. M. Richardson 'A Cabat for the National Gallery of Scotland: The true identity of Louis-Nicholas Cabat's Villa Medici', *Apollo*, CLI, 456, 2000, pp.48–51.

3. On the interest in Poussin at that time, see R. Verdi, 'Poussin's Life in Nineteenth-Century Pictures', *The Burlington Magazine*, CXIII, 1969, pp.741–50.

4. Miquel, p.490.

5. *Ibid.*, p.500.

6. Henri Lacordaire (1802–1861), a leading ecclesiastic in the Catholic revival in France following the Napoleonic period.

7. Richardson, pp.49–50.

8. Letter from Sylvie Brame, 11 December 1998, Gallery files.

56

1. Ossian, the 'Homer of the North', was a third-century Irish bard, son of Fingal, whose Gaelic poems were 'rediscovered' and 'collected' by James MacPherson, who 'relocated' them to Scotland and published them variously 1760–3 and in the complete *Works* of 1765. They enjoyed great popularity throughout Europe, inspiring both writers and painters (see H. Okun, 'Ossian in Painting', *Journal of the Warburg and Courtauld Institutes*, XXX, 1967, pp.327–56). Ingres's composition was generally inspired by the passage at the end of *The War of Inis-Thona*, 'I see the heroes of Morven; I hear the songs of the bards; Oscar lifts the sword of Cormalo; a thousand youths admire its studded thongs. They look with wonder on my son. They admire the strength of his arm. They mark the joy of his father's eyes; they long for an equal fame … But sleep descends in the sound of the harp; pleasant dreams begin to rise. Ye sons of the chase stand far distant, nor disturb my rest. The bard of other times holds discourse with his fathers, the chiefs of the days of old! Sons of the chase, stand far distant! Disturb not the dreams of Ossian!', J. Macpherson (intro. W. Sharp), *The Poems of Ossian*, Edinburgh, 1926 ed., p.392. (See also catalogue entry on Runciman, no.63.)

2. See, for example, G. Vigne, *Dessins d'Ingres: catalogue raisonné des dessins du musée de Montauban*, Paris, 1995, nos 1277–99 (including the compositional drawings in the museum's collection).

3. The most important discussions are D. Ternois, 'Ingres et le "Songe d'Ossian"', *Walter Friedlaender zum 90.Geburtstag*, Berlin, 1965, pp.185–92; H. Toussaint in *Ossian*, exh. cat., Paris / Hamburg, 1974, pp.102–6; R. A. Gross, 'Ingres' Celtic Fantasy "The Dream of Ossian"', *Rutgers Art Review*, II, 1981, pp.43–58; P. Condon, *In Pursuit of Perfection: The Art of J.-A.-D. Ingres*, exh. cat., Louisville / Fort Worth, 1983–4, pp.46–51.

4. Condon, no.8, colour illus. as *c*.1811–13.

5. Vigne, nos 1279, 1280.

6. Condon, p.46, fig.5.

7. Ingres later placed incorrect dates on many of these drawings, presumably a fault of memory.

8. H. Lapauze, *Les Dessins de J.-A.-D.Ingres au Musée de Montauban*, Paris, 1901, p.249 (dating the drawing to around 1824); Toussaint, p.103, no.VI, suggesting that *pinx.* refers to the painting, which Ingres mistakenly remembered as dating from 1811.

9. A. Magimel, *Oeuvre de J.-A.-D. Ingres … gravé au trait sur acier par A. Réveil, 1800–1851*, Paris, 1851, pl.22.

10. An investigation by the Highlands Society of Edinburgh, whose findings were published in 1805, proved inconclusive.The final debunking of Macpherson only took place in the 1850s to 70s with the publication of much authentic Gaelic poetry.

57

1. Acc.no.71 / 2, black and white chalk on blue-grey paper 53 × 43.5, signed lower left: *DC*. Purchased from Seiferheld & Co., New York, 1971.

2. *Master Drawings*, Bernard Houthakker, Amsterdam, 1971, no.17, illus. charcoal 32.1 × 25.7, signed lower left: *DC*. Acquired by Houthakker from Seiferheld & Co., New York, and subsequently sold to Winslow Ames, Saunderstown, Rhode Island.

3. Dewey F. Mosby, 'Decamps dessinateur', *La donation Baderou au musée de Rouen: Etudes de la revue du Louvre et des Musées de France*, 1980, vol.I, p.151, discussing the Toronto drawing, and letter in Gallery files, 31 August 1998.

4. R. P. Huet, *Paul Huet*, Paris, 1911, p.157.

58

1. J. Péladan, *Ernest Hébert. Son Oeuvre et son temps, d'après sa correspondance intime et des documents inédits*, Paris, 1910. For a recent appraisal of the artist, see P. Cooke, 'Ernest Hébert (1817–1908) and the Romantic Aftermath', *Apollo*, CXLVI, 1997, pp.32–6.

2. See the very full entry on this picture by Henri Loyrette in *Impressionnisme: Les origines 1859–1869*, exh. cat., Paris / New York, 1994–5, no.79

3. Péladan, p.125.

4. For the most recent account of Hébert's stay in Cervara, see René Patris d'Uckermann, *Ernest Hébert 1817–1908*, Paris, 1983, pp.97–104.

5. Georges Lafenestre, 'M. Ernest Hébert', *Gazette des Beaux-Arts*, 1897, p.353.

6. William R. Johnston, *The Nineteenth Century Paintings in the Walters Art Gallery*, Baltimore, 1982, pp.56–7, no.28, fig.37.133.

7. Lafenestre, pp.355, 359.

8. J. Claretie, 'Ernest Hébert, notes et impressions, artistes contemporains', *La Revue de l'art ancien et moderne*, 20, 1906, p.411.

9. *Ruelle orientale*, black chalk with white heightening, 31 × 18, Hôtel Drouot, Paris, 7 November 1990, no.41.

59

1. On this whole subject, see B. Foucart, *Le renouveau de la peinture religieuse en France (1800–1860)*, Paris, 1987.

2. P. Nicard, *Alexandre Hesse, sa vie et ses ouvrages*, Paris, 1882.

3. Nos 33 and 34 in *Les Dossiers du Musée d'Orsay 26: Dessins d'Alexandre Hesse conservés à l'Ecole nationale supérieure des Beaux-Arts*, catalogue by E. Brugerolles and D. Guillet, Paris, 1988. This represents the most up-to-date publication on the artist.

4. Portraits of *Mme Brisson* in 1835 and of *M. Adrien Brisson* in 1836 (both Private Collection) and the *Death of President Brisson 1591* (1840 Salon, no.832), *Procession of the League 10 February 1593* (1850 Salon, no.1517), *Henry IV leaving for the Hunt*, 1852, Nicard, pp.46, 140, 19, 69, 75.

5. Brugerolles and Guillet, pp.14–15, note 60.

60

1. The first inscription is possibly in the hand of Maximilian Luce (one of the compilers of Seurat's studio inventory), the second can be linked to the numbered inventory in the Signac archives where, under the category 'Croquis et Dessins', Signac noted '366–372 Baignade' (deduction based on information from R. L. Herbert, quoted in *Seurat and the Bathers*, exh. cat., National Gallery, London, 1997, p.65, note 3).

2. The context and creation of this masterpiece have been exhaustively studied by J. Leighton and R. Thomson in the London 1997 exhibition.

3. All were reassembled for the London 1997 exhibition, nos 2–14.

4. Until recently, ten related drawings were known: see César Mange de Hauke, *Seurat et son Oeuvre*, New York, 1961, nos 589–98 (but no.592's connection to the painting is doubted by many authorities). A further drawing for the so-called 'echo boy' has recently come to light and was included in the London 1997 exhibition, no.18, though its attribution to Seurat has been questioned.

5. Lecomte (1867–1958) was a writer and close friend of the critic Fénéon, with whom he shared anarchist sympathies, and he would have met Seurat many times. He ran the *Cravache* review for eighteen months as an avant-garde Symbolist newspaper and commissioned many important articles on modern art. Although he rather played down Seurat's importance in an article on Pissarro which he wrote for *Hommes d'aujourd'hui*, he made amends in another piece which appeared in *Art et critique* (S. Monneret, *L'Impressionnisme et son époque*, Paris, 1978, pp.323–4).

61

1. R. Brydall, *History of Art in Scotland*, Edinburgh, 1889, p.94. Daphne Foskett, however (*Miniatures, Dictionary and Guide*, Woodbridge, 1987, p.200), claims that she has 'not so far discovered one that could be attributed to him'.

2. Andrews and Brotchie 1960, p.156.

3. D. Foskett, *British Portrait Miniatures*, Feltham, 1963, p.171 and Woodbridge 1987, p.200; B. S. Long, *British Miniaturists*, London, 1966, p.330.

4. Poll Tax records for College Kirk Parish, Edinburgh, Scottish Record Office, E70 / 4 / 1 and Annuity Rolls 1697 / 8, pp.24 and 65, Edinburgh City Archives. I am grateful to my colleague Helen Smailes for this information.

5. A. M. Crinò, 'Documents relating to some portraits in the Uffizi and to a portrait at Knole', *The Burlington Magazine*, CII, 1960, p.260.

6. *Ibid*.

7. E. K. Waterhouse, *The Dictionary of 16th and 17th Century British Painting*, Woodbridge, 1988, pp.211–2.

8. Foskett 1987, p.200.

9. *Ibid*.

10. *Portrait Miniatures from the Collection of the Duke of Buccleuch*, exh. cat., Scottish National Portrait Gallery, Edinburgh, 1996, nos 49–51.

11. Andrews and Brotchie 1960, p.156; *Patrons and Painters: Art in Scotland 1650–1750*, exh. cat., Scottish National Portrait Gallery, Edinburgh, 1989, p.22.

12. See, for example, the oil by Peter Lely in the Scottish National Portrait Gallery (PG 2225).

13. National Portrait Gallery, London (No.2084), dated *c*.1666. A powerful plumbago portrait of the Duke by Paton, dated 1669, is in the collection at Ham House.

14. Edinburgh 1996, no.49. Signed and dated: *D. Paton fecit 1669. / S. Couper* [sic] *inventit 1665*.

62

1. J. Holloway and L. Errington, *The Discovery of Scotland*, exh. cat., National Gallery of Scotland, Edinburgh, 1978, pp.33–46; L. Herrmann, 'Paul Sandby in Scotland', *The Burlington Magazine*, CVI, 1964, pp.339–341.

2. See especially J. Roberts, *Views of Windsor: Watercolours by Thomas and Paul Sandby from the Collection of her Majesty Queen Elizabeth II*, exh. cat., Amsterdam / Portland / Memphis / Dallas / Manchester, 1996–97.

3. Obituary, *London Review and Literary Journal*, 8 November 1809, p.400.

4. See especially L. Binyon, *Catalogue of Drawings by British Artists … in the Department of Prints and Drawings in the British Museum*, London, 1898–1907.

5. J. D. Marwick, *List of Markets and Fairs now and formerly held in Scotland …* , published as an appendix to the *Report of the Royal Commission on Market Rights and Tolls*, London, 1890.

6. *The Scottish Domestic Scene*, exh. cat., Scottish National Portrait Gallery, Edinburgh, 1963, p.6.

7. I am grateful to Stephanie Davidson of the Edinburgh City Archives for helping to validate this point.

8. British Museum, London (BM 1904–8–19–2). Wrongly titled in Binyon 1898–1907 as Stirling Castle (LB 107).

9. British Museum, London (BM Nm–6–40).

10. British Museum, London (BM Nm–6–65).

11. Boitard's drawing is in the British Museum, London, entitled *Village Dancers* (BM 1853–8–13–56). See E. Bruce Robertson, *Paul Sandby and the Early Development of English Watercolours*, Ph.D. thesis, Yale University, New Haven, 1987, p.153. I am grateful to Dr Joe Rock for bringing this to my attention. New research by Dr Rock (as yet unpublished) suggests that Boitard may have been in Edinburgh in the mid-eighteenth century.

12. M. M. Stuart implies that The Black Bull inn in the Grassmarket was there by the mid-eighteenth century (*Old Edinburgh Taverns*, London, 1952, p.130). Another Black Bull, probably founded after 1850 and later known as the Old Veal Market Inn, was somewhere near the top of Cockburn Street. Edinburgh's most famous Black Bull Tavern, on Leith Street, was not established until 1780. I am grateful to John Burnett of the National Museum of Scotland for this information, and to John Morris for discussing the drawing with me.

63

1. See *The Norie Family*, exh. cat. Scottish Masters series, Scottish National Portrait Gallery, Edinburgh, 1994.

2. James Norie executed landscapes and ornamental work for Mavisbank House, near Lasswade, built in 1723–39 by the architect William Adam in collaboration with Sir John Clerk 2nd Bart. (1676–1755). Macmillan also notes that the Nories worked at Penicuik House on at least three occasions during Runciman's apprenticeship: in 1750, 1753 and 1754 (J. D. Macmillan, 'Alexander Runciman in Rome', *The Burlington Magazine*, CXII, 1970, p.23). For a general bibliography on the Clerks, see *The Dictionary of Art*, vol.7, pp.417–19.

3. A history of the building is given by A. Rowan in 'Penicuik House, Midlothian – I', *Country Life*, 15 August 1968, pp.383–87.

4. For Runciman's association with these artists, see *The Poetical Circle: Fuseli and the British*, exh. cat., Sydney / Auckland, 1979, pp.124–135; *The Fuseli Circle in Rome*, exh. cat., Yale Center for British Art, New Haven, 1979, pp.7–16.

5. See especially H. Okun, 'Ossian in Painting', *Journal of the Warburg and Courtauld Institutes of Art*, XXX, 1967, pp.327–56.

6. Runciman's decorations at Penicuik were destroyed in a fire in 1889. For a description and discussion of the project, see especially: W. Ross, *A Description of the Paintings in the Hall of Ossian at Pennycuik near Edinburgh*, Edinburgh, 1773; J. D. Macmillan, 'Truly National Designs: Runciman's Scottish themes at Penicuik', *Art History*, no.1, March 1978, pp.90–8; Okun 1967, pp.331–334.

7. Scottish Record Office, G.D. 18. R.H. 3242. See S. Booth, 'The Early Career of Alexander Runciman and his Relations with Sir James Clerk of Penicuik', *Journal of the Warburg and Courtauld Institutes of Art*, XXXII, 1969, pp.335–36; Macmillan 1970, pp.24–25, illus.

8. Scottish Record Office, G.D.18 / 4680. Quoted extensively in Macmillan 1970, pp.24, 27–28.

9. Listed and discussed in J. D. Macmillan, *The Earlier Career of Alexander Runciman and the Influences that Shaped his Style*, unpublished Ph.D. thesis, University of Edinburgh, 1974, pp.172 ff.

10. See especially drawings contained in albums D 5330A and D 5330B, accepted by H.M. Treasury in lieu of inheritance tax and allocated to the Gallery in 1992.

11. L. Errington, 'Gavin Hamilton's Sentimental Iliad', *The Burlington Magazine*, CXX, 1978, pp.11–13. One of the two surviving paintings, *Achilles Lamenting the Death of Patroclus* (NG 2339), and an oil sketch for *Andromache Bewailing the Death of Hector* (NG 2428) are in the National Gallery of Scotland.

12. For Runciman's association with Fuseli, see Macmillan 1974, Chapter XV.

13. Etching after the painted ceiling decoration at Penicuik House, Midlothian, c.1774. See Sydney / Auckland 1979, no.98, p.133; New Haven 1979, no.9, pp.12–13.

64

1. Runciman may have been an early teacher of Brown in Edinburgh. Their friendship is celebrated in a double portrait of 1784, on loan to the Scottish National Portrait Gallery, Edinburgh (PGL 31).

2. See also Brown's drawing of an elaborately coiffured woman, National Gallery of Scotland (D 4875). N. Powell, 'Brown and the Women of Rome', *Signature*, XIV, 1952, pp.40–50; *The Poetical Circle: Fuseli and the British*, exh. cat., Sydney / Auckland, 1979, pp.27, 92–95; *The Fuseli Circle in Rome*, exh. cat., Yale Center for British Art, New Haven, 1979, pp.54–63.

3. Examples of Brown's drawings from this trip are in the British Museum and the Yale Centre for British Art. See also Christie's, London, 16 November 1982, no.18. He exhibited a Sicilian view, *The Cave of Dionysius at Syracuse*, at the Royal Academy, London, in 1774, no.18.

4. Most of these are now deposited on loan with the Scottish National Portrait Gallery, Edinburgh. See B. Skinner, 'John Brown and the Antiquarians', *Country Life*, 12 August 1971, pp.392–6.

5. Now lost; recorded by Lord Buchan in 'John Brown with a Portrait', *The Bee*, Edinburgh, 8 May 1793, p.29.

6. P. McIntyre, 'John Brown and Thomas Gainsborough', *Gallery* (Monthly Magazine of the National Gallery Society of Victoria), April 1994, pp.16–18.

65

1. An extensive bibliography is given in the standard modern monograph on Ramsay by A. Smart, *Allan Ramsay: Painter, Essayist and Man of the Enlightenment*, New Haven and London, 1992.

2. H. L. Thrale, *Thralania. The Diary of Hester Thrale 1776–1809*, K. C. Balderston (ed.), Oxford, 1942, p.942.

3. National Gallery of Scotland, Edinburgh (NG 430). See *Allan Ramsay 1713–1784*, exh. cat., Scottish National Portrait Gallery, Edinburgh, 1992, no.66, pp.128–129.

4. Letter from Robert Adam to Helen Adam, Rome, 22 March 1755, Scottish Record Office, *Clerk of Penicuik MS*, GD18 / 4768.

5. A. Smart, 'A Newly Discovered Portrait of Allan Ramsay's Second Wife', *Apollo*, CXIII, 1981, pp.288–295.

6. The Baths of Ischia were renowned for their curative powers and apparently eased the pain in Ramsay's arm, allowing him to complete several drawings. See A. Smart, *The Life and Art of Allan Ramsay*, London, 1952, p.157; Edinburgh 1992, nos 105, 107 and 108.

7. Scottish National Portrait Gallery, Edinburgh (PG 1104).

8. J. D. Macmillan, *Scottish Art 1460–1990*, Edinburgh, 1990, pp.102–5; *Painting in Scotland. The Golden Age*, exh. cat., Edinburgh / London, 1986, pp.26–7.

9. For the Lady Murray of Henderland Bequest, see C. Thompson, *Pictures for Scotland. The National Gallery of Scotland and its Collection: a study of the changing attitude to painting since the 1820s*, Edinburgh, 1972, pp.9–13.

66

1. J. Fleming, *Robert Adam and his Circle in Edinburgh and Rome*, Cambridge, 1962.

2. The standard reference work on the brothers' practice is A. T. Bolton, *The Architecture of Robert and James Adam 1758–1794*, London, 1922.

3. W. L. Spiers, *Catalogue of the Drawings and Designs of Robert and James Adam in Sir John Soane's Museum*, Cambridge, 1979 (first published as an appendix to Bolton 1922); A. A. Tait, 'The Sale of Robert Adam's Drawings', *The Burlington Magazine*, CXX, 1987, pp.451–454; I. G. Brown, 'Robert Adam's Drawings: Edinburgh's Loss, London's Gain', *Book of the Old Edinburgh Club*, New Series, 2, 1992, pp.22–33.

4. Cullen's long and complicated building history is outlined by M. Binney in 'Cullen House – I' and 'Cullen House, Banffshire – II', *Country Life*, 19 December 1985, pp.1970–1974 and 26 December 1985, pp.2038–2042.

5. For the landscaping of the Cullen estate, see A. A. Tait, *The Landscape Garden in Scotland 1735–1835*, Edinburgh, 1980.

6. Drawing in Private Collection. References to designs in letters from John Adam to 5th Earl in Scottish Record Office, GD248 / 982 / 1.

7. Spiers 1979, pp.7–8.

8. Soane Museum, London, Adam vol.2 / 60, drawing dated 1775. Illus. in *Robert Adam. The Creative Mind: from the sketch to the finished drawing*, exh. cat., London / New York / Los Angeles / Washington / Edinburgh, 1997–99, no.25, pp.24 and 29.

9. Royal Library, Windsor. Illus. in *Robert Adam and Scotland. The Picturesque Drawings*, exh. cat. Scottish Arts Council Gallery, Edinburgh, 1972, no.24, plate 7.

10. Spiers 1979, p.13. The drawings are confusingly inscribed 'Findlater Castle', which gives the impression that they were designed for the site of the ancient castle of that name on the coast east of Cullen. A survey of the Cullen estate by White, however, dated 1789, incorporates a ground plan of Adam's new castle, and proves that these drawings were indeed for Cullen. See Binney December 1985, p.2041.

11. Illus. in *Drawings from Blair Adam*, exh. cat., National Gallery of Scotland, Edinburgh, 1983, no.31.

12. For the artistic collaboration between the two men, see A. A. Tait, 'Robert Adam and John Clerk of Eldin', *Master Drawings*, XVI, 1978, pp.53–57.

13. A. A. Tait, *Drawings and Imagination*, Cambridge, 1993, Chapter 5; 'The Picturesque Drawings of Robert Adam', *Master Drawings*, IX, 1971, pp.161–171. I am grateful to Stephen Astley of the Soane Museum for discussing this drawing with me.

67

1. Alexander Cozens's 'blottesque' method was first laid out in 1759 in his *Essay to Facilitate the Inventing of Landskips*. His final and best-known explanation, *A Method of Assisting the Invention in Drawing Original Compositions of Landscape*, was published in 1786.

2. Examples of these in the National Gallery of Scotland are *The Temple of Maecenas at Tivoli* (D 5023.52) and *The Colosseum from the North* (D 5023.13). See Edinburgh 1979, nos 10 and 13.

3. See especially *Dr Thomas Monro and the Monro Academy*, exh. cat., Victoria and Albert Museum, London, 1976.

4. For Cozens's association with Beckford see, C. F. Bell and T. Girtin, 'The Drawings and Sketches of John Robert Cozens', *The Walpole Society*, XXIII, 1934–35, pp.15 ff.; K. Sloan, *Alexander and John Robert Cozens. The Poetry of Landscape*, New Haven and London, 1986, pp.138–157.

5. Now in the Whitworth Art Gallery, Manchester. For their sale, see *Catalogue of Seven Sketchbooks by John Robert Cozens* (with an introductory essay by A. Blunt), Sotheby's, London, 29 November, 1973.

6. L. Melville, *The Life and Letters of William Beckford of Fonthill*, London, 1910.

7. Sotheby's 1973, p.18 – sketchbook vol.1, f.19.

8. Sotheby's 1973, p.18 – sketchbook vol.1, f.20. Finished watercolour illus. in A. Wilton and I. Bignamini, *Grand Tour: The Lure of Italy in the Eighteenth Century*, exh. cat., Tate Gallery, London, 1996, p.151, no.104.

9. *The Art of Alexander and John Robert Cozens*, Yale Center for British Art, New Haven, 1980, pp.43–48.

10. *English Landscape 1630–1850. Drawings, Prints & Books from the Paul Mellon Collection*, exh. cat., Yale Center for British Art, New Haven, 1977, p.48, cat.76; Andrew Wilton observes that 'These tracings were presumably made at some point shortly after Cozens's return to England late in 1783. They have been given that date for convenience but they could obviously have been done later' (New Haven 1980, p.43).

11. Tate Gallery, London, TB CCCLXXIV–15 (*Dr Monro's Album of Swiss and Italian Views*).

12. Wilton points to a Monro School study in the Yale collections, which was probably copied from a drawing lent to Monro by Richard Payne Knight (New Haven 1980, p.60).

68

1. Deposited on loan by the Trustees of the late Mrs Magdalene Sharpe Erskine (hereafter referred to as the Erskine Trustees).

2. Allan made multiple copies of these drawings but the finest and probably original set is in the collection of Aberdeen Art Gallery. For a discussion of these see F. Irwin, 'Drawn Mostly from Nature: David Allan's Record of Daily Dress in France and Italy, 1770–76', *Costume Society*, 32, 1998.

3. The National Gallery of Scotland has an extensive collection of Allan's Scottish genre drawings.

4. For an assessment of Allan's mature output, see especially G. Gordon, *Scottish Scenes and Scottish Story: The Later Career of David Allan, Historical Painter*, unpublished Ph.D. thesis, University of Glasgow, 1990.

5. J. Cameron, *Prisons and Punishment in Scotland*, Edinburgh, 1983, pp.20 ff.; C. Pearl, *Bawdy Burns, The Christian Rebel*, London, 1958, pp.86–93, illus. p.97 (facing).

6. Pearl 1958, pp.90–92.

7. On loan from the Erskine Trustees. See *The Artist and the Kirk*, exh. cat., National Gallery of Scotland, 1979–80, no.18, p.16.

8. Two prints, both dated 'Edr. 1784', but pulled from different plates, are in the National Gallery of Scotland. The first, on loan from the Erskine Trustees, is hand-coloured and inscribed 'Black Stool' (image size 29 × 34.4). The second, titled 'Presbyterian Penance', is more refined and was probably traced from the above (image size 29.7 × 35.4).

9. Illus. T. Crouther Gordon, *David Allan: The Scottish Hogarth*, Alva, 1951, p.74 (facing). Another watercolour, apparently undated, is in a private collection in Brighton.

10. Sotheby's, London, 21 May 1970, no.2 (pencil, 33 × 43.2). Also Christie's, London, 13 July 1993, no.12 (pencil and chalk, 34.3 × 45.7, and inscribed on verso '5 outlines on oil paper').

69

1. For the extensive literature on Turner see especially the bibliographies in M. Butlin and E. Joll, *The Paintings of J. M. W. Turner*, New Haven and London, 1977 (rev. ed. 1984) and A. Wilton, *The Life and Work of J. M. W. Turner*, London, 1979. For literature since 1984 see A. Wilton, *The Dictionary of Art*, vol.31, pp.466–76.

2. A. J. Finberg, *A Complete Inventory of the Drawings of the Turner Bequest*, British Museum, London, 1909.

3. Letter of 27 December 1847, quoted in A. J. Finberg, *The Life of J. M. W. Turner*, Oxford, 1961, p.419.

4. Wilton 1979, P259, illus. pp.55 and 328. Also P260, another version (untraced).

5. See, for example, A. Lyles, *Young Turner: Early Work to 1800. Watercolours and Drawings from the Turner Bequest 1787–1800*, exh. cat., Tate Gallery, London, 1989, nos 37 and 38; *Turner and the Sublime*, exh. cat., Toronto / New Haven / London, 1980–1, nos 4–6, illus. These works all measure around 53–55 × 75–78cms and are therefore comparable in size to our watercolour.

6. Finberg 1909, TB XXXIX and TB XLVI.

7. Finberg 1909, TB XLVI, f.1v.

8. See, for example, London 1989, nos 36–38.

9. I am grateful to John Ellis Roberts, Head Warden (North) of the Snowdonia National Park Authority for this identification.

70

1. F. Guillemard, 'Girtin's Sketching Club', *Connoisseur*, 63, 1922, pp.189–195.

2. T. Whitely, 'Girtin's Panorama', *Connoisseur*, 69, 1924, pp.13–20.

3. For Girtin's Jedburgh subjects (excluding those cited elsewhere in this entry), see T. Girtin and D. Loshak, *The Art of Thomas Girtin*, London, 1954, nos 165i, 165ii, 167, 187i, 187ii and 253. Undocumented by Girtin and Loshak: Watercolour of *Jedburgh Abbey from the South-East* [Prov: Sir John Ramsden Bart. (1755–1839); thence by descent: Sotheby's, London, 11 July 1990, no.91; Agnew's, London, *English Watercolours and Drawings*, 1991, no.59]; Pencil sketch of *Jedburgh Abbey from N-E* (Scottish Private Collection). Two views of the Abbey were exhibited at the Royal Academy, London, in 1797, nos 423 and 466.

4. Girtin and Loshak 1954, no.36.

5. Girtin and Loshak 1954, no.166i (British Museum). The inscription is ambiguous and may refer to either 2 or 11 October 1796.

6. J. Stoddart, *Remarks on Local Scenery and Manners in Scotland during the years 1799 and 1800*, London, 1801, vol.II, pp.82–3.

7. Girtin and Loshak 1954, no.166ii (English Private Collection). A contemporary copy of this watercolour by William Pearson, Girtin's closest follower, is in Manchester City Art Galleries (Acn. No.1939.70).

8. See Sotheby's, London, 12 April 1995, no.73. Also *Jedburgh Abbey from the South-East*, fn.3 above.

71

1. K. Garlick and A. MacIntyre (eds.), *The Diary of Joseph Farington*, vol.VI, New Haven and London, 1979, p.2362, diary entry for 26 June 1804.

2. See *Francis Towne*, exh. cat., London / Leeds, 1997, no.83, pp.156, 158.

3. A sketch from this tour of *Edinburgh from Donibristle* is in the National Gallery of Scotland (D 5375).

4. *Farington Diary*, vol.VI, p.2056, diary entry for 15 June 1803.

5. Examples of Abbott's drawings after engravings are in the Ashmolean Museum, Oxford. See also Christie's, London, 7 April 1992, nos 96–99; 14 July 1992, nos 69–72; 17 November 1992, nos 55–58.

6. Anthony Pasquin, *Liberal Critique*, 1794. For this quotation and a discussion of the critical reception of Abbott's paintings, see especially A. P. Oppé, 'John White Abbott of Exeter', *Walpole Society*, XIII, 1924–5, pp.67, 70–74, 82–84.

7. Clifford family collection, Ugbrooke. See London / Leeds exh. cat., nos 2 and 12–14.

8. For a particularly fine example, dated 1809, see Sotheby's, London, 12 April 1995, no.38.

9. Three examples were exhibited in *Three Exeter Artists: Francis Hayman, Francis Towne and John White Abbott*, exh. cat., Royal Albert Memorial Museum and Art Gallery, Exeter, 1951, nos 110 (dated 1822), 122 (dated 1789) and 124 (dated 1822). A view of Chudleigh, dated 1818, is in Exeter Museum and Art Gallery. See also Christie's, London, 14 July 1992, nos 59 (dated 1803), 73 (dated 1819), 74 (dated 1805), 82 (dated 1803); 17 November 1992, nos 45 (dated 1822), 49 (dated 1809); Sotheby's, London, 11 Nov. 1993, nos 82 (dated 1795) and 84 (dated 1816).

10. Christie's, London, 14 Nov. 1972, no.92. Another very similar drawing in pencil and watercolour, dated 1798, is in the collection of Mr. C. L. Loyd, Berkshire.

11. See, for example, London / Leeds exh. cat., nos 44 and 65.

12. M. Hardie, *Watercolour Painting in Britain*, vol.I, London, 1966, p.127.

13. Hardie 1966, pp.68 and 70.

14. *Catalogue of Fifty-five drawings by Old Masters of the Italian, German and Flemish Schools, belonging to Francis Abbott, Esq., lent to the National Gallery of Scotland*, May 1886, printed Edinburgh, 1886 (original MS National Gallery of Scotland archives).

15. National Gallery of Scotland D NG 723A and D NG 723B. In 1880 Francis also presented the British Museum, London, with several of his father's drawings and etchings.

72

1. Blake's rediscovery in the mid-nineteenth century led to the publication of the first full length biography by A. Gilchrist, *Life of William Blake: 'Pictor ignotus'*, London, 1863. Since then Blake's life and art has attracted an enormous amount of literature. For an extensive bibliography, see especially M. Butlin, *The Paintings and Drawings of William Blake*, London, 1981.

2. Butlin 1981, Text, pp.335–372, nos 433–526.

3. National Gallery of Scotland, Edinburgh (D 2281), William Findlay Watson Bequest, 1886.

4. Butlin 1981, Text, pp.317–335, nos 379–432.

5. S. Foster Damon, *A Blake Dictionary: The Ideas and Symbols of William Blake*, London, 1965, pp.216–23.

6. Butlin 1981, Text, pp.409–435.

7. Pierpont Morgan Library, New York.

8. Linnell watercolours, Fogg Art Museum, Harvard University.

9. A sketchbook containing twenty-seven preparatory drawings for the engravings is in the Fitzwilliam Museum, Cambridge. The original copper plates are in the British Museum, London.

10. Blake may have been made aware of this motif through his engraving after Fuseli's illustration of 1791, *The Fertilization of Egypt* – see M. Butlin, *William Blake: A Complete Catalogue of the Works in the Tate Gallery*, 1971, no.22. An alternative source may be Flaxman's *Giant on Mount Ida* – see C. H. Collins Baker, *The Sources of Blake's Expression*, reprinted from The Huntington Library Quarterly, IV, No.3, 1941, p.365.

73

1. For an account of this visit, see S. D. Kitson, *The Life of John Sell Cotman*, London, 1937, pp.76–93.

2. Morritt, from 1808 a great friend of Sir Walter Scott, is best known today as the one-time owner of Velázquez's *Rokeby Venus* (National Gallery, London), which he purchased in 1814.

3. A. M. Holcomb, *John Sell Cotman in the Cholmeley Archive*, Northallerton, 1980, p.69, letter from Cotman to Francis Cholmeley, 23 July 1822.

4. E. Baines, *History of the County of York*, 1822–3, vol.2, p.521.

5. *Early Drawings (1798–1812) in Norwich Castle Museum*, exh. cat., Norwich Castle Museum, Norwich, 1979, pp.60–61.

6. Michael Webb of North Yorkshire identifies the work as 'from the North bank of the Tees looking south and south-east across the river with the Greta joining it on the right' – letter November 1982, National Gallery of Scotland files.

7. *John Sell Cotman 1782–1842*, exh. cat., London / Manchester / Bristol, 1982–3, no.45, p.74; letter from Elizabeth Conran, The Bowes Museum, May 1996, National Gallery of Scotland files.

8. London / Manchester / Bristol 1982–83, no.45, p.74.

9. M. Hardie, 'Cotman's Water-colours: The Technical Aspect', *The Burlington Magazine*, LXXI, 1942, pp.171–176.

10. Kitson 1937, p.84.

11. Many of the elms on the banks of the Greta were felled in recent years because of Dutch Elm disease. The woodland around *Hell Cauldron* is consequently now much sparser than in Cotman's day.

74

1. For De Wint's association with the Society, see *The Royal Watercolour Society: The First Fifty Years 1805–1855*, Antique Collectors' Club, Woodbridge, 1992, and S. Fenwick and G. Smith, *The Business of Watercolour: A Guide to the Archives of the Royal Watercolour Society*, Aldershot, 1997.

2. 'Obituary, Mr. P. De Wint', *The Art Journal*, XI, 1849, p.260.

3. At the junction of Drury Lane and Union Road. See *Catalogue of the Peter De Wint Collection, Usher Art Gallery, Lincoln*, Usher Art Gallery, Lincoln, 1947, p.6.

4. See *Drawings and Watercolours by Peter De Wint*, exh. cat., Fitzwilliam Museum, Cambridge, 1979, no.81, p.34 and plate 47.

5. I am grateful to Neville Birch of the Society for Lincolnshire History and Archaeology for this information.

6. Cambridge 1979, no.5, p.3 and plate 3.

7. *Ibid*, no.6, p.3 and plate 3.

8. Edinburgh 1979, no.55.

9. V & A Museum (179–1898). See Cambridge 1979, no.4, p.2 and plate 2. A larger, more finished version of this watercolour is in a private collection, illus. in M. Hardie, *Watercolour Painting in Britain*, London, 1967, vol.II, fig.197.

10. V & A Museum (P58–1921). See *Catalogue of British Oil Paintings 1820–1860*, Victoria and Albert Museum, London, 1990, p.71.

75

1. Edinburgh / London, exh. cat., *passim*, 1995–6.

2. S. Lloyd, 'Fashioning the Image of the Prince: Richard Cosway and George IV', '*Squanderous and Lavish Profusion': George IV, his Image and Patronage of the Arts*, Dana Arnold (ed.), The Georgian Group, London, 1995, pp.5–14.

3. Lloyd, 'Richard Cosway, RA: The Artist as Collector, Connoisseur and Virtuoso', *Apollo*, CXXXVIII, 1991, pp.398–405; S. Lloyd, 'Forming the Taste of a Prince: Richard Cosway and George IV's Early Collection', *Apollo*, CXXXVIII, 1993, pp.192–4 [also published in a separate volume, *Buckingham Palace: A Complete Guide*, Robin Simon (ed.), London, 1993, pp.124–6].

4. S. Lloyd, 'The Accomplished Maria Cosway: Anglo-Italian Artist, Musician, Salon Hostess and Educationalist', *Journal of Anglo-Italian Studies*, II, 1992, pp.108–39.

5. F. B. Daniell, *A Catalogue Raisonné of the Engraved Works of Richard Cosway, R.A.*, London 1890.

6. G. C. Williamson, *Richard Cosway R.A. and his Wife and Pupils: Miniaturists of the Eighteenth Century*, London, 1897, ill. opp. p.44 (large paper copies only); 2nd edn., 1905, ill. opp. p.122.

7. For the auction of his library by Stanley's in 1821, see Edinburgh / London 1995–6, p.133, no.220. For Cosway's religious drawings, see *ibid.*, pp.127–8, nos 160–61 and 170–75; and *Maria e Richard Cosway*, Tino Gipponi (ed.), Turin, 1998, ills. *passim*.

8. Daniell, p.42, no.170. Macklin's Bible was published between 1791 and 1816, cf. M. D. Paley, *The Apocalyptic Sublime*, New Haven and London, 1986.

9. Gipponi, col. pl. between pp.68 and 69.

10. Royal Academy, London, MS Lawrence, LAW / 1 / 289, fols.1V-2r, quoted in Edinburgh / London 1995–6, *op. cit.*, p.80.

76

1. The Royal Regalia include the Scottish crown, datable to the time of Robert the Bruce; the Sword of State, presented by Pope Julius II to King James IV in 1507; and the Sceptre, made during the reign of James V.

2. Scottish National Portrait Gallery, Edinburgh (PG 2069). Given its much earlier date and horizontal format, this cannot be considered as a companion to *The Burial*.

3. See *George IV in Edinburgh*, exh. cat., Scottish National Portrait Gallery, Edinburgh, 1961.

4. Ashmolean Museum, Oxford. Illus. in *Sir David Wilkie of Scotland (1785–1841)*, exh. cat., North Carolina Museum of Art, Raleigh, 1987, no.62, pp.303–4.

5. Raleigh 1987, no.72, pp.323–324.

6. Illus. in *Dutch Art and Scotland: A Reflection of Taste*, exh. cat., National Gallery of Scotland, Edinburgh, 1992, fig.38, p.52.

7. Raleigh 1987, no.73, pp.325–6 and nos 76–9, pp.331–9.

8. One version of the *Adoration* is in the National Gallery of London (NG 47), purchased 1824. The *Entombment* is in the Alte Pinakothek, Munich.

9. While the lack of measurements in the Wilkie Sale catalogue makes it difficult to correlate the lots with known drawings, the sale prices give some indication of the measure of finish. No.115 sold for £27.6s, no.116 for £3.5s and no.376 for £4.15s. It seems reasonable therefore to match the National Gallery of Scotland's highly finished drawing with no.115.

10. The existence of several studies for *The Burial* complicates our drawing's provenance, which still remains uncertain. I am grateful to Professor Hamish Miles for his assistance.

77

1. Paton was the second of three children. His younger brother, Waller Hugh (1828–1895), became a respected landscape painter in a Pre-Raphaelite manner, while his sister, Amelia (1821–1904), who married the painter and pioneer photographer, David Octavius Hill, was known in her own right as a sculptress.

79

1. *Samuel Palmer and his Circle. The Shoreham Period*, exh. cat., Arts Council, 1956; R. Lister, *Samuel Palmer and 'The Ancients'*, exh. cat., Fitzwilliam Museum, Cambridge, 1984.

2. The standard modern biography is by R. Lister, *Samuel Palmer: A Biography*, London, 1974. For extensive bibliographies see also R. Lister, *Samuel Palmer: His Life and Art*, Cambridge, 1987 and R. Lister, *Catalogue Raisonné of the Works of Samuel Palmer*, Cambridge, 1988.

3. Lister 1988, p.192, no.602.

4. A. H. Palmer, *The Life and Letters of Samuel Palmer*, London 1892 p.133.

5. Lister (1988, no.602, p.193) points out that the motif of the shepherd and his flock on distant rising ground appears in works by other members of 'The Ancients', e.g. Edward Calvert's line engraving *The Bride* (1828) and George Richmond's line engraving *The Fatal Bellman* (1827).

6. According to A. H. Palmer, *Wrecked at Home*, exhibited at the Old Watercolour Society in 1862, [dimensions 191 × 425mm (?)] is an example of Palmer's 'Large Long' format. *Catalogue of an Exhibition of Drawings, Etchings by Samuel Palmer and other Disciples of William Blake*, exh. cat., Victoria and Albert Museum, 1926, no.99, p.42.

7. 'Men You Know', *The Bailie*, 12 March 1919, p.3.

8. The Gallery acquired J. N. Paton's important *Luther at Erfurt* (1861) and A. Christie's *The Pied Piper of Hamelin* (1881) from the 1919 Brechin Sale.

9. Lister 1988, p.213, nos 689 and 690.

10. For details on Brechin and the sale of his collection, see especially *The Bailie*, 10 February 1904, and 5, 12, 19 and 26 March 1919 and his obituary, *Glasgow Herald*, 16 December 1918. I am grateful to the work of Dr Elizabeth Bird and to George Fairfull Smith for this information.

80

1. Formerly collection of Mrs Alastair Campbell. Illus. in A. E. Mackay, *Arthur Melville: Scottish Impressionist (1855–1904)*, Leigh-on-Sea, 1951, plate 17.

2. A survey of Melville's association with 'The Glasgow Boys' is given in R. Billcliffe, *The Glasgow Boys*, London, 1985.

3. Frank Rutter in the *Sunday Observer*, quoted in Mackay 1951, p.121. Melville's career was recently reappraised by I. Gale in *Arthur Melville*, Edinburgh, 1996.

4. See V. Hamilton, *Joseph Crawhall 1861–1913: One of the Glasgow Boys*, Museums and Art Gallery, Glasgow, 1990, pp.45–73.

5. R. B. Cunninghame Graham, *Writ in Sand*, London, 1932, p.121–2.

6. R. E. Groves, 'Morrocco as a Winter Sketching Ground', *The Studio*, XLV, 1908, p.29.

7. N. Garstin, 'Tangier as a Sketching Ground', *The Studio*, XI, 1897, p.178.

8. J. L. Caw, *Scottish Painting: Past and Present 1620–1908*, Edinburgh, 1908, p.397.

2. His collection is now in the National Museums of Scotland. J. N. Paton, *Private Catalogue of Armour, Weapons and Other Objects of Antiquity in the Collection of Sir Noël Paton*, Edinburgh, 1879; M. Baker, 'A Victorian Collector of Armour', *Country Life*, CLVII, 1975, pp.232–6; H. Cheape and R. Marshall, 'The World of a Nineteenth-Century Artist in Scotland', *Review of Scottish Culture 3*, 1987, pp.84–86.

3. A Cavallo, 'Joseph Noël Paton: Designer of Damasks', *Connoisseur*, CLIII, 1963, pp.59–64.

4. A good bibliography is given in the modern monograph by M. H. Noël-Paton and J. P. Campbell, *Noël Paton 1821–1901*, Edinburgh, 1990.

5. Royal Scottish Academy, exh. cat., 1850, no.566, p.30.

6. Translation by Philip Wayne, Harmondsworth, first published 1949, p.114.

7. Hall was influential as the author and editor of *The Art Union* (from 1851 *The Art Journal*).

8. National Gallery of Scotland, Edinburgh (D 4252).

9. I am grateful to Robin Rodger of Perth Museum and Art Gallery for this identification.

10. The subject was treated again by Paton in a picture of *Faust and Marguerite Reading*, exhibited at the Royal Scottish Academy in 1854 (whereabouts unknown). A mixed media study of Mephistopheles in Faust's study passed through Sotheby's, London, 4 March 1980, no.52.

78

1. Nash's relations with the Old Watercolour Society did not always run smoothly. For details of his clashes with the President and Council, see S. Fenwick and G. Smith, *The Business of Watercolour: A Guide to the Archives of the Royal Watercolour Society*, Aldershot, 1997. His exhibited works up to 1855 are listed in *The Royal Watercolour Society: The First Fifty Years 1805–1855*, The Antique Collectors' Club, Woodbridge, 1992, pp.193–5.

2. For Nash's merits as a reproductive lithographer, see M. Twyman, *Lithography 1800–1850*, London, 1970, pp.213–16.

3. The principal source for Nash's career is J. L. Roget, *A History of the 'Old Watercolour Society'*, London, 1891, pp.240–45.

4. *A Letter to John Lewis Esq. Etc., Etc., President of the Society of Painters in Water Colours by Joseph Nash* (printed), Royal Watercolour Society Archives, London, J 65 / 10, letters of 21 and 26 April 1857, pp.4 and 6.

5. I am grateful to Simon Fenwick of the Bankside Gallery, London, for his assistance with this entry.

Abbreviations

ANDREWS 1968
K. Andrews, *National Gallery of Scotland Catalogue of Italian Drawings*, 2 vols., Cambridge, 1968.

ANDREWS 1985
K. Andrews, *Catalogue of the Netherlandish Drawings in the National Gallery of Scotland*, 2 vols., Edinburgh, 1985.

ANDREWS 1991
K. Andrews, *Catalogue of German Drawings in the National Gallery of Scotland*, Edinburgh, 1991.

ANDREWS AND BROTCHIE 1960
K. Andrews and J. R. Brotchie, *Catalogue of Scottish Drawings in the National Gallery of Scotland*, Edinburgh, 1960.

BARTSCH
A. Bartsch, *Le peintre-graveur*, 21 vols., Vienna, 1803–21 (See also Illus. Bartsch).

COLNAGHI 1966
Old Master Drawings A Loan Exhibition from the National Gallery of Scotland, exh.cat., Colnaghi's, London, 1966.

THE DICTIONARY OF ART
The Dictionary of Art, edited by J. Turner, 34 vols., London/New York, 1996.

EDINBURGH 1961
Fifty Master Drawings in the National Gallery of Scotland, exh. cat., National Gallery of Scotland, Edinburgh, 1961.

EDINBURGH 1976
Old Master Drawings from the David Laing Bequest, exh. cat., National Gallery of Scotland, Edinburgh, 1976.

EDINBURGH 1979
English Watercolours and other Drawings from the Helen Barlow Bequest, exh. cat., National Gallery of Scotland, Edinburgh, 1979.

EDINBURGH 1981
Drawings from the Bequest of W. F. Watson 1881– 1981, exh. cat., National Gallery of Scotland, Edinburgh, 1981.

EDINBURGH 1984
Rembrandt to Seurat. Drawings and Prints Acquired in the Past Five Years, exh. leaflet, National Gallery of Scotland, Edinburgh, 1984.

EDINBURGH 1986
The Study of Mankind. Three Centuries of Figure Drawing from the Permanent Collection, exh. leaflet, National Gallery of Scotland, Edinburgh, 1986.

EDINBURGH 1991
Saved for Scotland: Works of Art acquired with the help of the National Art Collections Fund, exh. cat., National Gallery of Scotland, Edinburgh, 1991.

EDINBURGH 1993
Bolognese Drawings in the National Gallery of Scotland, exh. leaflet, National Gallery of Scotland, Edinburgh, 1993.

EDINBURGH/LONDON 1985–6
Some Netherlandish Drawings from the National Gallery of Scotland, exh. leaflet, National Gallery of Scotland, Edinburgh and Hazlitt, Gooden and Fox, London, 1985–6.

EDINBURGH/LONDON 1994
From Leonardo to Manet. Ten Years of Collecting Prints and Drawings, exh. cat., National Gallery of Scotland, Edinburgh and Hazlitt, Gooden and Fox, London, 1994.

EXH. CAT.
Exhibition catalogue.

HOLLSTEIN
F. W. H. Hollstein, *Dutch & Flemish Etchings, Engravings and Woodcuts ca.1450–1700*, Amsterdam, 1949–87 (vols.1–31), Roosendaal 1988–93 (vols.32–43), Rotterdam 1994– continuing (vol.44–) (See also New Hollstein)

HOLLSTEIN G
F. W. H. Hollstein, *German Engravings, Etchings and Woodcuts ca.1450–1700*, Amsterdam, 1954– continuing.

ILLUS. BARTSCH
The Illustrated Bartsch, New York, 1978– (General editor: W. L. Strauss).

L
F. Lugt, *Les Marques de Collections de Dessins et d'Estampes*, Amsterdam, 1921; *Supplément*, The Hague, 1956.

LUGT
F. Lugt, *Répertoire des Catalogues de Ventes Publiques*, 3 vols., The Hague, 1938, 1953; 1964.

NEW HOLLSTEIN
The New Hollstein Dutch & Flemish Etchings, Engravings and Woodcuts 1450–1700, Rotterdam, 1993–continuing (no vol.nos).

WASHINGTON/FORT WORTH 1990–1
Old Master Drawings from the National Gallery of Scotland, exh.cat., National Gallery of Art, Washington and Kimbell Art Museum, Fort Worth, 1990–1.

Index of Artists

References are to catalogue numbers

PHOTOGRAPHIC CREDITS

Colour and black and white photography of works belonging to the National Galleries of Scotland was carried out by Antonia Reeve with the exception of nos. 1 and 13 which were taken by Jack McKenzie. The remaining photographs were supplied by the owning institutions with the exception of the following:

Fig.28 © Photo du Sénat, Paris

Figs.14, 32, 33, 35 and 39 © RMN, Paris

Figs.36 and 37 © Roumagnac Photographe

Fig.50 photographed by Prudence Cuming Associates Ltd, London